CRITICS
NOT
CARETAKERS

SUNY series, Issues in the Study of Religion
Bryan Rennie, editor

CRITICS NOT CARETAKERS

Redescribing the Public Study of Religion

RUSSELL T. McCUTCHEON

State University
of New York
Press

Published by
State University of New York Press, Albany

© 2001 State University of New York

Production by Susan Geraghty
Marketing by Mike Campochiaro

Printed in the United States of America

For information, address State University of New York Press,
90 State Street, Suite 700, Albany, NY 12207

Library of Congress Cataloging-in-Publication Data

McCutcheon, Russell T., 1961–
    Critics not caretakers : redescribing the public study of religion / Russell T. McCutcheon.
        p. cm. — (SUNY series, issues in the study of religion)
    Includes bibliographical references and index.
    ISBN 0-7914-4943-2 (alk. paper) — ISBN 0-7914-4944-0 (pbk. : alk. paper)
        1. Religion—Study and teaching. I. Title. II. Series.
    BL41 .M348 2001
    200′.71—dc21
                                                                                    00-041056

10 9 8 7 6 5 4 3 2 1

CONTENTS

*To all those who labor in the
part-time and adjunct trenches of the academy*

*And also to Marcia,
who helped to make those damp trenches a little cozier*

PREFACE

> I don't have any myself, but I believe in other people having
> religion.
>
> —David Lodge, *The British Museum Is Falling Down*

In April 1999, I delivered the introduction to this collection at the Eastern International Regional meeting of the American Academy of Religion (AAR)—a society to which I, like thousands of other North American scholars of religion *and* theologians alike, belong. Anticipating that
"theory-talk" might have an adverse affect on the audience—after all,
many in our field are against defining or theorizing religion—I opened
by quoting a passage from David Lodge's wonderfully comic novel
about conference-going British literary critics, *Small World* (1995
[1984]). The passage involved an exchange between: Angelica Pabst, a
mysterious young American who studies romances; Persse McCarrigle,
a slightly naive, underpaid Irish lecturer new to the conference circuit;
Philip Swallow, an English department head committed to the enduring
values of "Literature"; and Swallow's longtime friend, the provocative
literary theorist and plenary speaker Maurice Zapp. After recounting to
Persse the "hundreds of romances" she has read, Angelica says,

> "I don't need any more data, What I need is a theory to explain it all."
> "Theory," Philip Swallow's ears quivered under their silvery
> thatch, a few places further up the table. "That word brings out the
> Goering in me. When I hear it I reach for my revolver."
> "Then you're not going to like my lecture, Philip," said Morris
> Zapp.[1]

Unlike Zapp's theory-ladened lecture (whose most memorable line, to
me at least, was his critique of the hermeneut's endless quest for meaning: "Every decoding is another encoding")—where a number of people
either left or just fainted when he compared the act of reading to watching a striptease—no one stormed out on me, not that I noticed, anyway.
Also unlike Zapp's talk, after mine there were quite a few questions and
comments; one in particular still stands out in my memory. In fact, it
was the last question of the afternoon; it came from a woman near the
back of the lecture hall who asked, in a quiet voice, whether I was say-

ing that religion was *also* social, biological, political, economic, and so on, or whether I was saying that religion was *only* social, biological, political, economic, and so on. Her subtle yet significant distinction—*also* or *only*—nicely sums up the divide that continues to characterize the study of religion, a divide that I chronicle throughout this book. My answer? I leaned in close to the microphone at the lectern, and, in a voice familiar to anyone who has sat through a sound check before a rock concert, I simply said, "Only. Next question?"

After a brief pause for effect, I dropped the pretense and elaborated by saying that if in fact it was *also*, then the onus would be on her to articulate clearly just what this *also* entailed or to what in the observable, intersubjective world of human doings it referred. If it entailed some mysterious, other- or inner-worldly intuition of deep, unseen, or transcendent meaning, value, or revelation, then, I went on to say, there were literally thousands of theological institutions scattered throughout North America where this sort of presupposition is not only welcomed but also nurtured and reproduced. I concluded by saying that if religion is studied in a public university as part of the human sciences, then we have no choice but to study it as a *thoroughly human doing*, from top to bottom—which means that those things we name as religion are conceptualized as historical (i.e., social, political, gendered, economic, biological, etc.) all the way down, without remainder. I then ended with a rhetorical question: "How else could public scholars of religion conceive of it?"

Although some heads nodded in agreement—mostly, those heads were connected to the bodies of good friends with whom I had trained at the University of Toronto in the late 1980s and early 1990s—for a number of audience members, my answer was probably not all that convincing and, quite possibly, outright offensive. (Politely informing theologians at another institution some months later that I understood them to be data prompted the latter of these responses, though I later learned that the sharpest comments were reserved for the faculty meeting a few days after my talk.) Failing to understand the important difference between metaphysical reduction ("religion is nothing but . . ." talk—an approach shared by believers and disbelievers alike) and methodological reduction ("given my methods/theories, the discursive rules of our institution, and my particular set of interests and curiosities, religion turns out to be . . ." talk), many people in the audience likely saw me as discounting the believer's viewpoint. This could not be further from the point; like others in the field, I take the participant or insider's viewpoint utterly seriously (hence the epigraph I selected for this preface), but not in the way that believers might like. In other words, I do not see the participant as setting the ground rules for how his or her behavior ought to be studied by scholars. No other area of the human sciences is compelled to grant the people studied a monopoly on determining how their behaviors ought to be viewed, and I see no reason why such ownership of meanings should be granted in the study of religion. The participants' viewpoint, their behavior, and the institutions they build and reproduce are data for the scholar intent on theorizing as to *why* human beings expend such tremendous creativity and intellectual/social energy in discourses on the gods, origins, and endtimes.

This book may therefore not be directed to readers who cannot distinguish between methodological and metaphysical reduction. It is also not directed at readers who misread my work as an extended effort to deny that the notion 'religion' exists (Hart 1999: 9). Simply put, I have no interest in what religion *really is* (i.e., metaphysical reduction); instead, my interest has everything to do with *how* (i.e., description) and *why* (i.e., explanation) human communities divide up, classify, and ontologize their *ad hoc* social worlds in particular ways. Of all the categorizations that we as members of social groups employ, the "particular ways" of which I am interested have everything to do with the sociorhetorical function of such interrelated dichotomies as sacred/secular, religion/irreligion, tradition/spirituality, myth/history, private/public, insider/outsider, us/them, and so on. The group to which this collection of essays *is* therefore directed is that loosely organized group of readers who are willing to entertain the simple yet—judging from the criticisms prompted by earlier versions of some of the following chapters—surprisingly radical presumption that, *like all other aspects of human behavior*, those collections of beliefs, behaviors, and institutions we classify as "religion" can be conceptualized and then explained as thoroughly human activity, with no mysterious distillate left over. Should one assert that these activities we name "religion" are more than this—given the discursive constraints on public scholarship, I am at a loss to come up with a way of understanding any argument that says anything human can be more than this—then, one might better pursue such studies in a setting outside of the public university.

The chapters in this volume were all written over the past several years, and they examine the above thesis at a variety of rather ordinary sites in the study of religion. Many of them were written in a state of mind that was nicely summed up by Roland Barthes:

> The starting point of these reflections was usually a feeling of impatience at the sight of the 'naturalness' with which newspapers, art, and common sense constantly dress up a reality which, even though it is the one we live in, is undoubtedly determined by history. In short, in the account given of our contemporary circumstances, I resented seeing

Nature and History confused at every turn, and I wanted to track down, in the decorative displays of *what-goes-without-saying*, the ideological abuse which, in my view, is hidden there. (1973: 11)

I believe that it was this same impatience that I felt upon reading any number of articles published in some of our field's leading scholarly and professional periodicals—articles that naively presumed: (i) that religion equals morality; (ii) that scholars of religion have some special insight into the nature of 'the good'; and therefore (iii) that they have a responsibility for securing the fate of the nation-state or cooking up some therapeutic recipe for attaining self-knowledge or happiness. Because we all pick our battles, I would occasionally write a direct reply to such an article and, whatever the outcome, submit it to the journal. Yet other times, some article or a book—in the case of Burkert's and Saler's work, they are books with whose theses I generally agree—would act as a springboard into some larger topic. Because I have drawn some criticism in the past for the manner in which some of my work singles out the late and well-known scholar Mircea Eliade as an exemplar of the field's problems, the sites I have engaged in this collection are, as suggested above, all too ordinary. My hope is that this tactical change of focus will support my thesis that the study of religion, from top to bottom, needs rethinking. Having said this, however, I am not so naive as to think that some revolution is just around the corner. Because my approach understands the conception of religion as a privatized, internal, mysterious something to be intimately linked to the liberal humanist rhetoric used in reproducing the modern idea of the nation-state, then I'm pretty confident in saying that this conception won't be going away any time soon. And when it does (*if* it ever does) go away, it will only be after a lot of kicking and screaming on the part of influential people whose self-identity and stake in the social world are made possible by this rhetoric. With this in mind, I decided to open the book with an epigraph from the delightfully cynical movie critic Joe Queenan that notes the uphill battle facing any critic silly enough to tackle popular culture (in my case, as it is found within the academy). For every site I examine, there are at least ten more that could have equally attracted my attention. We all have to make choices.

The point I am trying to make throughout these chapters is exceedingly simple—the study of religion can be rethought as the study of an ordinary aspect of social, historical existence. Although the essays all explore this common theme and build what I consider to be a coherent argument, I recognize that each reader dips into books such as this at various points, reading with any number of different, tactical agendas in mind. While some may read the book front to back, most will likely hunt and peck throughout various chapters. For this reason I have tried to make sure that the argument of each chapter can be read on its own, so that those who always come late to the movie, or those who first flip to the end of a novel to see who did it, will still know what's going on; that is why I have placed the endnotes immediately after each chapter. I realize that approaching a book in this fashion means that there is an unavoidable amount of repetition, for, from the outset, each essay—no matter what its specific topic—much first engage in the same up-hill battle against the dominant—almost commonsense—model of conceptualizing and studying religion. Over the past several years I have found that the luxury of writing in our field's dominant tradition is that the ground rules, like the air we breathe, are accepted by your readership as obvious and in no need of statement. But for those of us interested in drawing attention to the troublesome nature of these seemingly self-evident rules and assumptions, each argument must always begin anew with a critique of first principles. As Noam Chomsky says, sound bites are impossible for those who hold oppositional viewpoints since sound bites make such commentators come off sounding like they're from outer space. Where possible, though, I have attempted to avoid unnecessary repetition.

From a general introduction written for a wide audience to a chapter that clearly lays out the theoretical basis of an alternative, sociorhetorical approach supported by a growing number of current scholars, the collection moves to what I—following the title of a review essay written by Tom Lawson several years ago—refer to as "dispatches from the theory wars." Each of these chapters uses one work of a specific writer as a point of entry into wider theoretical issues of importance to the field (those writers include Karen Armstrong, Walter Burkert, Benson Saler, Richard Roberts, and Garrett Green). Given the approach to studying religion that I develop throughout these dispatches, the two essays that follow then explore the social role of this brand of critical scholarship—a role dramatically different from the type of caretaking generally associated with scholars of religion who feel compelled to go public with their insights into the supposedly deeper nature of religion. Finally, because I have great difficulty with those who see scholarship and teaching as inhabiting two completely different worlds, I conclude the collection with four chapters specifically concerned with how we can address issues of theory and critical thinking at the one site where we have unimpeded access to the general public: the university classroom. If there is one place where we have the ability to persuade the public of the relevance of our field for understanding culture and our field's fundamental differences from theological scholarship, then it is surely in our classes.

Re-reading that last sentence, I cannot help but lament the fact that, finding ourselves at the centenary of Friedrich Max Müller's death in 1900—one of the most vocal early European apologists for a science of religion—scholars of religion still find themselves having to justify their place within the public university. On the personal level, almost all of us have stories of how our families, friends, or acquaintances did not quite understand how the study of religion differed from practicing religion. "Oh, I didn't know you were religious," invariably greets us when we answer the "What do you do?" question. Although many scholars relish the opportunity to discuss theological or moral issues with a seatmate on a long flight, I know a number of people who simply choose to say they practice some other occupation so as not to get into the long dance that often results when we talk about our work outside our so-called ivory towers. I recall how, on a flight from Denver to California, my seatmate—a pleasant lady with a number of questions about what a scholar of religion does—decided that I was rather sinful to do what I do. In fact, a few years back a good friend who has grown quite tired of this little dance played dumb while flying to the annual meeting of the American Academy of Religion/Society of Biblical Literature (SBL); seated beside someone who was obviously also traveling to the annual meeting (as he told the story, she was pouring over her copy of the program book, which is the size of my hometown's phone book), he naively asked, "What do you do?" and, for the next few hundred air miles, he learned all about what it was that a scholar of religion did. Unfortunately, it sounded to him more like what a liberal, Protestant theologian did. Although they were both on their way to the same professional meeting and were members of the same professional society, one—being deeply committed to a quest for meaning and coherence—comprised the data for the other. Given the deep confusion as to who is a colleague and who is a datum, there is little wonder, then, that the public and our university colleagues alike misunderstand scholars of religion.

Unlike the social role played by my friend's seatmate, this book argues that scholars of religion can become engaged public intellectuals, or culture critics, who neither study free-floating signifiers nor get sucked down never-ending hermeneutical vortexes (recall Maurice Zapp's advice: "Every decoding is another encoding"); instead, scholars of religion are equipped with tools to examine the means by which historically grounded human communities authorize and—to borrow a phrase from Burton Mack—act as mythmakers in efforts to construct and contest social identities that they are working to extend over time and place. In a word, the brand of scholarship on religion I propose is openly "redescriptive." I borrow this important term from an essay in Jonathan Z. Smith's influential book *Imagining Religion: From Babylon to Jonestown* (see "Sacred Persistence: Toward a Redescription of Canon" [1982: 36–52]). Building on the work of Max Black and Mary Hesse, Smith proposes that scholarship is a particular type of cognitive and social activity that involves provocative juxtaposition and building theoretical models by means of which "we may see things in a new and frequently unexpected light. A model, in short, is a 'redescription'" (1982: 36).

Redescriptive scholarship, as demonstrated by Smith, challenges us to distinguish clearly between emic or folk accounts and categories, on the one hand, and etic, scholarly accounts and categories, on the other. It challenges us to distinguish between the questions and anticipations we as scholars bring with us to the scene (e.g., theories, hypotheses, even guesses) and those aspects of the natural, observable world that either do or do not meet those expectations (making them data in need of explanation). Again, following Smith, the fact that we have data to study is evidence of our own curiosity concerning the way the world does not always conform to our anticipations. Unless, like phenomenologists, we are in the business of merely reporting on self-evidencies— something I call "couch potato scholarship"—there is no choice but for our studies of human behavior to engage in analysis and theory. Grouping together the moments separately identified as definition, description, classification, comparison, and explanation, we can talk of this alternative brand of scholarship simply as the activity of redescription.

A final word of caution; as suggested above, I am concerned with two things in these chapters: (i) Identifying the practical implications of the traditional way of classifying human behaviors as "religious" and then (ii) proposing an alternative way of studying and teaching about the rhetorical tools we employ to authorize and reproduce our social identities. It is a two-fold approach that, I believe, helps us to see something other than the timeless, unexplainable "sacred symbols" and "enduring values" that occupy the attention of many of our colleagues.

NOTE

1. My thanks to Ron Cameron for bringing this wonderful passage to my attention.

ACKNOWLEDGMENTS

I recall a lunch in a Montreal Greek restaurant in the Fall of 1998, where Luther Martin, barely able to contain his glee, toasted both my former teacher, Don Wiebe, and myself: as Luther so eloquently put it, he toasted Don for managing to publish a collection of his own essays and me for pulling one together decades sooner. With friends like that—well, come to think of it, these are the best sort of friends to have. They're the kind of friends who knew you when you were struggling to put together a good idea or get your first book review published. They don't take you too seriously, and, thereby, they prevent you from taking yourself too seriously. That way, you don't get "too big for your britches," as my mom used to say. For helping me not to take myself too seriously, I would like to thank the following people: Bill Arnal, Herb Berg, Ron Cameron, Michel Desjardins, Stephen Heathorn, Julie Ingersoll, Darlene Juschka, Gary Lease, Jack Llewellyn, Luther Martin, Tim Murphy, William Paden, Donald Wiebe, and Johannes Wolfart. My thanks also goes to Bryan Rennie for including this volume in his State University of New York Press series, the anonymous readers who assessed these chapters for the press, as well as SUNY's editorial and production teams.

In addition to these names I must single out three people whose writings have been rather influential of my thinking in recent years: Burton Mack, Jonathan Z. Smith, and Bruce Lincoln. It is directly from Mack's work that I borrow an idea that is central to this entire collection: the distinction between "caretakers" and "culture critics." Although Mack's work on Christian origins is in a very different area than my own work, we share an active interest in developing a thoroughly social theory of religion, demonstrating an important point: scholars are united by means of their curiosities, questions, theories, and methods, not necessarily by their shared data. This observation should make clear that my work has been influenced a great deal by the many essays written by Jonathan Z. Smith. This past year I used two of Smith's works in my own graduate courses—*Drudgery Divine* (1990b) and his essay on pedagogy, "Less Is Better" (1991)—which prompted me to re-read two works that I have not read for some time. To state it bluntly, when reading through the following chapters as a group, I was amazed to see just how profoundly my research and teaching have been shaped by Smith's work—not so much his data but his style of scholarship. I therefore see the works collected in this volume as an extended argument for rethinking the study of religion along lines first—and best—outlined by Smith himself. Finally, the chapter that stands in the middle of this collection and that has, so far, provoked the most vocal reactions from readers—"A Default of Critical Intelligence? The Scholar of Religion as Public Intellectual"—was written just after delivering the final manuscript for my previous book, *Manufacturing Religion: The Discourse on Sui Generis Religion and the Politics of Nostalgia* (1997c) to the press—a book, I was later to learn, for which Bruce Lincoln had acted as the press's outsider reader. Given the critique I level at the field in that book and that I extend in these essays, I fear what would have happened to that manuscript had anyone but Lincoln been invited by a publisher to read it. While finishing that manuscript I reviewed Lincoln's *Authority: Construction and Corrosion* (1994) and, along with his earlier works on the sociopolitical role played by myths and rituals, coupled with Mack's thoughts on caretakers and critics, it all coalesced into my argument for a very different public role for the scholar of religion. My understanding of religion as a sociorhetorical practice (both the cultural practices we collect under the name *religion*, as well as the very act of naming acts as religious) is therefore derived directly from my reading of Lincoln's work. Although I try very hard to cite all relevant sources whenever I can, the influence of Mack, Smith, and Lincoln weaves throughout these chapters, sometimes to such an extent that I have difficulty remembering who first came up with a certain idea—me or them. My default assumption is always them.

In addition, my sincere thanks also goes to my former and current students, first at the University of Tennessee in Knoxville (1993–1996) and now at Southwest Missouri State University in Springfield. Several of the following chapters first came into the world as inglorious, off-the-cuff examples used in classrooms—examples that, over the course of several weeks or months, developed into initial drafts that my students then critiqued and debated, putting to bed that tired old distinction some people still draw between research and teaching. Despite the fact that most of my undergraduate students suffer through my classes to get a general education credit, the enthusiasm for the study of religion that I have encountered in a number of my students causes me some optimism for the future of the field. Although the shape of the current academic labor market suggests that *not* pursuing a Ph.D. could be the wisest decision a person ever makes, I fear that the field would lose something important should some of the students I have known and had the privilege to work with decide to go into other professions.

Also, I must acknowledge the support of the dedicated members of the North American Association for the Study of Religion (NAASR), an admittedly small group that is now fifteen years old and that has continually offered me an informal context for exploring issues of both theory and critique. Case in point: a much earlier form of the second chapter of this book was originally presented at a 1997 NAASR session in San Francisco (along with papers by Tim Fitzgerald and Gary Lease), and its published version served as one of several discussion papers for one of NAASR's 1999 sessions in Boston. As well, the editors with whom I have had the good fortune to work over the past ten years on NAASR's journal, *Method & Theory in the Study of Religion* (Ann Baranowski, Willi Braun, Darlene Juschka, and Arthur McCalla), as well as the editorial team at the quarterly *Bulletin of the Council of Societies for the Study of Religion* (Pam Gleason and David Truemper), whose team I joined in 1996, also deserve my thanks for allowing me to be part of creative groups figuring out how it is that we can talk about religion in a publicly accountable context. I have had the luxury of meeting many people through my editing; although I have sometimes jokingly stated that all good things have come to me through my work on *MTSR*, I really must say here that this is no understatement.

Of all these people, however, I must single out my sometimes co-editor, all-time good friend, and all around nice guy, Willi Braun. Willi is my constant conversation partner; I first became aware of the work of Smith and Mack because he told me to read them, and virtually all of the following essays have benefitted in countless ways from his critical eye, his tinkering and fine tuning, and our many conversations, either over the phone, by email, or in hotel rooms while killing time at conferences. If there is a person whose influence lurks anonymously almost everywhere in this collection, it is surely him.

I also wish to acknowledge the various groups to which I was lucky enough to have read earlier versions of some of these essays in the volume: the XVIIth Congress of the International Association for the History of Religions (Mexico City, August 1995); the central States regional meeting of the Society for Biblical Literature (Kansas City, April 1997); the Department of Religious Studies at the University of California, Santa Barbara (November 1997); the Humanities Lecture Series at Bishop's University, Quebec (November 1998); the Department of Religious Studies at the University of Tennessee, Knoxville (February 1999); the Department of Religious Studies at the University of Vermont, Burlington (March 1999); the eastern international region of the American Academy of Religion, which invited me to present its 1999 plenary address (with special thanks to Bill Cassidy, Susan Henking, and, for his kind introduction, Tom Peterson); the School of Religion at the University of Iowa (October 1999; with thanks to Rob Stephens, an alumnus of SMSU, for arranging my visit); the faculty of theology at Georgetown University (November 1999; with thanks to Fran Cho for inviting me); and Truman State University (March 2000; with special thanks to Mike Ashcraft for inviting me to another school in the "show me" state).

Finally, my love and gratitude go to my wife, Marcia, and my thanks go to her good friends and colleagues—Karen, Terri, Susan, Wendy, and Kelly (in Indianapolis), Lisa and Eileen (in Springfield), and Vicki and Vivian (in Toronto). Most of these chapters were written while Marcia and I lived apart, pursuing our separate careers, far from our "home and native land." This is a situation required of a number of working couples, making our story all too ordinary. However, it makes relationships with good friends extraordinarily important. Our story has turned out well, so I will not dare to complain (too much). But I would be a fool not to realize that it has turned out well precisely because of Marcia's optimism, patience, sacrifices, energy, and great love of life.

COPYRIGHT
PERMISSIONS

For granting permission to print the revised versions of the following essays, I would like to acknowledge and thank these periodicals, books, editors, and/or publishers:

"A Default of Critical Intelligence? The Scholar of Religion as Public Intellectual," *Journal of the American Academy of Religion* 65/2 (1997): 443–468.

"The Economics of Spiritual Luxury: The Glittering Lobby and the 1993 Parliament of Religions," *Journal of Contemporary Religion* 13/1 (1997): 51–64.

"The History of God: 'Just the Same Game Wherever You Go'," as published in *Queen's Quarterly* Vol. 104, No. 4 (1997): 617–633.

"Methods and Theories in the Classroom: Teaching the Study of Myths and Rituals," *Journal of the American Academy of Religion* 66/1 (1998): 147–164.

"'My Theory of the Brontosaurus . . .': Postmodernism and 'Theory' of Religion," *Studies in Religion* 26 (1997): 3–23.

"Redescribing 'Religion and . . .' Film: Teaching the Insider/Outsider Problem," *Teaching Theology and Religious Studies* 1/2 (1998): 99–110.

"Redescribing 'Religion' as Social Formation: Toward a Social Theory of Religion." In Thomas A. Idinopulos and Brian C. Wilson (eds.), *What Is Religion? Origins, Definitions, and Explanations*, 51–71. Leiden: E. J. Brill, 1998.

"Talking Past Each Other—Public Intellectuals Revisited: Rejoinder to Paul J. Griffiths and June O'Connor," *Journal of the American Academy of Religion* 66/4 (1998): 911–917.

"Taming Ethnocentrism and Trans-cultural Understandings," *Method & Theory in the Study of Religion* 12/1&2 (2000): 294–306.

[M]ainstream American culture is too daunting an enemy to fight. . . . [It] comes at you in waves, so even if you do manage to fend off "Gilligan's Island," "Ironside," and Loggins & Massina, you'll still have to reckon with "The Partridge Family," "The Brady Bunch," and Seals & Crofts. To paraphrase the old "pony soldiers multiply like blades of grass" chestnut, for every Tony Orlando that you polish off, ten Tony Danzas will spring up in his place.

—Joe Queenan, *Red Lobster,*
White Trash, and the Blue Lagoon

PART I

Redescribing Religion
as Something Ordinary

Religion as mythmaking reflects thoughtful, though ordinary, modes of ingenuity and labor. . . . [B]oth religion and the study of religion are concerned with the human quest for intelligibility, with taking interest in the world and making social sense.

—Ron Cameron (1996: 39)

CHAPTER 1

More Than a Shapeless Beast: Lumbering through the Academy with the Study of Religion

"Isn't religion people's attempt to connect with what's out there— or in here?" My right hand swept . . . toward the marbled ceiling where God possibly lived, then fell to rest on my heart. "No!" thundered Cameron. . . . "Religion is a social way of thinking about social identity and social relationships."[1]

—Allen (1996)

So went an exchange between Charlotte Allen and Ron Cameron, a scholar of Christian origins, that opens Allen's *Lingua Franca* cover article on the conflict between two approaches to the study of religion.[2] This seemingly inconsequential exchange with Cameron soon found Allen on the edge of what she describes as a "fault line of an academic debate"; it is a line drawn between, on the one hand, attempts to understand religion to be essentially about finding meaning, either "out there or in here"—a pursuit Allen associates with the largest North American professional society for scholars of religion and theologians, the American Academy of Religion (AAR)—and, on the other hand, efforts to explain this very effort to construct meaning as a product of human biology, psyches, history, or society—work typified, in Allen's estimation, by the much smaller and younger North American Association for the Study of Religion (NAASR). In Allen's words, the fault line is drawn between NAASR's "tiny David" and the "AAR's Goliath."

Finding the study of religion to be the feature article in a national periodical is well worth celebrating—given the economic constraints facing many North American universities in general, and their religious studies programs in particular—a little PR is never a bad thing. However, as accurate as it may be for Allen to describe the study of religion as "a shapeless beast, half social science, half humanistic discipline, lumbering through the academy with no clear methodology or *raison d'être*," in my opinion it is hardly a compliment. Because those who carry out their scholarship within religious studies departments have, for some time, experienced this frustrating ambiguity, and because our colleagues in the university often misunderstand the contributions to be made by the academic study of religion, I think it will benefit us to revisit the old question of this field's identity and try to clarify the issue by redescribing the academic study of religion.

RELIGION AS A PRIVATE AFFAIR

The dominant position in the field today is based on a tradition that goes back at least to the late-eighteenth-century German romantic Friedrich Schleiermacher; responding to the Enlightenment's commitment to rationality and objectivity and its conclusion that religion was little more than an instance of primitive superstition that somehow had survived into the modern era, Schleiermacher defended religion against its so-called cultured despisers by re-conceiving of it as a nonquantifiable individual experience, a deep feeling, or an immediate consciousness. (See Fiorenza [2000] for a theologian's reassessment of Schleiermacher's influence on current debates on "religion.")

Although the leading, contemporary representatives of this tradition agree with Schleiermacher in placing religion within personal consciousness and emotion, they refer to the object of this consciousness differently; for Paul Tillich, it took the form of a personal value judgment (as he phrased it, one's "ultimate concern"), for Rudolf Otto and Mircea Eliade, it was an unexplainable and irreducible element of human consciousness (the object of which was variously named the "holy" or the "sacred"), and for Wilfred Cantwell Smith, it was the capacity of persons to have what he referred to as "faith in transcendence"—a phrase very much at home with such seemingly nontheological, liberal humanistic notions as the triumph of the human spirit. Regardless what its object is called, the conception of religion as an inherently meaningful, nonempirical, uniquely personal experience that transcends historical difference and evades rational explanation is generally shared across a surprisingly large segment of the field today.[3] Moreover, it is a folk conception that is shared by many of our colleagues within the university, along with many of the people that we as scholars of religion study. To argue for a different conception of religion, one that enables us to name something public and observable, is certainly to swim against the prevailing currents.

The main problem with using this folk conception of religion as an analytic, scholarly tool is that it takes what is all too public and social and tries to secure and protect it within the private and inscrutable realm of subjectivity and pure consciousness. Because we as scholars cannot actually get our hands on these primary dispositions and aesthetic feelings—or so the standard argument goes—we are left simply with describing and empathizing with their secondary manifestations, expressions, and historical artifacts—hence our field has a host of descriptive handbooks on cross-cultural religious symbolism. Their logic: the diverse symbols characteristic of religion worldwide all point to a common inner experience shared by humans *qua Homo religiosi.* The premise that guides such scholarship is that, while religion is an independent variable and a cause of other events, it can never be considered simply to be an all too ordinary effect of events in the historical, social world.[4] In other words, from the outset what I call the "private affair" tradition presupposes that religion cannot be *explained* as a result of various cultural or historical factors and processes; instead, it is argued that the deeper meaning of religion can only be deciphered and understood to make manifest in culture certain essentially religious or transcendent values and feelings. Religions therefore manifest religious feelings. Despite the troublesome circularity of this sort of unilluminating reasoning, such a position continues to dominate popular *and* scholarly imaginations alike.

Martin E. Marty, perhaps the best known scholar of religion in the United States, provides a current example of this perspective in his *Academe* defense for teaching and researching on religion in the university (Marty 1996).[5] Despite the fact that he at first appears to critique those who ignore what he terms religion's "public side" and, instead, see it simply as a "private affair," Marty continually refers to such things as "religious impulses," "religious sensibilities," "faith," and "piety"—terms all firmly placed within the "private affair" tradition inherited from Schleiermacher. Because such presumed sensibilities and impulses are nonempirical scholars of religion are left with studying what Marty refers to as their "expressions" (a term that significantly implies that the impulses originate from some sort of intentional source) and "artifacts" (a term that equally significantly implies that the source is alive and not to be confused with the inert evidence that remains after its departure from the scene). What we see here is none other than the common presumption that religion, or the sacred, is itself somehow pure, internal, intentional, creative, socially autonomous, and efficacious and can therefore only be studied through its various secondary, symbolic manifestations. In a word, religious feelings can be considered to be a cause, but never simply an effect. This is the undefended assumption that commonly grounds the widely used phenomenological method, a method uniquely suited, or so some would argue, for describing, comparing, and thereby determining the common essence that underlies historically and culturally varied beliefs, behaviors, and institutions (in a word, its many manifestations).

Marty goes so far as to suggest repeatedly that such "things" as religious impulses and sensibilities deserve study in their own right as causal agents. Instead of seeing the rhetoric of unseen impulses as a potent rationalization used to privilege what are in fact historically motivated actions, on a number of occasions Marty discusses how religious impulses motivate people to do activities as diverse as killing or healing. Writing in the same issue of *Academe*, the onetime editor of the *Journal of the American Academy of Religion*, William Scott Green, adopts the Weberian stance to assert that "religion [or 'religious convictions,' as he also calls them] has been and yet remains a tremendously potent force in American social, political, and economic life" (1996: 28).[6] For both Marty and Green, as for many scholars of religion, religious feelings are used to explain other aspects of human behavior, but religious feelings can themselves never be explained as the result of other aspects of human behavior.

What is   THE NATURALISTIC TRADITION ?

Over against this position there are a number of scholars of religion currently working in public universities who are not content with simply studying religion in terms of supposedly self-evident impulses and private sensibilities. Instead, they take these very claims of self-evidency and privacy as deserving of study; they maintain that the privilege that results from this rhetoric of religious impulses and private experiences needs to be studied as the product rather than the cause of other human beliefs, behaviors, and institutions.

For example, while it may be accurate to *describe* liberal religious participants such as Marty as reporting that religious systems are based on special, authoritative, and private experiences, accurately *repeating* on such circular, self-authorized reasoning hardly exhausts all forms of scholarship on religion. When we read, for instance, one scholar—Charles Long—writing that religious experiences constitute "a mode of release from the entanglements of the social and the existential" (1986: 35), we must never fail to understand such *purely descriptive scholarship* as always incomplete until it *redescribes and historicizes* (in a word, *theorizes*) such claims of sociohistorical autonomy and privilege. *After all, the premise that makes the human sciences possible in the first place is that human behaviors always originate from within, and derive their culturally embedded meanings from being constrained by, historical (i.e., social, political, economic, bio-*

logical, etc.) entanglements. Despite what the people we study may
assert, as scholars of religion we always begin from the premise that
there can be no release from the historical. As our first step toward
redescribing the study of religion, then, we would be well advised to
put into practice the advice of the literary critic Frederic Jameson—
"always historicize."

To begin such historicization, we need to start pretty close to
home by identifying the very real interests that are served by the private affair tradition's most basic tool, the category of "religious experience" itself.[7] As the scholar of Buddhism Robert Sharf has recently
phrased it in a wonderful article on the term *experience,* "[*religious
experience*] is often used rhetorically to thwart the authority of the
'objective' or the 'empirical,' and to valorize instead the subjective,
the personal, the private" (1998: 94).[8] The philosophically idealist
rhetoric of 'experience' presumes that pristine, prereflective moments
of pure self-consciousness (or, along with Schleiermacher, we could
call it "God-consciousness") somehow float freely in the background
of the restrictive conventions of language and social custom, what
Jonathan Z. Smith, quoting Nietzsche, has called the "myth of
immaculate perception"; it is a position comparable to that which
once fueled literary studies, insomuch as Literature was thought by
some to embody essentially transcendent themes and values. In the
study of religion, Smith has traced this romantic rhetoric of experience to what he terms "the regnant Protestant *topoi* in which the category of inspiration has been transposed from the text to the experience of the interpreter, the one who is being directly addressed
through the text." Smith concludes, "As employed by some scholars
in religious studies, it must be judged a fantastic attempt to transform
interpretation into revelation" (1990b: 55).

As both Sharf's and Smith's critiques should make clear, the rhetoric
of experience has come under hard times; simply put, some now understand experience as a thoroughly sociopolitical construct. I think here of
the historian Joan Wallach Scott, who has directly addressed this very
issue in a powerful essay, "The Evidence of Experience." In her conclusion she writes:

> Experience is at once always already an interpretation *and* something
> that needs to be interpreted. What counts as experience is neither self-
> evident or straightforward; it is always contested, and always therefore
> political. The study of experience, therefore, must call into question its
> originary status in historical explanation. This will happen when his-
> torians take as their project *not* the reproduction and transmission of
> knowledge said to be arrived at through experience, but the analysis of
> the production of that knowledge itself. (Scott 1991: 797)

Fitzgerald agrees: experiences are always public, he suggests, for "the semantic context for having and interpreting an experience is necessarily also a social, institutional context" (2000: 129). Or, as Sharf phrases it,

> the rhetoric of experience tacitly posits a place where signification comes to an end, variously styled "mind," "consciousness," the "mirror of nature," or what have you. The category experience is, in essence, a mere placeholder that entails a substantive if indeterminate terminus for the relentless deferral of meaning. And this is precisely what makes the term experience so amenable to ideological appropriation. (1998: 113)

Scholarship in public universities entails pushing beyond mere description of subjective self-disclosures and reports on this or that experience, as if these experiences somehow predate the sociohistorical world; scholarship requires one to generate theories of human minds and societies, to engage in cross-cultural comparison of the human doings that our theories help us to see as significant, to contextualize our subjects' reports on their doings within the larger settings that make both the doings and their reports possible and meaningful in the first place, and then to explain *why* just these similarities or just those differences exist between various human communities, their doings, and their self-perceptions.

As I use the term, this is the work of the scholar of religion as public intellectual, an admittedly trendy term that can be used in countless and contradictory ways; as noted in a recent *Lingua Franca* article, "any term that embraces both [the semiotician] Umberto Eco and [the conservative U.S. political pundit] Arianna Huffington can safely be said to have a problem" (Scocca 1999: 8). Putting together the comments of Wallach Scott and Sharf, we can say that the work of the public intellectual entails the task of identifying the sociorhetorical mechanisms that authorize, normalize, and homogenize what are in fact divergent and highly contestable 'experiences' of the world in which we live. This is what I mean by a public intellectual. It doesn't necessarily mean publishing in *The New York Review of Books*, being a regular panelist on Bill Maher's "Politically Incorrect," or acting as a consultant for government. As I will argue in chapters 8 and 9, the scholar of religion as public intellectual holds no philosopher's stone that will turn lead into gold and, in the process, solve the world's problems; for those who think there *is* some sort of easy solution, that the world is basically a simple place, and that a hermeneutic key will someday be found to unlock the meaning of life, this sense of a public intellectual is surely far too limited and therefore downright unsatisfying. I, however, happen to agree with

Edward Said when, recently commenting on the CNN coverage of King Hussein's funeral, he flatly stated that "reality is a confusing, complex dynamic of events, processes, [and] personalities" (1999). Presuming just such a complexity, my public intellectual comes not to inform the world as to *how it ought* to work but studies the manner in which *how it happens to work* is actively portrayed as *the only way it can work.* Appeals to the rhetoric of experience are perhaps the most effective means human communities have so far developed for enabling slippage between *is* and *ought*, between *complexity* and *simplicity*, between the *local* and the *universal*, and, as the French critic Roland Barthes once phrased it, between *History* and *Nature.*

For the public intellectual, then, experience is sociopolitical and never pure; as scholars working in the human sciences, we should never fail to see it as the interpretive and therefore always contestable by-product of a stratified, diverse community, a by-product always in need of contextualization when studied. This is an important point, I think: it is not so much that the expression of an experience is sadly constrained by the limits of the languages that we have no choice but to employ in its expression (a point associated with romanticism and phenomenological analysis alike); rather, the 'it' of personal experience is likely possible only in light of preexistent linguistic, social, and other structural conventions and constraints. Although it may sound counterintuitive, *experiences are always public*; as Wallach Scott concludes, in this approach, experience is not the origin of our explanation, "but that which we want to explain." Experience is the localized depository of complex and often virtually transparent messages communicated through, and made possible by, social life; the rock singer John Mellencamp knew as much when, in his 1985 hit "Small Town," he sang that he was not only "educated in a small town," but he was "taught to fear Jesus in a small town."

This is *precisely* the point that many scholars of religion miss altogether: believing religion somehow to provide privileged access to some posited transcendent realm of meaning, they search for their hermeneutic philosopher's stone and fail to understand feelings such as fear or awe as 'taught' and therefore products of social life. Ironically, I am reminded of the founding narrative of Gautama: scholars of religion often expend wasted effort, an expenditure that sustains the illusion of social autonomy and fuels the myth of the immaculate perception. For scholars of the private affair tradition to claim religious experiences and emotions as the pristine source or cause of religious behaviors is therefore to fall considerably short of the requirements of scholarship in a public university. Instead of seeing religion as an undefinable experience that mysteriously manifests itself first here and then there, we could instead understand the discourse on experience as an all too human construction that accomplishes specific rhetorical work in specific social groups.

It should be clear that the implications of these two views on 'experience' cut to the very heart of how we study religion in a public university, how we distinguish the academic study of religion from theological studies, and how we organize departments for the academic study of religion. Whereas scholars once relied on a conception of religion as *sui generis* (i.e., self-caused) to form the basis of institutionally autonomous religion departments (their argument: an autonomous datum requires an autonomous site for its study), some scholars now question what sense it makes to argue that any aspect of human behavior could be unique, distinct, or in any way free from the unending tug-and-pull of historical change, social influence, and even genetic determination. Moreover, many now understand that the very efforts to privilege and protect any object of study, let alone the community of scholars that studies it, come with generally undetected social and political baggage.

"RELIGION" REDESCRIBING A FOLK CATEGORY

As part of our redescription of the study of religion, we must acknowledge that not just 'experience' but also 'religion' is a slippery signifier, *not* because, as Cantwell Smith once suggested, it is the limited, inevitably reified and insufficient manner in which outsiders signify a prior, undescribable, and interior faith (1991), but *because many of the peoples that we study by means of this category have no equivalent term or concept whatsoever.* "Religion" is an emic folk category scholars acquire from a rather limited number of linguistic/cultural families, a category that we simply take up for the sake of etic analysis and use *as if it were* a cross-cultural universal.[9] So, right off the bat, we must recognize that, in using this Latin-derived term as a technical, comparative category, even the most ardently sympathetic religious pluralist is, from the outset, deeply embedded in the act of intellectual, if not cultural, imperialism or theoretical reduction. (Although we disagree on most matters, see Griffiths [2000] for a useful survey of the Latin origins of "religion.")

While I do not mean to invoke some extreme notion of political correctness or cultural relativism by suggesting that scholarship in the human sciences must be driven by indigenous folk categories—if it were, it would mean the end of the human sciences as we now know them!—this does raise a crucial methodological point: *all scholarship, whether it is simply a well-intentioned and even sympathetic descriptive restate-*

*ment or a rigorous, explanatory analysis of indigenous systems of clas-
sification and collective representations, is by definition a reduction or a
translation.*[10] With this in mind, those who rely on caricatures of reductionism as the basis for their protests against social scientific analysis of
religious discourses will need to reconsider seriously their conception of
how their own scholarship actually proceeds.[11] Despite the best intentions of self-reflexive ethnographers, human subjects under study generally do not "speak for themselves"—instead, they simply go about living their lives, with little or no interest in either self-consciously
reflecting on the meanings, motivations, and implications for living just
that life, in just that social world, or re-presenting these systematic
reflections for the benefit of a cross-cultural collection of nonpartici-
pants in that life. It should come as no surprise, then, that many now
agree that all ethnographies are products of outside queries that are
mediated through vocabularies and media foreign to the lives of the participants under study. If this were not the case, we would not have
reports on the 'religions' of people living outside the Latin-based language family.

Moreover, even within societies whose members *do* employ the category of religion when generating folk classifications that they use to
distinguish, arrange, and value various aspects of their daily social lives,
its popular usage is intimately linked to a people's own self-descriptions
and self-identity (e.g., "I'm saved; are you?"), therefore suggesting that
the term is deeply embedded within conflicting systems of social classification and value. It is therefore questionable to what extent 'religion'
can be of use to scholars who wish not simply to reproduce these systems of classification and value but, instead, who aim to explain the
findings that result from their cross-cultural study of observable human
social practices and institutions.[12]

With the slippery nature of our categories in mind, a second
methodological point emerges: *scholars must be careful to distinguish,
on the one hand, between reporting on folk descriptions, accounts, and
classifications concerning how the world operates and, on the other,
developing their own theoretically grounded redescriptions of these very
same folk accounts and taxonomies.* An important, though somewhat
ironic, point is apparent here: scholars of religion do not actually study
religion, the gods, or ultimate concerns; rather, they use a folk rubric,
'religion,' as a theoretically grounded, taxonomic marker to isolate or
demarcate a portion of the complex, observable behavior of biologically,
socially, and historically situated human beings and human communities
that talk, act, and organize themselves in ways that the scholar finds
curious and in need of analysis. Accordingly, and I think this is also
worthwhile to note, *what counts as religion for one theorist is hardly*

religion for another—not, as some of our colleagues might say, because one definition has a better grasp of the *real* nature of the object of study, making one definition a better "fit" with reality, but because each observer arrives on the scene with different interests, different questions, and different anticipations—all of which come home to roost in their classification tool "religion." To count as scholarship, these interests and anticipations must be organized into a coherent theory that can be applied and debated publicly. Acknowledging that the world does not come already classified and prepackaged in little styrofoam containers, ready for our experiential consumption, means we must decline to advance the couch potato model of scholarship whereby scholars sit back and empathetically chronicle 'that which presents itself' (á la phenomenology). Instead, it is our responsibility as scholars constantly to propose, explicate, analyze, and critique our schemes and our theories, for it is around these—rather than the supposed self-evidency of our data—that all academic pursuits are developed and organized.

With a tip of my hat to the stories told about Socrates' wisdom being rooted in the recognition of his ignorance, I can say that in owning up to the fact that we do not have *a priori* knowledge as to what religion 'really is' or where to find it, we are far wiser than many of our predecessors; unlike many of them, we acknowledge that pretheoretical values and social institutions are the contexts in which we propose, test, and defend theories, that theories make the generic stuff of unreflective human experience stand out as data, and that the data of religion is therefore of our own making.[13]

In a word, we manufacture zones of significance and value in the so-called real world by means of our label *religion*; moreover, depending on the definition and theory of religion we employ, we often manufacture goods of questionable value. It is little wonder, then, that our field continually suffers from a lack of identity and is so often misunderstood by our colleagues in the university: we lack agreement concerning the general theoretical parameters that enable us to make claims about this thing religion in the first place; and, more daunting than anything else, we attempt to engage in a theoretically precise analysis of human social life from within the very social worlds we seek to understand. These are important points, I think; at the root of the problem of definition is the fact that many in the field avoid the requirements of explicit theory building, testing, and public critique, and instead opt for simply repeating folk understandings by means of nuanced description and reporting. However, as I have already suggested, this latter sort of scholarship—if indeed it constitutes scholarship as opposed to mere color commentary—forgoes critical analysis and thereby fails to ask what Smith has simply referred to as the "So what?" question (1990a: 10).

THE IMPOSSIBILITY OF AN ACADEMIC STUDY
OF UNDEFINABLE ESSENCES

Because few descriptivist scholars actually formulate an explicit theory of religion that allows them to justify why a particular practice or symbol attracts their attention, let alone an explicit definition to direct their research, more often than not the category of religion as used in scholarly studies has little theoretical currency whatsoever. Instead, as already suggested, many scholars of religion and theologians alike take religion to be a self-evident human impulse in no need of definition, let alone explanation. Based on this assumption, they proceed inductively, as if observation of self-evidences followed by generalization is sufficient. There may be no better example of what I understand as an antitheoretical stand than the comments of the current executive director of the AAR, as cited in a *New York Times* article that ran on the opening day of the AAR's 1996 annual meeting in New Orleans: "Dr. DeConcini, for one, objected that trying to forge a definition of religion would threaten to exclude teachers whose specialties run outside the conventional bounds" (Niebuhr 1996: 13). Such an argument against definition (which is, after all, implicitly an argument against theory; definitions are simply theories in miniature) is puzzling, for without a commonly accepted definition of religion—some way of demarcating this category and the social domain to which it refers from others—how is it that we can even determine these so-called conventional bounds, let alone how could one even fall outside them? Without a definition that can be rationally articulated, applied, critiqued, and defended, how do any of us know precisely what our colleagues are talking about when they make claims about this thing 'religion'? Without a definition of religion, what, precisely, do members of our field study? Moreover, without an agreed upon manner in which we can not only propose but publicly test and critique definitions, how will we know when any sort of progress has taken place in the field? And finally, how can one have a scholarly field when the leadership of the main professional organization seems to place sanctions on defining and thereby coming clean as to just what we are studying when we study religion.

Despite such clear dangers, a surprising number of people in the field hold such a view on the evils of definition and theory; they yet maintain that religion is an undefinable mystery that can only be experienced and appreciated. However, they fail to consider the logical and institutional outcome of this ill-considered position; according to the anthropologist Weston La Barre, if religion is conceived as a personalistic mystery, then it defies all attempts not only to analyze it but even to describe it; moreover, the academic study of religion ceases to exist as a scholarly pursuit. In La Barre's words:

> If God is unknown, then theology [as well as the study of undefinable religion] is a science without subject matter, and the theologian [as well as the scholar of *sui generis* religion] is one who does not know what he is talking about. [However,] if he has only forgotten what he was talking about—the premises lurking hidden in his unconscious connotations and denotations—then these must be made explicit if we are to discuss them meaningfully. We can proceed only if we have more verifiable meanings attached to our terms. (1972: 2)

Without explicit and public definitions of religion, without explicitly formulated, publicly criticizable theories of religion (as opposed to private intuitions, feelings, guesses, or hunches), all we are left with is the lumbering, directionless academic study of undefinable essences where scholars are united only in their presumably unified yet unarticulated intuitions. Failing to confront such issues, we continue to construct departments on a long-outmoded seminary model, as if the very people we study (the religious) somehow had privileged access concerning how their self-reports ought to be studied and understood.

CONCLUSION: MORE THAN A SHAPELESS BEAST

If one takes religion, religious impulses, sensibilities, and private convictions at face value and as self-evident, extraordinary causes of other human phenomena, one conveniently avoids ever confronting that religion may well turn out to be among the more enduring and powerful means humans have developed for legitimizing, contesting, and monitoring social cohesion and identity. After all, do not many people trace our term *religion* to Latin roots meaning either careful observation or the act of binding together? Avoiding this one possible redescription of religion by placing religion firmly within the private confines of individual experience, where religion is conceived as an essentially good or pure impulse, efficiently serves to protect an aspect of the social world from the types of study by which scholars in other fields routinely redescribe human constructs, behaviors, and institutions. It assumes religion somehow to be extraordinary, deriving from or expressing some unseen inner or outer world, and thereby avoids risking that religion—like all other aspects of human social life—may well turn out to be all too ordinary. As Cameron states in this section's epigraph, "Religion as mythmaking reflects thoughtful, though ordinary, modes of ingenuity and labor. . . . [B]oth religion and the study of religion are concerned with the human quest for intelligibility, with taking interest in the world and making social sense" (1996: 39). I would argue that it is only when we start out with the presumption that religious behaviors are ordinary social behaviors—and not extraordinary private experiences—that we will come to understand them in all their subtle yet impressive complexity. With this recommendation in mind, please be clear on one thing: understanding religion as ordinary hardly means our work will be any easier. As the French sociologist Pierre Bourdieu so nicely observes, "[t]here is nothing more difficult to convey than reality in all its ordinariness" (1998: 21).

If we redescribe so-called religious beliefs, practices, and institutions as thriving yet all too public and ordinary sites where people manufacture, authorize, and contest ever-changing social identities, then the study of religion finds itself at the very core of the modern university's Humanities' mission. As Gary Lease said in his 1998 University of California Santa Cruz humanities lecture,

> [In the humanities we find] the opportunity to conduct an intensive conversation with the traditions, present and past, that help make us who we are, and above all who we will be. . . . This linkage of past, present, and future; . . . this ability to communicate effectively with others both inside and outside of your culture . . . ; this pursuit of knowledge about yourself and others: These make up the core of humanities. (1998: 92)

Although some programs in the study of religion are housed within the social sciences, the vast majority of programs generally contribute to the work of the humanities. As some understand them, the humanities document and celebrate the beauty inherent in 'the human condition' and the resiliency of 'the human spirit', goals rightly associated with the liberal, private affair tradition in the study of religion. But, as identified by Lease, the key topic addressed across the humanities is the relationship between those three things members of a social formation narrativize as their collective 'past,' 'present,' and 'future'; to put it another way, we can simply talk about all three by means of the abstract notion of a 'tradition'. Despite the fact that religious studies programs sometimes struggle to maintain only a marginal status in their colleges, studying the mechanisms that enable traditions to be invented, authorized, reinvented, and contested *are the very topics that scholars of religion know something about* (for a good example, see Braun 1999a). If we can agree on anything, it would have to be the fact that humanists study the manner in which social groups recreate themselves by focusing their collective attention in the here and now. Scholars of religion in particular study the way groups manipulate such focusing devises as discourses on origins, endtimes, and nonobvious beings. Or, to put it another way, myths and rituals are mechanisms whereby groups exercise and manage what Smith terms an "economy of signification." As scholars, we therefore examine the many narrative, behavioral, and institutional devices groups employ to represent and contest differing conceptions of themselves—and to allocate access to resources based on those conceptions.

In setting out to redescribe religion in this way—as but one set of ordinary strategies for accomplishing the always completed yet never ending work of social formation—we will be able to communicate with other scholars about an observable and enduring aspect of human behavior rather than isolating ourselves within a seemingly privileged yet marginalized discourse concerned with studying nonempirical experiences. It means that as scholars and teachers we have little choice but to go public and leave the private realm of privileged experience to the rhetoricians and theologians who can afford their idle lumbering. Moreover, redescribing religion necessarily entails redescribing the field that studies 'it': religious studies. Therefore, the two questions that Allen poses in the opening to her *Lingua Franca* essay turn out to be *the* central issues facing this field today: "What is religion, anyway, at least as a subject of study at the American university? And does it have anything to do with God?"[14] To these questions we can now offer two very different answers. On the one hand, the study of religion is the generally liberal pursuit of universal and yet deeply personal feeling gained largely through paraphrasing texts, claims, and behaviors inspired by, or which somehow are said to manifest, essential meanings and values, all of which is derived from experiences of God, the gods, the sacred, the wholly other, the numinous, or the *mysterium*. On the other hand, the study of religion is but one instance of the wider, cross-disciplinary study of how human beliefs, behaviors, and institutions construct and contest enduring social identity—talk about gods and talk about mythic origins are but two strategies for doing this. Although the former employs such methods as phenomenology and hermeneutics to study normally unattainable deep essences by means of surface descriptions, the latter employs social scientific tools to study how human communities construct and authorize their essentialist myths (by they grouped together and named as nationalist, ethnic, or even religious).

Despite the fact that these two approaches appear to be competing, lined up, as they are, on either side of what Allen characterizes as a fault line, the former turns out to be but one piece of data to be studied by means of the methods and theories of the latter. Or, as Don Wiebe is quoted in the same *Lingua Franca* article, the former constitutes the *religious* study of religion—itself a religious pursuit—whereas the latter constitutes the *academic* study of religion. Or, as aptly phrased by J. Z. Smith on a panel at a recent AAR annual meeting, theologians are quite simply the data for scholars of religion (Smith 1997).

That the religious study of religion should be the datum for academic scholars working in publicly funded universities is slowly dawning on more members of the field who are no longer content to study mysteries, essences, and private experiences. Redescribing what we mean by 'religion' therefore means redescribing how we carry out scholarship and teaching in a public context where we are accountable to widely operating scholarly standards of evidence, argumentation, and refutation—"the rules of the game," to borrow the words of DeConcini, who was also interviewed for the *Lingua Franca* essay. However, because she immediately goes on to maintain that there is "no gap between theology and [such academic] research," it seems that she has confused two very different discursive games with significantly different sets of institutional standards and evidential rules.

This confusion even makes its way into Allen's *Lingua Franca* essay, when, near its close, she suggests that it "may be a good thing for religious studies to be a shapeless beast, half social science, half humanistic discipline, lumbering through the academy with no clear methodology or *raison d'être*." It is a good thing only if we presume that religion is essentially a multifaceted mystery that gets shortchanged when understood exclusively as a human doing. Contrary to Allen, and given the dominance of the liberal humanistic and theological approaches, the *raison d'être* of this lumbering beast is more than clear, and, to my way of thinking, it is far from good: it takes religion at face value simply as a self-evidently meaningful, apolitical, unique phenomenon that causes other things to happen but is itself uncaused since it is an indescribable impulse and personal conviction; it is, accordingly, a phenomenon in need of nuanced description and sympathetic appreciation *but not* explanatory analysis and redescription. As I read it, this is what theologians are in the business of doing; they need no help from us. An apology for the study of religion in the modern university that presumes scholars of religion to be empathetic caretakers and naive, well-meaning hermeneuts is doomed from the outset, for it fundamentally confuses a distinction that lies at the base of all human sciences, between theoretically based scholarship on assorted aspects of human behavior and those very behaviors themselves.

NOTES

1. This is a paraphrase of Burton Mack's own words: "[F]or [J. Z.] Smith, what has come to be called religion is actually a social mode of thinking about social identity and activity" (Mack 1988: 20 n. 9). My thanks to Ron Cameron for pointing this out to me.

2. For other views on the *Lingua Franca* article, see the *Bulletin of the Council of Societies for the Study of Religion* 26/4 (1997) for Tim Murphy's introductory essay (1997) and the nine invited replies (representing the opinions of scholars of religion from the United States, Canada, the United Kingdom, and South Africa); see also Allen's rejoinder (1998).

3. See McCutcheon 1997c for a study of the diverse sites where this understanding is evident, from the debate on the politics of Eliade to world religion textbooks. See the work of Tim Fitzgerald (1997, 1999) for a confirmation of my findings.

4. Such a presumption even underlies many of the articles published by social scientists in the *Journal for the Scientific Study of Religion*. For a critique of such studies that presume religion to be an independent variable, see Krymkowski and Martin 1998.

5. *Academe* is the publication of the American Association of University Professors (AAUP); the issue in which Marty's article appeared was devoted to the study and practice of religion in public universities.

6. This article is a revised version of an essay Green originally published in a special issue of *JAAR* (62/4 [1994]), an issue that surveyed the state of the study of religion. For articles in that issue that take a rather different approach to the field, one that faults its members for their lack of theoretical sophistication, see Gill (1994) and Penner (1994).

7. I have attempted just this in a forthcoming essay on the history of the study of religion in the United States, entitled, "Autonomy, Unity, and Crisis: Rhetoric and the Invention of the Discourse on *Sui Generis* Religion."

8. Within the study of religion, I know of few essays better than Sharf's when it comes to problematizing what he aptly terms the "ideological nature of the rhetoric of experience." See also Fitzgerald (2000).

9. On the use of the emic/etic distinction in the study of religion, including a discussion of the terms' origin in linguistics and subsequent application in anthropology, see the introduction to chapter 1 in my own, *The Insider/Outsider Problem in the Study of Religion: A Reader* (1998b; see also Headland et al. 1990, Harris 1979, 1987, and Pike 1967). For an excellent example of how such a common ethnographic category as "marriage" is a descriptive or interpretive category and not an explanatory one, see the first chapter of Dan Sperber's *Explaining Culture* (1996: 18–21, 29–31).

10. As noted in the preface, it is crucial to distinguish a *metaphysical reduction* (one that claims to have identified the essence of the data, á la Marx, Freud, and even Eliade) from a *methodological reduction* (one that only claims to have reduced the data based on the frame of reference provided by the researcher's theory). As should be clear, within the human sciences, only the latter option makes any sense at all, for the former presupposes the possibility of a contextless theory of everything.

11. See Dan Sperber (1996: 152): "Any attempt to analyze social and cultural phenomena in a scientific manner, in particular any naturalistic attempt, is sure to meet with accusations of reductionism. Of course such accusations could be brushed aside. It is not hard to show that the label 'reductionist' is doubly misused: on the one hand, nobody is really proposing a reduction of social phe-

nomena; on the other, should such a proposition be made seriously, it would deserve interest rather than scorn, since true reductions are major scientific advances."

12. Despite the growing number of writers commenting on the limited value of "religion," let alone the sociopolitical loadings of the category (see also King 1999), Ivan Strenski (1998a, 1998b) has recently penned two essays arguing that writers such as Tim Fitzgerald, David Chidester, Gary Lease, and myself are naively overconfident concerning the influence comparativists' works wield in centers of "real" decision making. Although I escape much of his wrath, concerning my work in particular Strenski claims that it is part of an "inbred clique" whose work, in his estimation, is "alternatively an exercise in naivete, bad faith, or ignorant mischief, or indeed, all of the above" (1998a: 118). Given that Strenski's past writings suggest that he too is interested in explaining religion, it is utterly perplexing why he has attacked the above group—hardly a cabal or a clique—by resurrecting Schleiermacher's reactionary romantic rhetoric (i.e., labeling us as religion's "despisers"). However, as I argue in a later chapter, there is a very real threat to all modernist, liberal ideologies (whether they are politically liberal and naturalistic [as in Strenski's case] or romantic and conservative [in Schleiermacher's case]) when one radically historicizes the kind of claims to individual autonomy that come prepackaged in the rhetoric of experience and in presumptions of religion's autonomy. In formulating an answer to Strenski's critique, then, we can say that it is not a matter of overestimating the influence individual scholars of religion have in determining such things as a government's foreign policy; rather, it may have more to do with recognizing how the choices and interests of scholars are shaped by and conform to preexisting structures of power and privilege. Focusing, as Strenski does in much of his work, on individual action and accountability, rather than examining structural circumstances in which subjectivity and accountability are made possible, may allow us to continue to convince ourselves that the state-sponsored profession of defining, describing, sorting, and interpreting human behavior somehow floats free of its sociopolitical preconditions. After all, our object of study in such a neutered science reinforces a number of liberal assumptions concerning the autonomy of the individual, the importance of free choice, the evils of structure, and the universal nature of the Human Condition. In other words, as long as we play our assigned role as experts on disembodied, believing minds, symbols, and customs, there may be little need of governmental agencies in liberal democracies to pay attention to our work. (See Chidester and Lease's responses to Strenski in *JAAR* 66/2 [1998]; wisely, Fitzgerald seems not to have bothered to reply to Strenski's *ad hominem* attack on his work in particular.)

13. Observing that religion is the product of the scholarly imagination is, of course, a point I borrow directly from Jonathan Z. Smith. On Smith's use of theory in directing research, see Sam Gill's detailed and helpful essay: "It is not that religion has some inherent nature or essence, it is that religion takes on this profile according to the way Smith chooses to construct the data he considers relevant to his theory of religion" (1998: 287 n. 7); "Again, it is important to note that Smith's understanding of myth is a product of his self-conscious choices of theory. It is not a claim about some essence or nature of myth. Also, it is impor-

tant to note that Smith's view of myth would, I think, be broadly and soundly rejected by most religious adherents" (295 n. 18).

14 In the same *New York Times* article cited above (Niebuhr 1996), the AAR's former executive director, Jim Wiggins, "suggested that religious studies faculties would benefit from trying to answer a central question: What is religion?"

CHAPTER 2

Redescribing 'Religion' as Social Formation: Toward a Social Theory of Religion

> A society can neither create nor recreate itself without creating some kind of ideal by the same stroke. This creation is not a sort of optional extra step by which society, being already made, merely adds finishing touches; it is the act by which society makes itself, and remakes itself, periodically. . . . A society is not constituted simply by the mass of individuals who comprise it, the ground they occupy, the things they use, or the movements they make, but above all by the idea it has of itself.
> —Emile Durkheim (1995 [1912]: 425)

As should by now be clear, I identify with a growing group of scholars who are open to scrutinizing the history of their categories, the theories that ground them, and the social contexts in which scholarship takes place—they have rediscovered the need to engage issues of definition and category formation. Such a change in attitude is important, for it signals that what a previous generation of scholars took for transparent self-evidencies are now recognized as tools developed over time, tools with a history that come with theoretical, even political, baggage, tools that are used to classify, sort, and analyze human behavior.

Once, the vast majority of scholars followed such influential writers as Max Weber, when, in a suitably inductivist vein, the first sentence of his influential *Sociology of Religion* (1922) states: "To define 'religion,' to say what it *is*, is not possible at the start of a presentation such as this. Definition can be attempted, if at all, only at the conclusion of the study" (1993: 1). Contrary to Weber, take Brian K. Smith's opening to his study of Vedic ritual, where, after noting Weber's view, he suggests just the opposite:

> To define is not to finish, but to start. To define is not to confine but to create something and . . . and eventually redefine. To define, finally, is not to destroy but to construct for the purpose of useful reflec-

tion. . . . In fact, we have definitions, hazy and inarticulate as they might be, for every object about which we know something. . . . Let us, then, define our concept of definition as a tentative classification of a phenomenon which allows us to begin an analysis of the phenomenon so defined" (1989: 4–5).

Unfortunately, not all of our colleagues agree, for a number of them continue to employ categories that have questionable analytic use. For instance, we still find courses and monographs on primitive religion, cult experts populate daytime TV and news telecasts whenever marginalized social movements get into the newspapers, and social movements that call themselves "world religions" are continually portrayed as socially autonomous (i.e., *sui generis*) systems of 'faith' and 'salvation'. What fuels the continued use of such terms is the general confusion of phenomenological *description* with social scientific *analysis*; for the descriptive value that most of our categories possess is largely the result of their being derived from, and fully inscribed within, the vocabularies and belief systems of the groups we study *rather than* the analytic vocabularies of scholarship. Sadly, the study of religion has yet to shake off its largely Protestant theological roots. Moreover, conflating these two domains of inquiry—or failing to see any role for analysis in the first place—is evidence of the theoretical bankruptcy of the modern study of religion, a bankruptcy that comes with a political price to be explored in subsequent chapters.

When seen as an end in itself, phenomenologically based description confuses data with colleagues—which is one reason why, in some of the later chapters, I find it so attractive to make this sort of confused scholarship my own datum. So-called scholarship on religion ought to be our subject of study when it fails to posit emic claims and behaviors as data, data that becomes meaningful to a scholarly discourse once it has been redescribed by means of theoretically driven etic categories (on the distinctions between description and explanation, see Carter 1998; McCutcheon 1998b). To appeal to Marvin Harris, writing nearly twenty years ago, "[r]ather than employ concepts that are necessarily real, meaningful, and appropriate from the native point of view, the observer is free to use alien categories and rules derived from the data language of science" (1979: 32). That this point is not widely accepted by scholars of religion is troubling indeed. So, right off the bat, let me say that future scholarship in our field needs to address two related issues: the problem of articulating explicit working definitions and the problem of theoretically based analysis of the data created by our acts of classification. In a word, future scholarship on religion must be redescriptive.

As noted earlier, I borrow the term *redescription* from Jonathan Z. Smith, in particular his essay "Sacred Persistence: Toward a Redescription of Canon" (1982: 36–52). Applied to the study of religion, redescription sums up the complicated work of scholarship, work that a former generation thought simply involved accurate or nuanced descriptions of what was simply given or that which presented itself. Redescriptive scholarship, as consistently demonstrated throughout Smith's body of work, avoids presuming a perfect fit between the concepts we use and the world we encounter through those concepts. As argued in his essay, "The Bare Facts of Ritual" (1982: 53–65), there is an incongruity not only between words and deeds of the groups we study, but also between human expectations of events and the events that actually transpire. In the words of Gay Becker (1997)—a medical anthropologist writing on personal responses to health issues—human life can be characterized as a series of disruptions against which we construct coherent plots and narratives of what is in fact an ever-changing past and an anticipated yet inevitably frustrated future. With such incongruity or disruptions in mind, redescriptive scholars are aware that, to quote Harris once again, the "road to etic knowledge . . . is full of pitfalls and impasses" (1979: 39).[1]

To engage in this sort of scholarship, we need to redescribe or, as Smith might say, rectify, a number of our key categories so that, as Harris suggested, their usefulness is based in the vocabularies of scholarship rather than the vocabularies of the communities we study. The first candidate is the term *religion* itself. Because many of our colleagues invest this term with an ontology of its own, they are able to gloss over the fact that most of the people they study by means of this category actually have no functional equivalent to the term whatsoever. By means of this gloss, they effectively avoid confronting the hazards of the insider/outsider problem, for they perpetrate the supreme, imperial act of reduction: they declare that, regardless of what those under study may think, everyone is religious in just this or that way. Precisely because some of our colleagues presume religion, or, more properly, religious experience, to be a universal human impulse of fundamental, deep, real, and therefore self-evident value, they lack the ability to see that their comments on, for example, Chinese religions or the religion of Islam are already highly abstract redescriptions of indigenous social systems and categories. Accordingly, the very ones yelling loudest about the need to "take religion seriously" have, so far, been the least serious in how they treat the most fundamental category in our scholarly lexicon.

Despite 'religion' possessing some descriptive value—for even to me it makes eminent sense, at least on an initial, descriptive level, to distinguish talk of the gods from talk of the family or talk of the nation state—we must confront the fact that the category "religion" has no explanatory value whatsoever. Taking religion to be a self-evident, eter-

nally existing phenomenon of deep importance, most of our colleagues
have failed to recognize just how intriguing the behaviors they call "religious" are; they fail to inquire as to just why it is that human beings
sometimes expend such great amounts of energy in activities that engage
invisible agents and immaterial states of existence. Accepting indigenous
systems of meaning at face value, they fail to inquire as to why—in our
own culture, at least—it is entirely sensible to out grow beliefs in some
nonempirical, immaterial beings (e.g., the Tooth Fairy, Easter Bunny,
Santa Claus, etc.), but not other *equally nonempirical, immaterial
beings* (God, for one, Satan for another). What on one level is a useful
descriptive marker that demarcates a species of beliefs and behaviors
turns out, on another, simply to highlight a collection of data in need of
explanation.

As is probably clear by now, I favor developing a social definition
and social theory of religion. Despite the promise of other equally interesting theoretical frameworks, it is on the level of constructing, legitimizing, and contesting power and privilege that I find so-called religious systems to be of most interest. Therefore, for me, on the
redescriptive level religion turns out to be but one subspecies of larger
sociohistorical, ideological systems (see Lease 2000). The challenge,
then, is to develop a coherent, theoretically based vocabulary capable of
placing religion firmly within the social world, with no leftover residue
that prompts supernaturalistic speculations. Although the category
"society," at least as it is often used, may deserve a place in what Willi
Braun has called the "museum of scholarly categories," unlike some of
its fellow exhibits, it can be effectively rehabilitated for future use in our
social theory religion. Instead of the naively monolithic connotations of
'society',[2] the category "social formation" provides us with a more useful tool for classifying and organizing for the sake of study those ways
in which human communities construct, maintain, and contest issues of
social identity, power, and privilege through what, for the sake of initial
description, we can term "religious discourses."

In this chapter, I would like to pull together a number of contemporary writers who are making significant contributions toward a social
theory of religion, thereby laying the theoretical foundation not only for
some of the critiques I offer in subsequent chapters but also for my closing suggestions on including discussions of theory in our classrooms. The
originality of this chapter is therefore limited to being among the first to
repeat (with appropriate citations of course) the good ideas of other people, but repeating them in proximity to other equally good ideas, hopefully working toward a coherent theory of religion as social formation.

Jonathan Smith anticipated the current use of 'social formation' in
his programmatic essay, "The Social Description of Early Christianity"

(1975). Smith identifies the need for a sociological model to help over-come the excessive focus on literary-historical and theological approaches in the study of Christian materials: "We have been seduced into a description of a *Sitz im Leben* that lacks a concrete (i.e., non-the-ological) 'seat' and offers only the most abstract understanding of 'life'" (1975: 19). He rightly castigates scholars for producing studies that "have been written in a theoretical vacuum in which outdated 'laws' are appealed to and applied" (1975: 19), studies that "have been clouded in the majority of cases by unquestioned apologetic presuppositions and naive theories (1975: 20).[3] Of the four possible directions Smith outlines for such a social description (or what we would now term a *redescrip-tion*), the third entails investigating "the *social organization* of early Christianity in terms of both the *social forces* which led to the rise of Christianity and the *social institutions* of early Christianity" (1975, 20).[4] Simply put, Smith recommends treating religion as a social formation.

Although "social formation" is a category that can be traced directly back to the French Marxist Louis Althusser (1971; see also Resch 1992), and even though it can easily be found in the work of a number of contemporary scholars of religion, popularizing the category seems to have been the doing of Burton Mack (see Mack 2000 for his most systematic statement on this topic). It is a complex category and one that we unnecessarily limit if we mean by it only the factors that ini-tially form or bring a social movement into existence. 'Social formation' is of use not only in the study of how new social organizations develop but also when studying how they are institutionalized, maintained over time and place, how they are contested, and, eventually, come to an end. If we see society as a continually reemerging, shared, and contested con-struct, then 'social formation' nicely represents not only the ongoing work of bringing an imagined social group into existence but also the sleight of hand in making it appear always to have existed.

When used to redescribe religion, 'social formation' refers to a spe-cific and coordinated system of rhetorical acts and institutions that con-structs the necessary conditions for shared identities. By coordinating discourses on such things as nonobvious beings (a term I derive from Walter Burkert; see chapter 4), absolute origins, and ultimate endtimes within highly rule-driven systems of practice, we create a system of sociorhetorical strategies that facilitate the development of enduring social and self-identities. However, I must be clear on one important point: there is no such thing as a specifically *religious* social formation; it is just that among the host of mechanisms available to social groups in their ongoing efforts to define and reproduce the conditions (both intellectual and material) that have allowed them to be a them in the first place, discourses on nonobvious beings, origins, endtimes, and control are sometimes used and are often found together in interrelated systems of belief, behavior, and institution. For purely descriptive, taxonomic reasons, such social formations are often termed "religion." Given the degree to which 'religion' often denotes an ontologically distinct, *sui generis* phenomenon (a word I use purposefully here), it may not really help—in fact it may obscure the more important theoretical matter entirely—to refer to this one subset of social formations as religious.

Unlike Catherine Albanese, who has recently employed the category "religious formation" in her discussion of the relations between religion and popular culture (1996: 734), our category "social formation" suggests that there is nothing specifically religious, spiritual, or mystical about the social groupings we describe as religions or world religions. Where 'religion', 'world religion', 'mysticism', and 'spirituality' all operate on the phenomenological or descriptive level of analysis, 'social formation' is openly redescriptive and operates on a higher logical level of analysis. It is for this reason that Albanese's discussion of "spiritual structures" not only holds little promise for future analytic research but actually threatens the advances we have already made (1996: 735). In fact, by invoking the Tillichian juxtaposition of 'culture/religion', Albanese perpetuates a longstanding confusion noted earlier: for the redescriptive scholar, religion is an aspect of human social organization and not an uncaused force that operates over against culture; so-called religious beliefs, behaviors, and institutions are merely a few of the many sites where social formations develop and are contested. To maintain otherwise, to suggest that religion is somehow separate or free from social and historical causation, is to rely upon the intellectually and politically suspect notion of *sui generis* religion. Therefore, because it is a merely descriptive category that is itself in need of further analysis, there is little theoretical value to the category "religious formation." In fact, according to Gary Lease, there can be no such thing as a religious formation or even the history of a religion, strictly speaking, *"for the simple reason that there is no religion: rather such a history can only trace how and why a culture or epoch allows certain experiences to count as 'religion' while excluding others"* (1994: 472; italics added). To investigate the *how* and *why* Lease mentions will require us to lay bear the strategies that enable the conditions of social formation. It should be clear, then, that 'religion' is not a clean theoretical construct and, accordingly, provides the field with a questionable basis.

Social formations, then, are active processes that never arrive and are never completed. In one sense, the process implied by social formation simply suggests the active constitution and reconstitution of a social group. But in another sense, *a* social formation denotes the continually changing results of these active processes and the context in which these processes take place—in this case social formations are more *things* than *processes*. What is crucial is to recognize that both senses are necessarily related; despite the ever-present danger of mistaking our abstract concepts for real things, the utility of 'social formation' is precisely its ability to avoid the traps of reification, all of which comes from its status as a gerund.[5] In other words, social formation is not a thing or an it.

Therefore, when we examine social formations, we are not studying stable, self-evident things so much as analyzing systemwide strategies whose result is to portray the many as one and heterogeneity as homogeniety. The social formations we are able to study are therefore always analytic constructs and therefore mere shadows of their former shadows; they are abstractions of what are in reality constantly changing processes. So, when we study social formation, we are studying something that has neither an absolute origin nor an absolute end. When we study social formation, we are also not studying a unified, intentional process with a *telos*. Taking seriously that human social formation actually makes possible the conditions necessary for such things as linear narratives of distinction (then, now, and later) or value (bad, better, best), we will instead study the means by which human groups respond to the inevitable disruptions and plain old accidents of historical existence. Taking these accidents and disruptions seriously, we will avoid positing a smooth, linear development to social formations, as if they were the outcome of individual actors' intentions, careful planning, and coherent organization.

We will avoid all this because a thoroughly social theory of religion posits individual actors' intentions, plans, and organizations not as *causes* of but as *artifacts* that result from social formation, as the evidence of preexistent, communally shared intellectual and material conditions beyond the scope or control of the individual. In fact, it is only in light of such preexistent conditions that one gets to count as an individual in the first place. As Smith has stated so succinctly when commenting on early Christian social formation, "[t]here is no post-Easter experience which then is 'given voice' in Christian discourse; the experience is contained in and by that discourse" (1996: 274). However, we must not lose sight of the fact that the preexistent intellectual and material conditions determinative of our current social existence and identity are certainly the result, to whatever degree, of individual decisions and actions carried out by our predecessors. However, we must not fail to recognize that our predecessors were themselves operating, as we are, in complex, inherited social worlds not of their making.

We might say, then, that because of, as well as despite, our best intentions, social formation not only happens, but in fact it happens to us. Social formation is therefore complex, interactive, partially intentional, yet a blind process. We should therefore not approach its study lightly, for social formation simultaneously makes us and is made by us. Agency and structural constraints come together in a complex process in all social formation. In this way, our work on social formation will combine the best insights of such seemingly divergent theorists as Louis Althusser, on the one hand (who, although coining the very notion of social formation, emphasized structure at the expense of agential human beings, whom he understood as mere "supports" for modes of production [Giddens 1984: 217]) and, on the other, the historian E. P. Thompson (who disagreed quite publicly with Althusser's emphasis on structure and who, instead, understood social life as "unmastered human practice").

There may be no more apt way of communicating this complexity than to refer to the opening lines of Thompson's *Making of the English Working Class*: what we are engaged in "is a study in an active process which owes as much to agency as to conditioning. The working class [a social formation, we might add] did not rise like the sun at an appointed time. It was present at its own making" (Thompson 1991 [1963]: 8). Borrowing a term from the British sociologist Anthony Giddens (1984), we can better get at this reciprocal process by talking about "recursive reproduction." As explained by Braun:

> Its key point is that social action, even in times of high degrees of social change, is bounded by and dependent on the structures (material, economic, political, etc.) and resources (means of communication, myth-making, etc.). The full package of a society's constitution thus is both means and outcome of social actions and practices. Analogy: even a "novel" sentence is a reproduction of the rules of grammar and the bounded vocabulary of the language in which the sentence is uttered. (1999b: 220 n. 14)

In Giddens's own words, "human beings act purposefully and knowledgeably but without being able either to foresee or to control the consequences of what they do" (1984: 217–18). The study of social formation, then, "is involved in relating action to structure, in tracing, explicitly or otherwise, the conjunction or disjunctions of intended and unintended consequences of activity and how these affect the fate of individuals. . . . For the permutations of influences are endless, and there is no sense in which structure 'determines' action or vice versa" (1984: 219). In studying social formation, then, we will have to attend to the interface of individual actors and the systemwide constraints in which they live.

For purposes of scholarship, we will likely wish to arrive at a vocabulary capable of comparing and detailing what we take to be significant

differences and similarities between, and developments within, analytically distinguishable social formations. In other words, why is it that we
might refer to the English working class as existing now rather than
then? Or, in Braun's example, what makes this sentence "novel" from
that? I recently re-read parts of Kurt Rudolph's 1983–1984 Haskell Lectures, *Historical Fundamentals and the History of Religions* (1985),
where, over a decade ago, Rudolph anticipated our current interest in
pursuing a thoroughly redescribed social theory of religion by rehabili-
tating some of our vocabulary. In the last lecture, entitled "Development
as a Problem for the History of Religions" (1985: 81–98), after tracing
the rich history of evolutionist thinking in the early field, Rudolph nicely
reclaims the category "development" to refer not to a preprogrammed,
unfolding process but to a complex set of analytically separable, historical stages. In other words, because social formation is always under
way, we will only be able to study its strategies and movements by halt-
ing it artificially. According to Rudolph, then, to be interested in the
development of any given religion—or, as we would say, social formation—means one will likely examine a number of interrelated sites:

> [T]he beginning phase, the phase that gives to each its characteristic
> features or "habitus," . . . that is, the stage of founding or consolida-
> tion; the stages of adaptation and assimilation ("syncretism"), of sub-
> stitution (as in the interpretation of the names of foreign gods), or of
> isolation; the stages of deformation and "encrustation"; of revolution
> or reformation; a stage of heresies and schisms; and stages of secular-
> ization and dissolution. The stage of dissolution, however, can also be
> a stage of transformation. (1985: 93)

Borrowing from the British Marxist literary critic Raymond Williams
(1977: 121–27), we can simplify Rudolph's overly complex stages by
identifying three phases in the life of any social formation: *dominant*
(when a social system reproduces its authority effectively in the midst of
ongoing natural disruptions),[6] *residual* (when, due to changing natural
conditions, a social system formed in the past is no longer able to reproduce its authority and legitimacy yet remains effective in the present),
and *emergent* (when, in the wake of natural disruptions, novel or experimental forms of authority and attendant social organization are developing). Although the first and last more than likely are self-explanatory,
'residual', may require some brief explanation: since all social formations develop from chronologically prior groups and institutions, a
social theory of religion will avoid questions of absolute origins (i.e., we
do not inquire as to where society *per se* came from) but will, instead,
examine the social and natural conditions that attend the demise of one
social formation and the role residual social formations play in the emer-

gence of new forms of identity and organization (i.e., we only ask how this particular social formation emerged when and where it did). Dominant, residual, and emergent social formation will always be found to occur together.

For example, I think of Jack Lightstone's insightful comments concerning the role played by the turn-of-the-era residual, intellectually elite Jewish scribal class in the emergence of text-based Judaism:

> [I]n the main what one has is a scholarly refinement of rabbinic literature's own account of its own literary history. This [the rabbis' own] account, distilled and refined, becomes the [modern scholarly] description of the early rabbinic and proto-rabbinic social formation, in terms of which the literary history and character of the early rabbinic documents are explained, and in which framework their meaning is elucidated. "Catch-22!" (1997: 278; as quoted by Braun 1999b: 229)

Combining both Lightstone and Smith, Braun phrases it as follows:

> the end of the Temple in 70 C.E. meant that a large priestly-scribal sector lost not only jobs, but its fundamental social, intellectual, and ritual *reason d'être*. The sector's 'burden of alienation and deracination' can hardly be overestimated. We know the imaginative remaking of this group of itself as the formation of the rabbinic colleges which reconstituted a Judaism in which "temple" and judiciary values based on temple ritual becomes replacement ritual. (1999b: 229)

To study the social formations we normally call "religions" or "religious traditions" amounts to writing their natural history—from their emergence to their eventual dissolution and, possibly, reconstitution. Related to Smith's comments on the incongruity of lived experience and the need to rationalize the disruptions and accidents that invade our systems of signification is Gary Lease's attempt to delineate just such a natural history. (The work of Bruce Lincoln and Burton Mack of course comes to mind at this point as well). For Lease, religions, much like nationalisms, attempt "to be totally *inclusive* of all paradoxes by establishing *exclusive* meanings." Because historical life is rather more complex than the interpretive models of any totalized system, Lease predicts that, despite our best attempts to rationalize their appearance, the dissonances and conflicts that inevitably arise will eventually cause "the societal system to *breakdown* and the 'structures' which allowed such a paradoxical mutuality to dissolve" (Lease 1994: 475). Embarking on a natural history of social formations will therefore examine a religious system not as an ahistoric given but as a historical product that has a specific history, a limited future, and a wealth of possibilities.

If we follow Lease, then, to write the natural history of a religion as a social formation would be to create a "catalog of strategies for *main-*

taining paradoxes, *fighting* over dissonances, and *surviving* [and recovering from] breakdowns" (1994: 475). Such a catalog would amount to a map of the many social sites where myths are developed and deployed for one of the primary ways in which social formations are constructed, maintained, contested, and rebuilt is through the active process of mythmaking. According to Mack:

> Social formation and mythmaking are group activities that go together, each stimulating the other in a kind of dynamic feedback system. Both speed up when new groups form in times of social disintegration and cultural change. Both are important indicators of the personal and intellectual energies invested in experimental movements. . . . [S]ocial formation and mythmaking fit together like hand and glove. (Mack 1995: 11)

Although he did not employ these specific categories in his early study of religion, the reciprocal relationship between social formations and mythmaking was made clear as early as Durkheim's *Elementary Forms*. To repeat a portion of this paper's epigraph:

> A society can neither create nor recreate itself without creating some kind of ideal by the same stroke. This creation is not a sort of optional extra step by which society, being already made, merely adds finishing touches; it is the act by which society makes itself, and remakes itself, periodically. (Durkheim 1995: 425).

In keeping with, but improving upon, this Durkheimian tradition, we could say that a social formation is the activity of experimenting with, authorizing, and reconstituting widely circulated ideal types, idealizations, or, better put, mythifications that function to control acts and sites of signification.

Based on my readings, this is what Lease seems to imply by his notion of religions as totalized systems of meaning, what Smith seems to be saying about ritual functioning to classify and clarify by exercising an "economy of significance" (1982: 56), and what Roland Barthes seems to be saying about myths authorizing History (i.e., contingency) as Nature (i.e., necessity) (1973: 11). Moreover, these interrelated strategies of routinization, normalization, domestication, universalization, and idealization—all of which are ways in which significance is managed and controlled by means of myth and ritual—are themselves ideological mechanisms. This is precisely what Bruce Lincoln meant when, a decade ago in *Cosmos, Myth, and Society*, he employed some classic Marxist vocabulary to note that

> an ideology . . . is not just an ideal against which social reality is measured or an end toward the fulfillment of which groups and individu-

als aspire. It is also, and this is much more important, a screen that strategically veils, mystifies, or distorts important aspects of real social processes. Like any other ideology, myth largely serves to create false consciousness in many members of society, persuading them of the *rightness* of their lot in life, whatever that may be, and of the total social order. (1986: 164)

Therefore, mythmaking is none other than idealmaking, where the term *ideal* is conceived not as an abstract, absolute value but as a contingent, localized construct that, by means of rhetorical, even ideological, mechanisms represents and simultaneously reproduces certain specific social values *as if they were universal.*

Social formation, then, is explicitly caught up in the ideological strategies of totalization, naturalization, rationalization, and universalization; to appeal to Benedict Anderson, we could say that social formations are based on mythic "ontological reality [that is portrayed as] apprehensible . . . through a single, privileged system of re-presentation" (1991: 14). Accordingly, Durkheim's thoughts on the creation and authorization of "some kind of ideal" find their modern equivalent in the works of the authors just named. Social formations are the ongoing results of mythmaking activity (where I see mythmaking as a discourse involving acts and institutions, as well as narratives), an activity that unites into a totalized system of representation what Mack refers to as the "epic past, the historical past, the historical present, the anticipated historical future, and the hoped for epic future" in one narrative, behavioral, and institutional system. Where but in so-called religions do we see this happening most effectively?

To return to Lincoln's thoughts, and as Mack has also suggested, mythmaking takes place from a specific sociopolitical position and supports a specific judgment about the here and now. Ideals, myths, and rituals therefore do not simply project consensually reached agreements; each of these does not communicate some substance so much as give shape and authority (i.e., significance) to this or that message. Accordingly, myths present one particular, contested viewpoint as if it were an "agreement that has been reached" by "we the people" (a phrase that is part of a powerful mythic rhetoric). For instance, to take up Mack's use of the contemporary American situation as an example, rhetoric that brings together references to the founding fathers (what Mack might refer to as the "epic past"), with the image of the patriarchal nuclear family of the 1950s (historical past), with current crime rates, teenage birth rates, abortion rates, and divorce rates (one particular present), with projections for budget reductions in the next ten years (historical future), all of which contributes to the future well-being/security of the American experiment/idea/nation (epic future) is the consummate art of mythmaking. By means of mythmaking, the historicity and specificity of each of these is collapsed into one monolithic, unfolding narrative. To appeal to Barthes once again, by means of myth, History has effectively become Nature. Or, to appeal to the American literary critic Frederic Jameson, by means of a disguised or undetected ideological slippage, "is" becomes "ought," the myth of presence and self-identity is established, and value-neutral "change" takes on the significance of being either good or bad (1988: 17). And, even though the British Marxist literary critic Terry Eagleton sadly defines myth in a very traditional way (i.e., narratives about such things as "sacred times, places, and origins"), he nonetheless correctly understands myths to be "a particular *register* of ideology, which elevates certain meanings to numinous status" (1991: 188–89). All of these writers therefore appear to agree that by means of mythmaking, local, symbolic worlds of significance are authorized and naturalized by being mistaken for, or actively portrayed as, universal, literal ones.

Because one of the premises of all social scientific scholarship is that all behavior is contextualized within historical (i.e., social, political, economic, etc.) pressures and influences, we understand all such perspectives and points of view as partial and linked to certain views and behaviors not shared by all members of a social grouping.[7] This ensures that we not lose sight of the fact that all social formation relies on a kind of sleight of hand whereby all-inclusive systems arise from premises that are fundamentally exclusive. Social formation, then, is the art of manufacturing and reproducing totalized systems of re-presentation. Because the social values, truths, and ideals are hardly universal, because, as Durkheim noted, the "mystery that appears to surround them is entirely superficial and fades upon closer scrutiny . . . , [when one pulls] aside the veil with which the mythological imagination covered them" (1995: 431), there is an inherent contradiction embedded at the core of social formations. Accordingly, there is much at stake in maintaining the mythic status of the system of representation and signification. As Lease comments concerning the inherent contradictions of all totalizing practices, "a society cannot live without them, nor can it live with them" (1994: 475). It is precisely the mythmakers (in our case, they sometimes go by the name *colleagues*) who develop discourses that obscure and thereby manage these contradictions.

Mythmaking, then, is the business of making "particular and contingent world-views appear to be ubiquitous and absolute" (Arnal 1997: 317). Social formation by means of mythmaking is nothing other than reasonable responses to the inevitable social disruptions, contradictions, and incongruities that characterize the historical, human condition. Systems of social significance, encoded within narratives of the epic past and the anticipated future, coordinated within behavioral and institutional systems of cognitive and social control, characterize our responses to the various incongruities and disruptions that come with historical existence; "myth both unites the group and provides an interpretive framework for coping with the exigencies of, and threats from, the natural world" (Giddens 1984: 265); so-called religious systems are perhaps the preeminent site for creating continuity (cognitive as well as social) amidst the discontinuities of life. In setting out to redescribe religion as but one set of strategies for accomplishing the always completed yet never ending recursive reproduction of social formation—a project that, as the following chapters will demonstrate, will involve critique as well as constructive work—we will be able to communicate with other scholars about an observable, public, and enduring aspect of human behavior.[8]

APPENDIX: MYTHMAKING AND SOCIAL FORMATION[9]

Toward the end of my paper "Redescribing 'Religion' as Social Formation: Toward a Social Theory of Religion," I quoted Gary Lease, for whom religions, much like nationalisms, attempt "to be totally *inclusive* of all paradoxes by establishing *exclusive* meanings." Because he presumes that contingent, historical life is rather more complex than the static models provided by totalized systems, Lease predicts that, despite our best attempts to rationalize social dissonance and contradiction, conflicts will eventually cause "the societal system to *breakdown* and the 'structures' which allowed such a paradoxical mutuality [to exist will then] . . . dissolve" (1994: 475). It was at this point in my paper that I suggested that we can combine Lease's thought with the work of such scholars as Bruce Lincoln, Burton Mack, and Jonathan Smith, not to mention scholars outside the study of religion, such as Eric Hobsbawm, E. P. Thompson, and Anthony Giddens; for to write the natural history of a social formation—from its emergent to its dominant and residual forms—is to create what Lease terms a "catalog of strategies for *maintaining* paradoxes, *fighting* over dissonances, and *surviving* breakdowns" (1994: 475). In my reading, this is precisely the common effort that engages this group of writers. Taken together, their work amasses a catalog that collects and classifies some of the many techniques for the strategic deployment of meaning—what Smith (1982) has so nicely termed "exercising an economy of signification." Following Mack, I understand this collection of strategies and tactics to be loosely grouped together as mythmaking practices.

As one possible bridge between my paper's somewhat abstract theorizing on the role religious discourses play as mythmaking devices in the service of social formation, on the one hand, and the work of scholars studying the historic beginnings and transmission of the social movement we have come to know as Christianity, on the other, I would like to turn to Judith Perkins's *Suffering Self: Pain and Narrative Representation in the Early Christian Era* (1995). Perkins examines a change in the manner in which the self or subjectivity was represented and conceived in the early Roman empire. Unlike Rodney Stark (1996),[10] who argues that Christianity won out in the competitive religious economy of antiquity because of its superior theology, Perkins argues that Christianity was launched into a social world where the possibility of self-understanding was changing from the prevailing Greco-Roman image of the human self as a rational soul/mind controlling a physical body that hampered the perfection and liberation of the soul/mind, to the representation of the self as a soul/mind inextricably joined to a body that was, by definition, liable to pain and suffering, a suffering that required the attention or intervention of some outside source. Contrary to Stark's circular thesis, which explains Christianity's rise as a result of factors internal to Christianity itself, Perkins's argument accounts for its success by presupposing the ad hoc nature of all social life, making the rise of any given social group a function of factors that likely lay outside of itself. As I read her, she argues that the Christian understanding of human society as a community of sufferers was in the right place at the right time; its spread was made possible by a discourse focusing on bodies in need of attention. It was, according to Perkins, "around one of these represented 'subjects,' the suffering self, that Christianity as a social and political unity would form and ultimately achieve its institutional power" (1995: 3).

What strikes me as a gain in Perkins's analysis is that she places the social factors that made Christianity possible outside of Christianity itself, thereby snapping that self-serving, closed feedback loop that, as Mack has told us, dominates the history of scholarship on Christian origins. And this is what I believe the Ancient Myths and Modern Theories of Christian Origins seminar is working toward. But her book also made me think of another issue the group is concerned with: the problem of scholarship that simply reproduces emic categories as if they were cross-culturally and analytically useful—in other words, the theoretical, social, and political implication of classification.[11] With this in mind, what most struck me, a novice when it comes to the study of early Christianity, was Perkins's reference to Tertullian's mention of a particular judge—Arrius Antoninus—who was rather reluctant to punish early Christians. In one case, after letting most of them go, he is quoted as having said: "[W]retched men, if you wish to die, you have cliffs and ropes to hang yourselves" (1995: 21; citing *To Scapula* 4, 5). Although we know that some early Christians did indeed go to their deaths confessing the faith, too quickly creating an analogy between "martyrdom" and "suicide" suggests that the judge had, in the first case, somehow misread the social significance and ongoing rhetorical utility of ritualized public death while, ironically, correctly reading and thereby undermining the early Christians' intentions insomuch as he denied them their public opportunity to engage in an extreme act of social signification. So there is indeed much at stake for too quickly classifying the emic act known as martrydom as mere suicide. Whereas martyrdom functioned as a highly politicized, oppositional ritual around which new, experimental social identities formed, suicide—much like marriage as Perkins demonstrates in her analysis of the early Greek romance genre—supports expected social roles, thereby reinforcing specific dominant worlds. In the case of Greek romances, Perkins finds that "the character chose to die to avoid violating social rules, such as chastity, or out of sorrow for the loss of a spouse and the end of a significant social relation that entailed, or when their social roles were concluded." She concludes that, much like the happy ending afforded both then and now by marriage, "[s]uicides functioned in this genre to underscore the primacy of social relationships and to reinforce the reading of romance[s] as a celebration of communal strength and meaning found in the social community that is idealized in this genre" (103).

I find this all very illuminating; as with all of our categories, there is something at stake for miscategorization. But there is also something at stake for being satisfied with simply reproducing the emic vocabularies—and with them, the worldviews and values—of the groups we study. In other words, carefully distinguishing the classification "suicide" from "martyrdom" is indeed crucial, but failing to theorize those acts we come to know as martyrdom as being potential sites of social formation is equally problematic. After all, if in their historic context martyrs functioned as politically oppositional sites around which social identity was in part built, how is it that Christians, having long ago attained discursive hegemony in many parts of the globe, can still make reference to the self-sacrificial acts of the martyrs? Clearly, the social significance of martyrdom must be retooled. This retooling I take to be the role of mythmaking.

So, to repeat the problem at hand: presuming that in their original historic context (that of an *emergent* social formation), such ascetic behaviors as martyrdom functioned as public, ritualized, and politically oppositional acts, how is it that, having attained *dominant* status, social formations continue to draw on these accounts in a rhetorically efficacious manner? Does not social success reduce the usefulness of cosmogonies, insomuch as social success removes members ever more from the actual oppositional worlds that created and used such tales in the first place? To answer these questions, we must draw on our knowledge of Lease's catalog of "strategies for *maintaining* paradoxes, *fighting* over dissonances, and *surviving* breakdowns." For, although the present historic context of a dominant social formation is radically different from the historic context of the emergent social formation that it takes to be its precursor, reproducing specific portions of its origins discourse is one mechanism that enables an ongoing, dominant social formation to represent itself to its members as a homogenous tradition. With social success comes an ever-dwindling collection of historical affinities, a lack that is compensated for by an ever-increasing catalog of mythmaking strategies.

As I read him, this is precisely what Smith addressed in his essay "Sacred Persistence: Toward a Redescription of Canon" (1982): it is the problem of practical limitation and imaginative ingenuity. One topic we can illuminate by means of these interrelated tools, mythmaking and social formation, is the problem of how it is that dominant social formations so smoothly represent themselves as marginalized and oppositional, much as contemporary Republicans rely on the well-oiled assumption that wealthy white males are somehow an endangered species. My guess is that this technique is crucial in the successful reproduction of any social identity.

NOTES

1. As I phrased it elsewhere (McCutcheon 1999b: 92), four of the presumptions that direct this research are:

(1) The natural world (i.e., the world we bump into when we try to cross either a forest or the hotel lobby at the AAR/SBL meeting) is an incredibly complex place and I presume that no human community knows what is *really* going on in it. Instead, we all have hunches, recall just this or that past event, and anticipate future events—some of us even build explicit theories—all in an effort to talk about and act within this world. I would therefore be the last to champion ontological reductionism as an explanatory option; following Don Wiebe, I advocate methodological reductionism.

(2) Because of the utter complexity of the world, a variety of methods is necessary to start talking about it in an academic manner. I therefore support pluralistic methodological reductionism. It would be quite mistaken to think that, once the work of studying social formations is exhausted (as if it could ever be exhausted), *either* there would be nothing left for colleagues using other scales of analysis to study *or* there would remain some refined distillate called experience, consciousness, belief, the sacred, or Human Nature, that we could only study by means of some special methodology from outside the human sciences.

(3) Any system of thought and practice that fails to presume 1 and 2 is a candidate for the status of data. Reflection on the deeper truth or meaning of religion (whether that reflection is theological *or* humanistic) attempts to bypass the historically grounded nature of all human attempts to know the world around us, making them instances of mythmaking in need of theorization. It is for this reason that I think it sensible to exclude certain approaches from the pluralistic methodologically reductionist study of religion as carried out in the public university.

(4) There are no final explanations. Scholars in the human sciences are just as deeply involved in the art of rhetoric, contestation and social formation as anyone else. It is a useful rule of thumb to say that it is the people we study who typically propose final, universal explanations.

2. Ronald Inden outlines a variety of reasons why we should be weary of using "society" uncritically. As he puts it: "Social scientists . . . have relied heavily on the term 'society', to talk about the human world. It has become the term used in social scientific discourse to talk about virtually any complex agent—tribe, village, clan, nation-state, linguistic or ethnic group that occupies, or is seen wishing to occupy, its own territory. These are the entities likened to the machine or organism of the physical and biological sciences. This usage masks the empirical complexity of these agents by treating them (or ideal types of them) as if they were unitary, determinate objects, the manifestations of some underlying essence of product of some subtantialized agent, a pure class of persons who share some permanent something despite their actual (dis)organization at any one time. Another voluntarist usage of the term 'society', is evoked in the same breath as this mechanistic one, gives the almost opposite impression—that these compound agents are purely purposive organizations, all of whose members have consciously and freely joined their wills to its. Both are also implicit in the metaphor of the body politic as a machine" (1990: 27).

3. Compare Smith's comments to those of the sociologist Rodney Stark from two decades later: "For far too many sociologists, 'work' is a form of ancestor worship. That is, theory is believed to consist of the opinions, prejudices, insights, analyses, and metaphors about social life contained in the works of dead founders" (1997: 20–21).

4. The other three consisted of describing the social facts or *realia*, the social history, and the social world. Smith finds in Peter Berger's work an example of the last, a description of "the creation of world of meaning which provided a plausibility structure for those who chose to inhabit it." More recently, the work of William E. Paden provides an excellent example of the ways in which religious systems build meaningful worlds inhabited by their participants (1992, 1994, 1996a, 1996b, 2000).

5. My understanding of *social formation* as a gerund has befitted tremendously from my correspondence with Burton Mack over the past few years.

6. Fearing that the term *social* will only reproduce the problems that accompany most uses of *society*, Inden opts for *imperial formation* rather than *social formation* (1990: 29ff.). Although his introduction of power into the equation is very important, there is no need to see 'social formation' as incapable of including the imperializing roles of interest to Inden. In fact, adapting

Williams's three types or stages nicely communicates that power and control must be central to our understanding of social formation.

7. Or, as phrased by J. Z. Smith, "there is no primordium—it is all history" (1982: xiii).

8. Portions of this discussion of mythmaking are reproduced, and elaborated on, in McCutcheon 2000.

9. This brief appendix was presented as a discussion paper to the annual meeting of the North American Association for the Study of Religion, 19 November 1999, Boston, MA—a session co-sponsored by the Society for Biblical Literature's Seminar on Ancient Myths and Modern Theories of Christian Origins. The other panelists were Willi Braun, Burton Mack, Luther Martin (chair), and Jonathan Z. Smith.

10. For review essays on Stark's thesis, see the essays by Willi Braun, Burton Mack, Randall Collins, and myself in *Religious Studies Review* 25/2 (1999): 127–39.

11. On classification, see Smith 2000.

PART II

Dispatches from the Theory Wars

If "religion" is substantively empty—or infinitely fillable with aeolian qualities . . . let us abandon the eschatological hope, so tenaciously persistent in our field, that by some brilliant hermeneutical can-do we will spook the true genie out of the bottle of "religion." If "religion" is substantively empty, then there is no genie in the bottle!

—Willi Braun (2000: 8)

CHAPTER 3

Writing a History of God: "Just the Same Game Wherever You Go"

In all great religions, seers and prophets have conceived strikingly similar visions of a transcendent and ultimate reality. . . . The monotheistic faiths, however, call this transcendence "God."
—Karen Armstrong (1991)

So wrote Karen Armstrong in the introduction to her biography on the prophet Muhammad (1991). Two years later, in her best-selling book *A History of God* (1993), Armstrong explored this hunch, investigating what she claims to be the evolution of the concept or experience of God that occurs in three historically related social formations: Judaism, Christianity, and Islam. In spite of her research, however, it is not entirely clear whether members of each religion are indeed experiencing the same god—or any god for that matter. As it turns out, what is more interesting than investigating the deep similarities of certain devotees' reports is to investigate just why it is that people seem continually drawn to generating nonempirical sameness where empirical differences dominate. In other words, just why is Armstrong's history of God so popular among readers?

In an effort to understand the allure of Armstrong's quest for sameness, it is worth our while to reflect on the astounding popularity of one of her intellectual predecessors, Joseph Campbell. Before his death in 1987 at the age of eighty-two, Campbell was well on his way to gaining a large following of readers interested in his particular thematic approach to the cross-cultural study of myths. It was Campbell's understanding that at the base of the many diverse stories we tell to one another, there exists a common structure that transcends history, geography, ethnicity, and so on—in a word, historical, material difference. As is well known, Campbell relies on a three-part quest motif of "departure/confrontation and change/return" that he believes comprises heroic stories told the world over in virtually all ages. Furthermore, based on his understanding of the theories of Carl Jung, Campbell asserts that the proper analysis of stories as varied as the adventures of Odysseus and the televised images of the Apollo astronauts splashing down in the ocean can provide evidence of certain fundamental aspects of the human psyche—Human Nature, if you will—and our common need to, in his words, "follow our bliss." Perhaps there is no more useful summary of the practical application of Campbell's thought than this last phrase, taken from his interviews with journalist Bill Moyers, entitled *The Power of Myth*, first broadcast on PBS a year after Campbell's death.

After his death and amidst Campbell's growing fame, a debate began on the political implications of his methods for the study of myths and symbols. Furthermore, a number of stories about Campbell's private life and the derogatory public remarks he would often make at the expense of, among others, various minority groups, began to circulate, all of which called into question the significance of his seemingly consoling yet individualistic advice about following one's bliss. In September 1989, Brendan Gill, the longtime writer for *The New Yorker* and friend of the late Campbell, published a very critical opinion piece in the *New York Review of Books*. For some, Gill's article constituted an inappropriate personal attack on a defenseless dead man. Such a reaction is understandable, for, by this time, Campbell had already been transformed from a somewhat obscure teacher and researcher from Sarah Lawrence College in New York State into one of the great intellectual gurus of the twentieth century. Gill entered this debate, it seems, precisely because after the Moyers interviews were aired—the interviews and the Doubleday book they produced continue to be very popular, a staple of every bookstore's usually meager "mythology" section—the individual he had once known who advocated surprisingly troubling personal attitudes had, almost overnight, become a respected authority for a generation in the late 1980s that, in Gill's estimate, was searching for some sort of justification for social and economic egotism.

Campbell's work may have been useful as just such a justification because he used a decontextualized method of comparison borrowed from nineteenth-century scholarship; Campbell's work on myths therefore provided the perfect rationale for the reduction of complexity and diversity to simplicity and unity. For Campbell, regardless of the material conditions of their composition, all myths functioned in the same psychological manner: as an expression of the inherent human need and desire to follow our heart's desire, whatever that may be. For example, in the Moyers interviews, Campbell likens both Vietnam War protestors and American soldiers to heroes on quests. Regardless of the dramatically different sociopolitical implications of their actions, they are all, according to him, on a quest for personal fulfillment. That each type of quest in this case exacts a considerably different price in human lives is not an issue of importance to his approach. Like all good heroes before us, we are all simply following the bliss of self-realization. In other words, Reaganomics had found its spiritual and psychological legitimation.

Admittedly, I have taken a rather circuitous route to get around to addressing Karen Armstrong's *New York Times* and *Washington Post* best seller from a few years back, *A History of God*, but I believe it was defensible digression. The lessons we learn from the criticisms of Campbell's work must surely also shed some light on the possible reasons for the great popularity of books such as Armstrong's. For, like Campbell, Armstrong presumes that through careful yet largely uncritical analysis of "their" and "our" sacred stories (presuming, of course, that "we" all have them), we will come to the conclusion that an utter unity persists despite the seeming diversity of the empirical evidence. For example, despite the many differences in human conceptions of a monotheistic creator deity—certainly there are radical differences both within each of the three religions she examines and between them—Armstrong maintains that the same "transcendent reality" underlies all these limited and partial conceptions (possibly even distortions). In keeping with Carl Raschke's recommendation that scholars of religion "apperceive [the] essential make-up of things" as the basis for differentiating between normal and abnormal religion (1986: 136), she advocates a highly individualistic and normative "mystical" form of religious experience as the next step in "our" ever-evolving conceptions of transcendence.

Of course Armstrong might be right. From the outset, we must acknowledge that one or another religious devotee may very well be right in maintaining, for example, that a relationship with "Jesus Christ as your personal lord and savior" is the sole avenue to bliss or that Krishna is one of the many manifestations of the great god Vishnu. Not only this, however, but one must also be prepared to admit that, instead of just one of these rather exclusivistic claims being right and true, some usually overlooked—overlooked even by devotees themselves—essence or common structure may reside behind or beneath these various claims, making them all simply different responses to the same experience. But in saying this one must be prepared to admit that, not simply Campbell or Armstrong, but instead Billy Graham, Sun Myung Moon, David Koresch, or, most recently, Marshall Applewhite might have (had) access to this essence and that "we" are all terribly mistaken. This is precisely what the members of Heaven's Gate seem to have believed. Of course I can simply dismiss them (and others like them who disagree with me) as "crazy," but that would be too easy.

The trouble is that as an outsider to the claims made by the above-

named people, one needs to investigate what criteria one might employ
to distinguish between the various claims they make—Campbell dug
deep into the Jungian collective unconscious to find this invisible yard-
stick. In other words, how might one distinguish between the Southern
Baptist's claims and Armstrong's, or between the accuracy of the Buddha's analysis of reality (that it really is not "out there" in the way we
normally think it is) and Jim Bakker's onetime popular message that the
love of a personal God is evidenced, at least in part, by one's material
success? The difficulties should be more than apparent. The criteria
whereby we normally distinguish between truth claims do not necessarily lend themselves to the analysis of religious claims concerning such
vague entities as philosophical essences, spontaneous intuitions, and
unique religious experiences. Take, for example, Armstrong's thoughts
on the so-called fundamentally religious nature of all human beings—an
assumption crucial to her evolutionary thesis that the time has come for
Jews, Christians, and Muslims to unite and transcend their personalized
and limited notions of deity. Armstrong writes that

> my study of the history of religion has revealed that human beings are
> spiritual animals. Indeed, there is a case for arguing that *Homo sapi-
> ens* is also *Homo religiosus*. Men and women started to worship gods
> as soon as they became recognizably human; they created religions at
> the same time as they created works of art. This was not simply
> because they wanted to propitiate powerful forces; these early faiths
> expressed the wonder and mystery that seem always to have been an
> essential component of the human experience of this beautiful yet ter-
> rifying world. Like art, religion has been an attempt to find meaning
> and value in life, despite the suffering that flesh is heir to. Like any
> other human activity, religion can be abused, but it seems to have been
> something that we have always done. It was not tacked on to a pri-
> mordially secular nature by manipulative kings and priests but was
> natural to humanity. Indeed our current secularism is an eminently
> new experiment, unprecedented in human history. We have yet to see
> how it will work. (1993: xix)

Armstrong is not alone in holding that we are, fundamentally, *Homo
religiosi*, looking for (as opposed to inventing) meaning and value. In
this century, this assumption is best associated with a tradition of scholarship stretching from the late German theologian Rudolf Otto to the
late Romanian expatriate, Mircea Eliade; Armstrong is simply the pop-
ularizer of a well-entrenched scholarly consensus. All three writers assert
that religion is an utterly unique and fundamental aspect of all human
experience. And, in yet another instance of how the study of religion is
often appropriated by those who work in the area of religious pluralism,
both scholars are used by Armstrong to support her own case (given

both Otto's and Eliade's interests in issues of pluralism, such an appropriation is not all that surprising). However, there are just as many scholars who would describe human beings in rather different terms. For such scholars, myths, rituals, institutions, and so on are not the expressions or manifestations of fundamentally basic and distinct aspects of human beings. Instead of promoting this liberal humanist presumption concerning a deeply personal human nature, these assorted acts are redescribed as some of the very sociorhetorical mechanisms that enable humans to think themselves as humans and as members of coherent social groups to begin with.

To assert (rather than hypothesize), as does Armstrong, that humans have a basic religious aspect is already to have decided that religion—like all aspects of culture—is not in fact a historic invention; and to have decided this begs the question of evidence: how does one know this? In other words, how does Armstrong know that religion "was not tacked on to a primordially secular nature by manipulative kings and priests but was natural to humanity"? Moreover, just why do we immediately presume that the good old "sacred/secular" distinction holds water and is not—as is more likely—simply a rhetorical artifact from a certain way of demarcating us from them, and allowed from disallowed. Just because the self-conscious division between the so-called sacred and secular spheres is a relatively recent development in the history of European political philosophy, this does not necessarily mean that the view of society as a "sacred" whole is accurate, right, or better, as Armstrong seems to suggest. Because assertions about human nature—whether they are concerned with the religious or psychological guilt that we all carry beneath our overcoats—cannot easily be verified or falsified, contemporary scholars of religion tend to avoid such discussions altogether.

For some time now, scholars of religion have been making the distinction between making such claims as, God loves me, or the Buddha gained enlightenment, on the one hand, and the task of redescribing, analyzing, and theorizing such claims, on the other. The academic study of religion entails the description and comparison of myths, rituals, and so on, conceived as human doings, suggesting that such acts have a meaning for the scholar that they do not necessarily have for the devotee him- or herself. As interesting as it may be, *A History of God* is not part of this particular tradition of scholarship. Despite appearances, it is the work of a devotee addressed to other rather liberal-minded religious readers.

Armstrong's previous books have been based on her own experiences as a nun (the British best seller *Through the Narrow Gate*), a study of the Christian creation of sex and gender in the West entitled *The Gospel according to Woman*, and, as already mentioned, her biography of the Prophet Muhammad. In Britain, Armstrong is a well-know print-media and television figure, having made a successful six-part television documentary on the life of Saint Paul and as a routine contributor to the *Times* and the *Observer*, among other papers. She was educated at Oxford (where she read literature), spent seven years as a Roman Catholic nun, and has taught at a Jewish seminary in London, England. To give her credit, she acknowledges from the outset that *A History of God* is the result, in part, of her own religious quest for a more adequate conception of the monotheistic deity. In her introduction she writes that at the start of this quest, some thirty years ago, she would have appreciated knowing that a "few highly respected monotheists would have told me quietly and firmly that God did not really exist—and yes that 'he' was the most important reality in the world" (xx). These opening words anticipate Armstrong's conclusion, where, after surveying the history of "God," she finally settles on the genderless deity of the mystics, an abstract, monistic conception that can be experienced personally but cannot be adequately expressed in the limitations of language.

Armstrong's erudition and learning are certainly evident in the wide range of her knowledge. The book begins with the early movement from polytheism in the ancient Mediterranean world to what she terms the "tribal deity named Yhwh." Accompanied by the ancient Hebrew development and apparently successful use of an exclusivistic tribal or civic deity, Armstrong traces the further development of the notion of a paternal and personal deity eventually understood by Christians as Father (and member of the complex concept of the Trinity). And, beginning in the sixth and seventh centuries of this era, she tells how Muhammad, a former worker in the thriving Arabian spice trade, reported having Isaiahlike visions of an angel, Jibril, commanding him to "Recite."

What seems to unite these diverse conceptions is that each is concerned with communicating with a personalized deity, one that can be described by the devotee in terms appropriate for other human beings. For example, Yahweh, God the Father, and Allah are all considered to be just, powerful, loving, and sometimes rather angry, and each is usually conceptualized as male. However, in Islam the sin of *shirk*, which we can characterize as the sin of associating Allah with lesser qualities or, more generally, the sin of anthropomorphizing Allah (projecting human qualities onto Allah), is perhaps the gravest of transgressions. Conversely, it is more than clear that, for the vast majority of people (at least of a certain generation of Christians in North America), Charlton Heston—complete with his noble, chiseled features; out-stretched arms; long, wind-blown hair and beard; and conservative politics—is a far more powerful metaphor or image for this deity. Certainly, some contemporary feminist theologians are actively challenging these conceptions—and Armstrong can be conceived as part of this challenge—but the pervasiveness of male pronouns, metaphors, and occupants of positions of institutional power within these three social formations continues.

After chronicling this history, Armstrong offers a critique of the now widespread conception of a personalistic deity. She writes that because "Judaism, Christianity, and—to a lesser extent—Islam have all developed the idea of a personal God, . . . we tend to think that this ideal represents religion at its best. . . . Yet a personal God can become a grave liability." Using the supposed gender of this deity as her example, Armstrong argues that the development of a personal and/or a personalized notion of deity has its limitations:

> The very fact that, as a person, God has a gender is also limiting: it means that the sexuality of half the human race is sacralized at the expense of the female and can lead to a neurotic and inadequate imbalance in human sexual mores. A personal God can be dangerous therefore. Instead of pulling us beyond our limitations, "he" can encourage us to remain complacently within them; "he" can make us cruel, callous, self-satisfied, and partial as "he" seems to be. Instead of inspiring the compassion that should characterize all advanced religion, "he" can encourage us to judge, condemn, and marginalize. It seems, therefore, that the idea of a personal God can only be a stage in our religious development. The world religions all seem to have recognized this danger and have sought to transcend the personal conception of supreme reality. (209–10)

In Hinduism, a complex tradition known for its multitudinous gods and goddesses, there is also the abstract concept 'Brahman', a word that denotes the utter unity of not only all people but all life—gods and goddesses included—as a whole. In the above quotation, it would seem that Armstrong has something like Brahman in mind when critiquing the intrinsically "limited" nature of conceptions of a monotheistic and personal deity. In spite of the fact that the authors and editors of the ancient Hebrew texts ensured that the face of their god (even the pronunciation of the divine name) was never directly seen by the prophets, this deity is nevertheless portrayed throughout this tradition as having an inexplicable and sometimes seemingly ruthless allegiance to a small group of nomadic people in search for a homeland. In the case of Islam, the ban against the creation of artistic visualizations of Allah, a reluctance that seems to lead to the expression of the artistic imagination in architecture and calligraphy, still did not prevent contemporary Muslims from employing their conception of a monotheistic deity as a rather powerful symbol of cultural and national autonomy. And as for Christians, it should be more than obvious that their God can take on such personalized forms as variations on Father Christmas, a crucified, bearded man, and, in the case of American civil religion, can be communicated through such images as the presidential seal and the bust of George Washington with "In God We Trust" etched beside.

In place of such "limited" personal conceptions of this deity, Armstrong advocates the future development of "mystical" conceptions of God as a transcendent rather than humanlike deity. Following such writers as Raschke, she harshly critiques what she bluntly labels as the "idolatrous" outcomes of the notion of a personalized and exclusivistic deity.

> To make such human, historical phenomena as Christian "Family Values," "Islam," or "the Holy Land" the focus of religious devotion is a new form of idolatry. This type of belligerent righteousness has been a constant temptation to monotheists throughout the long history of God. It must be rejected as unauthentic. The God of Jews, Christians, and Muslims got off to an unfortunate start, since the tribal deity Yahweh was murderously partial to his own people. Latter-day crusaders who return to this primitive ethos are elevating the values of the tribe to an unacceptably high status and substituting man-made ideals for the transcendent reality which should challenge our prejudices. They are also denying a crucial monotheistic theme. Ever since the prophets of Israel reformed the old pagan cult of Yahweh, the God of monotheists has promoted the ideal of compassion. (391)

Her criticisms of the "primitive ethos" and the "murderously partial" conception of deity indicative of the ancient Israelites may strike some of her readers as offensive. No doubt it is just such an audience that Armstrong hopes to reach. For unless one employs a rather questionable interpretive strategy, significant portions of all three of these religions' traditional tales do indeed portray an often violent image of deity leading warriors to battle. Concerning the sometimes murderous images of these deities, there is no better example than the Gulf War where, it would appear, each side was championed by a deity; for George Bush and Saddam Hussein both invoked religious rhetoric in support of their geopolitical causes.

More specifically, the trouble with "interpreting-away" such possibly offensive stories and images is that one can never really be sure which stories ought to be interpreted allegorically and which are literally true. For example, although many contemporary Christians would find Paul's remarks about women not speaking in churches and his language of "expiation" in the letter to the early Christian community in Rome (God's need for a blood sacrifice to appease him and compensate for human sinfulness) at the most to be only metaphorically useful today, they would nevertheless find it utterly unacceptable to interpret metaphorically his other assertions concerning Jesus actually being the second Adam or the incarnation of a deity.

When it comes to interpreting, it is never entirely clear on what basis one "keeps this" and "drops that." And as for Biblical literalism, a tradition of importance in some Christian circles, it should be apparent that, when reading a document that reflects the entrenched cultural and historical context of people half a world away and reaching back thousands of years, it is utterly impossible to take the entire document literally. In spite of the fact that the Hebrew text calls for a regular and total redistribution of debt, property, and goods every fifty years (known as the Jubilee year in Leviticus 25:8ff.), and that the Christian Scriptures routinely make judgments on the immanent end of the world and a radical renunciation of property and wealth, Jews and Christians throughout the world are somehow able to thrive in capitalist economies. In other words, when Jesus says that Peter is his "rock," literalists do not maintain that Jesus mistook Peter for inert, inorganic material. Somehow, readers are able to negotiate this metaphor smoothly and are able to distinguish this text from those that, to them at least, are most certainly not metaphoric. Those Protestant groups who handle rattle snakes during their services of worship, groups that can be found in some areas of the Appalachian region of the United States, are some of the few groups who take literally certain (but, once again, not all) portions of the Christian text. In this case, they put great emphasis on a certain portion of the Gospel of Mark (16:18) where true believers are distinguished not only by their ability to speak in tongues and to heal, but also by their ability to drink poison without being harmed and to handle deadly snakes (though the passage unfortunately doesn't elaborate on whether or not they'll get bit). That people *are* occasionally bit, and that, from time to time, they do indeed die from such bites and from drinking the poison, does not deter them. It should be clear, then, that the apparent ease with which Armstrong is able to make decisions concerning the shape of normative faith is rather misleading.[1]

This tendency to anthropomorphize, to project human qualities on what might otherwise not only be totally nonhuman, but what might actually be an inert and immaterial external world, may very well not be a limitation, as Armstrong maintains. Assuming a variation on nineteenth-century theories on social evolution—religious evolution, in this case—she characterizes the tendency to anthropomorphize as a somewhat primitive limitation that humans can, in the near future perhaps, transcend. However, another interesting book on religion, Stewart Guthrie's *Faces in the Clouds: A New Theory of Religion* (1993; see also Guthrie 2000), proposes a very different evolutionary account of anthropomorphism. For Guthrie, humans and most animals project their own characteristics onto the world at large in an effort to make sense of their environment. David Hume already said as much: we always find "human faces in the moon [and] armies in the clouds." But Guthrie redescribes such projection, whether it be seeing faces in the clouds or human characteristics in the natural world, as an evolutionarily developed coping or survival mechanism common to virtually all higher order, sentient life. "Uncertain of what we face," he writes, "we bet on the most important possibility because if we are wrong we lose little and if we are right we gain much. Religion, asserting that the world is significantly human-like [i.e., that it is controlled by superhuman forces with intentions and plans not that dissimilar to our own], brings this strategy to its highest pitch" (38). According to Guthrie, this tendency, then, is more a necessary survival strategy than a limitation, as Armstrong would put it. Even cats toy with yarn as if it were prey, and dogs are notorious for treating cars as intentionally challenging their territory. And virtually everyone I know can work up a considerable temper over rain that arrives just as the barbecue is about to begin, as if the rain or the sky were somehow an intentional agent that could be held accountable for its "actions." If Guthrie is correct, then Armstrong's hope for humans transcending their supposedly limited conceptualizations of deity (whether or not deities are actually out there) is misdirected.

A History of God is an ambitious, phenomenologically based chronicle of how a diverse collection of cultures have posited and then conceptualized a singular and powerful creator deity. The study, like the work of a number of scholars in Armstrong's tradition, ought not to be confused with the kind of redescriptive scholarship accomplished by scholars of religion such as Guthrie. This is a book that is a highly readable and interesting personal quest for a more adequate conception of deity for the religiously and culturally pluralistic late twentieth century written by a liberal religious devotee and intended for an audience of equally liberal religious devotees. Much like the classical Christian proofs for the existence of God, one must already believe in the concept prior either to proving it or describing it in the manner of Armstrong. Her assumption that common personal experiences of one "transcendent reality" are the basis for not only the three seemingly diverse conceptions she examines in detail (Yahweh, God the Father, and Allah) but also the many gods of Hinduism, the more abstract Hindu concept 'Brahman', as well as the abstract nontheistic forms of Buddhism, places Armstrong's work squarely within the company of other caretakers who posit a nonempirical reality either "out there" or "in here." For culture critics, however, such concepts as 'God' or 'Brahman'—let alone reports of religious experiences—are historically and socially entrenched data, deserving of study in their own context. To make claims concerning the common essence that lies beyond the grasp of the usual tools of empirical research marks the end of scholarly research and the beginning of a personal quest.

On this note, one can question Armstrong's emphasis on the very term *God*—after all, the book purports to be a history of God that encompasses all three (and more) religions—and investigate just how the use of that term is evidence of an attempt to harmonize or homogenize data that might otherwise be understood as significantly different. For the majority of English-speaking persons of any of the three religious traditions examined by Armstrong, 'God' is more than likely a useful and generic term for the monotheistic deity they worship. However, the term is more properly relevant only to English-speaking Christians, for, in most cases, it denotes a male creator deity who happens to be either one element of a trinity or itself symbolized in the form of a three-part manifestation: the Father, the Son, and the Holy Spirit.

Unfortunately for Armstrong, is it not so easy to harmonize these fundamentally important characteristics of the Christian conception of deity with those of either the Jewish or the Muslim traditions. Although all three social formations are historically related to one another, insomuch as the Christian tradition virtually appropriates the entire Jewish myth and, several centuries later, Abraham, Moses, Mary, and Jesus, among others, figure prominently in the Qur'an, each system is distinct in many other crucial ways and has a particular interpretation of this seemingly common textual tradition that necessitates a strict division between the religions. For instance, take the character of Abraham. For Jews, he is undeniably the first Jew, the first person who answered the deity's invitation to form a covenant or agreement. However, in light of the new covenant that is symbolized in the very blood of the crucified Jesus, Abraham and the entire patriarchal and prophetic tradition of the Israelites is drastically reinterpreted as mere foreshadowing for the eventual arrival of Jesus, later understood as the Christos, the anointed one. In the hands of Muslim writers and theologians, Abraham is reinterpreted again as the first true believer, the first to submit to the will of Allah. Only with the arrival of Muhammad, the "seal of the prophets" and the communication of the will and words of Allah through the eminently beautiful Arabic language, would this message be finally and adequately communicated to humankind.

Accordingly, the use of 'God' for all three of these monotheistic conceptions is itself evidence of a somewhat imperialist attitude on the part of commentators who occupy positions of cultural privilege, assuming all too easily that their local is most obviously universal. Some writers have even gone so far as to describe Brahman, itself an impersonal, abstract concept, as constituting "God in Hinduism"—a wholly misleading description that fails to take many Hindu insider reports seriously. If this argument has not convinced the reader, then think, for a moment, of informing one's Christian friends that, whether they know it or not, they are actually worshiping Yahweh, Elohim, or Allah for that matter. What would devout Jews make of the suggestion that they are the chosen people of Allah, and how would Muslims feel about learning that Muhammad is the prophet and messenger of God the Father? Unless one is addressing a rather liberal devotee in each of these cases (liberal in the sense of European political philosophy), one will find an immediate reaction that suggests that to the devotee there is a rather important distinction between these various folk terms/conceptions. Possibly because of the recent role that English plays as the default *lingua franca* of the world (a privilege that is hardly innocent), coupled with the general success of European-Christian culture in spreading throughout the world by means of its economic, political, and military dominance (again, hardly innocuous), and the fact that modern research on the issue of religious pluralism is largely a Christian phenomenon, 'God' is widely accepted as a plastic, contentless yet all-inclusive term capable of being stretched to include both its role as signifying the specific deity of Christianity and its role as a generic substitute for "their" deity's name as well. However, to be sensitive to the historical particularities of each religion—just as phenomenologists have often lectured their colleagues—researchers involved in the act of description ought to employ the vocabularies relevant to the devotees themselves, unless, of course, one is engaged in the further scholarly task of redescription, when such folk terms are replaced by analytic concepts of the scholar's own making.

Although it ought not to be confused with the academic study of religion as it is practiced in universities throughout the world, Karen Armstrong's *History of God* is an informative introduction to a wide body of literature on the topic of 'God'—from the creation myths of Babylon to the writings of the twentieth-century European philosophers—that will continue to attract liberal-minded readers. This popularity, however, is the more interesting fact; it is itself evidence of the age in which we live when people of relative privilege seem intent on reducing empirical diversity and multiplicity to ethereal and essential unity and simplicity—a unity and simplicity that follows a rather strict party line. This is nothing more than the ideological strategy of universalization. As in the case of liberal discourses that posit human freedom, individuality, and equality as shared or common essentials, the problem is that in our sometimes fevered attempts to find commonality amidst diversity, we construct abstract images of sameness that overlook, ignore, and sometimes deny and belittle the very concrete ways in which human communities continually divide and distinguish among themselves, ways that are themselves some of the primary strategies that bring about severe material and social imbalances. After all, racism and sexism flourish within the liberal democracies in spite of the rhetoric of equality and freedom. Or, to put it in the words of James Taylor in his song "Slap Leather" (1991), what we find in Armstrong's *History of God* is none other than a history of concocting sameness, where we "turn the whole wide world into a TV show; So it's just the same game wherever you go; You never meet a soul that you don't already know; One big advertisement for the status quo."

In the end, then, and in spite of its impressive command of the data, *A History of God* is yet another instance of the liberal attempt to unify diversity by glossing over concrete difference of culture, politics, economics, and so on, in favor of a presumably abstract, nonhistorical—and, in this case—so-called religious or spiritual sameness. Armstrong's best seller is not a history of the concept of God but is an unknowing history, and practical example, of the on-going human effort to create social identity and homogeneity by means of rhetorics of unity, a rhetoric that purchases social identity at the expense of those who do not quite fit the dominant pattern. As important as it is to recognize what "we" have in common, it is sometimes more important to investigate who does and does not constitute this "we" and who gets to decide on the criteria whereby something is understood as "same" and "different."

NOTE

1. That we all know people who have died in car accidents on our highways does not deter us from driving, now does it? This wonderful juxtaposition was proposed by my teaching assistant in 1999, Stephen Hopkins. He was trying to persuade his B.A. students that systems of meaning, such as that of the snake handlers, have an internal coherence lost on those who come to their study with the presumably normative status of a different sociosemantic system. Contrary to the liberal humanist assumption, there is simply no "common sense" that can be appealed to when one seeks to adjudicate safe from unsafe or useful from useless. After all, is not speeding down a highway's on ramp comparable to attending a snake handling ceremony, insomuch as in both cases the very real and present dangers are known and accepted?

CHAPTER 4

Explaining the Sacred: Theorizing on Religion in the Late Twentieth Century[1]

> The observation that practically all tribes, states, and cities have some form of religion has been made repeatedly, ever since Heroditus. Ancient philosophers made this "consensus of nations" proof for the existence of the gods. The question is not whether ethnographers may still find a few exceptions to that consensus; it is the universality of the consensus that is to be explained.
> —(Burkert 1996: 1)

So begins the published form of Walter Burkert's Gifford Lectures from 1989, *Creation of the Sacred*. Like any good book, its opening lines, just quoted, anticipate the territory over which the attentive reader can expect to travel. In these three sentences, Burkert makes it clear that the focus of his book is on the specific problem of *explaining* what he later terms the "acceptance, persistence, and preponderance" of this universal human phenomenon, religion. His words bear repeating: "the question is not whether ethnographers may still find a few exceptions to that consensus; it is the universality of the consensus that is to be explained." Or, as he phrases it soon after, "the remarkable fact is not the existence of ecstacy or other forms of altered consciousness," both of which he identifies as particular types of experience that facilitate interaction with culturally postulated, nonempirical beings; instead, "it is [the] acceptance and interpretation [of such states as ecstacy] by the majority of normal people" that is remarkable and therefore in need of explanation (1996: 6). To accomplish just such an explanation, Burkert engages in comparatively based, cross-culturally applicable, cross-disciplinary theorizing. Coming near the close of the twentieth century, when cross-cultural generalizations and naturalistically based theorizing in the study of religion have consistently been avoided by many working in the field— when, in Quentin Skinner's words from a decade ago, grand theorizing is generally "treated as little better than a confused and old-fashioned failure to keep up with the scientific times" (Skinner 1987: 4)—Burkert's aim is a bold one, which, in my opinion, deserves consideration.[2] That the return to grand theorizing in our field lags behind the other human sciences by about three decades is something we will need to address on another day.

So, just how bold is Burkert's book? Without even having to bring up the name of Charles Darwin, a controversial enough figure for those rightly troubled by the Social Darwinism of an earlier century, one need only mention that Burkert is an unabashed naturalist who takes seriously the role played by theory in the study of human behaviors. If we correctly understand definitions of religion to be representatives of one's theory of religion—for, as Lawson and McCauley have correctly pointed out, "definitions are only as good as the theories that inspire them" (1993: 217)—then Burkert represents one of two opposing poles in the modern field: whereas the inductivist/phenomenologist understands theorizing to get in the way of intuitively based description of self-evident religious facts, the deductivist finds in prior theorizing the necessary preconditions that make mere things into facts.

With this crucial difference in mind, I can say that, over the course of a few short academic generations, we have come a long way in understanding just how to practice the academic study of religion as a comparative human science. Whereas we entered this century trying to recover from the metaphysically reductive grand theorizing of an earlier century, as a new century dawns, Burkert is among a small but growing number of scholars attempting to avoid the dangers of metaphysical reduction while theorizing on such grand themes as the origins of religion and its persistence in human nature and society. Given the degree to which most contemporary studies of religion simply avoid posing the kinds of questions that Burkert raises (confirming that a spirit of anti-intellectualism lies near the very core of our field), and given the number of years many of us have waited for such questions to reemerge as credible sites of academic discourse, there is much at stake in this rebirth of theory in the study of religion. But to help bring this about, there are a couple of issues that need to be addressed, and Burkert's book provides us with an opportunity to reflect on wider issues of theory in the study of religion.

Throughout this century a number of intellectual "-isms" have come and gone; although some were surely mere cultural fashions, to borrow Eliade's rather condescending but still useful term, some have had tremendous impact inside and outside the walls of our classrooms and conference halls; few have had more impact than structuralism's successor, postmodernism. Whether we mean by this slippery signifier an utter "incredulity toward [such] metanarratives [as] the dialectics of the Spirit, the hermeneutics of meaning, the emancipation of the rational or working subject, or the creation of wealth" (Lyotard 1984), we can easily see the troubled waters in which contemporary theory building navigates. The years that intervene between Weber's matter-of-fact distinction between the university lectern and the church pulpit and Burkert's attempt to apply sociobiology to study religion's persistence have seen the rise of radical critiques of aligning essences with historical origins, a historiography devoid of teleology, and a self-consciously playful attitude toward the production of meaning. Surely anyone familiar with even a small bit of such critique will tread lightly when making claims about such things as human nature.

Burkert correctly understands that if he is to persuade his readers that there is still a place for general theorizing in the human sciences— or, we could go so far as to say whether there is still a place for this thing some of us call the "human sciences"—then we must successfully negotiate the sometimes severe critiques of postmodern relativity. For, as he observes early on, within the postmodern university, there is little or no room for claims concerning Nature: "it has been dispelled as a concept and is physically vanishing from our sights under the heap of man-made construction and refuse" (1996: ix). Instead, as he notes a little later, "the principle [now] held by the leading schools of contemporary social sciences [is that] each culture must be studied in its own diversity and relative autonomy. In consequence [he goes on to conclude], the very concept of human nature has come under attack . . . [and] nature is excluded from cultural studies." Appealing to Clifford Geertz, Burkert notes that this exclusively culturalist approach, one that conceives of cultures as closed systems of signification, presumes that "humanity is as various in its essence as it is in its expression" (Geertz 1973: 35f.). However, if we reason that religion, no less than language, art, or our ability to sort, value, and exchange objects, is part of the universally shared activity—as opposed to an essential, ethereal quality—that has developed within human communities and by human minds, then to study religion contextually, as many postmodern and even postcolonial religionists wish, means not only to study it within its cultural and local political settings, but also to study it within its biological settings or, as Burkert phrases it, within the "specific 'landscapes' conditioned by the age-old evolution of human life" (1996: 21). After all, if we are to avoid the pitfalls of metaphysical reduction while profiting from the knowledge to be gained by means of methodological reduction, we need to agree that there are many scales of naturalistic analysis within our academic house.

Burkert's reasoning is rather straightforward: if we presuppose that contemporary human minds and social systems are not *sui generis* phenomena and are, instead, the inherited result of almost countless complex biological events, then a truly multidisciplinary, social scientifically based study of religion has little choice but to include sociobiological theorizing to try to explain why it is that human beings, to recall David Hume's famous phrasing, have seen, and continue to see, "human faces in the moon [and] armies in the clouds." Along with Burkert we must begin this journey by presuming that religion is an aspect of the ordinary, but far from simple, world where human beings, who share an identifiable set of biological characteristics and environmental contexts, are busy trying to reproduce and thereby pass on their genes to a new generation. If we presume this, then we can hardly limit the study of religion to the study of distinct, autonomous cultural settings and practices for all throughout human communities we find appeals to what Burkert refers to as "nonobvious entities." If, along with Sam Preus (1987), we place Hume at the early watershed point of the naturalistic tradition of scholarship on religion, then Burkert is surely one of its more notable recent members.

As already suggested, to renew this tradition of naturalistic theorizing in the human sciences, we must overcome the sometimes paralyzing critiques of the exclusively culturalist approach. Although I am of the generation whose introduction to the academy entailed an early dose of postmodernism (meaning that I happen to think that, from time to time, it is rather healthy for members of a scholarly field to tell emperors and colleagues alike that beneath their constructs they are as naked as the rest of us), I also happen to think that we will only come to know something about this complex natural world in which we live if we are able to make our presuppositions, assumptions, and theoretical models (our "worlds"; see Paden 2000) public, testable, and therefore critiquable. So, while being influenced a great deal by such writers as Michel Foucault and Terry Eagleton (one a postmodern genealogist and the other a Marxist literary critic sympathetic to the best of what postmodern critique has to offer), I am also indebted to those writers who comprise the naturalistic tradition in our field, a tradition that, for some time, has doggedly worked to develop theories for studying religion not as an uncaused *sui generis* feeling or impulse but as a social fact of historical, human existence. In fact, that we no longer place much weight on a number of early naturalistic theories (going so far as to acknowledge that few were actually sound theories to begin with) has to be seen as a bit of a victory for those who see something to be gained by means of theory building, testing, and public criticism. Therefore, it is on the relationship between these two different levels of analysis—theory building, on the one hand, and critique, on the other—that a future study of religion has to be based.

To get us going on this, I suggest that instead of seeing the relationship between the naturalistic and the postmodern study of religion as antagonistic, we should perceive it as self-reflexive or dialectical: whereas one comprises the necessary activity of building models by means of which we apprehend and then try to understand the complexities of the world around us (for none of us has unmediated access to reality, whatever that actually means—not postmodernists and, despite their best claims to the contrary, certainly not religious devotees), the other is a metatheoretical activity whereby some members of our profession critique the model builders and sign makers for being so bold as to think that, as many before me have phrased it, their maps are adequate representations of the actual territory. When we lack the second level of self-reflexive critique, when we presume that our categories and "worlds" are completely adequate presentations of the world around us, we are left with the peculiar modernist view of the world, which, in an utter irony, is shared by religious and positivist scholars of religion alike.

This self-reflexive, postmodern component of metacritique, which must not be confused with the necessary and prior activity of theory building, steers us clear of the kind of metaphysical reduction so feared by some members of our field *while at the same time* ensuring that the study of observable events is the point of demarcation between the study of religion and its practice. After all, if anything can distinguish our field from the institutions we study, it is the manner in which participants in the latter attempt to insulate their claims and institutions from historically grounded analysis and critique. Therefore, despite the fact that some in our field understand postmodernism to imply an end to all discursive boundaries and institutionally formative rules—thereby effectively re-authorizing openly theological discourses in the public university (a position that I examine in a latter chapter)—issues of theoretical, methodological, and institutional demarcation continue to have utmost relevance in the postmodern study of religion. Simply put, we do a tremendous disservice to the critical potential of postmodernism if we leave it to theologians to set the ground rules for how postmodern critique enters the study of religion.

Given the clear limitations of a previous generation's appeals either to *sui generis* religion (as the ground for the humanistic history of religions) or to pure objectivity and value neutrality (as the ground for the science of religion), we can no longer presume that the old ways in which we distinguished the study of religion from its practice remain convincing. What is required is a more persuasive argument that can take into account the ironic fact that pretheoretical values and institutional constraints condition all efforts to know. I believe that identifying the relations between theory building, application, and testing, on the one hand, and metacritique, on the other, holds some promise for demarcating the study of human behavior from the straightforward participation in that behavior. So, when *Creation of the Sacred* opens by immediately drawing the reader's attention to the quagmire—or, in his words, a battlefield—of intracultural theorizing, we should enter it knowing that, although it might be a bit of a mess to get through, it will be well worth the effort.

If members of the field are successfully to make it through this quagmire and maintain the distinction between the study and the practice of religion, they will not only need to clarify how theory is related to critique, they will also need to understand what is involved in generating productive, cross-cultural comparative categories; as argued earlier, the very category "religion" is the most obvious one that we need to consider. This is not lost on Burkert, for, after arguing for the place of cross-cultural theorizing, he sets about defining this central comparative category. For Burkert, religion entails "formalized ritual behavior appropriate for veneration; the practice of offerings, sacrifices, vows, and prayers with reference to superior beings; and songs, tales, teachings, and explanations about these beings and the worship they demand" (1996: 4). Or, to put it another way, religion, like all human activities, operates within the biologically determined landscape as a form of socially symbolic communication sanctioned by appeals to nonobvious entities (things you don't bump into, e.g., gods, ancestors, demons, ghosts, etc.), all of which is undertaken with deadly seriousness (1996: 4–8). In fact, if anything distinguishes religion as symbolic communication from such other equally symbolic systems as art or games, it is this element of seriousness, or even outright fear, and the anxiety it focuses and thereby displaces. Religion, as a mode of communication, therefore helps to construct "an uninterrupted chain of tradition, taking over the mental worlds of [our] elders, working on them and passing them along. . . . [B]y virtue of its seriousness [religion] claims preeminence" (1996: 24).

Apart from the category of religion, then, we see a host of other easily recognized and therefore familiar comparative categories in Burkert's work: veneration, sacrifice, worship, ritual, myth, prayer, and superior beings, to name but a few. Like any good scholar, Burkert tries to tell us precisely what he means by each of these categories; for example, ritual "entails fixed behavior patterns marked by exaggeration and repetition and often characterized by obsessive seriousness—patterns which are prominent even in most modern varieties of religious communication" (1996: 19); and a myth is a tale that is the "generalized, . . . common possession of a group or tribe that helps to constitute its conscious group identity" (1996: 57). Here we must be clear on one crucial point:

contrary to what a previous generation of phenomenologists presumed, Burkert correctly understands that all comparative categories have significance *only in the context of* an overall theory of what it is that is being compared—in this case he is setting out to explain the commonalities in a component of social behavior shared by all human beings, this component he terms "religion." The fact that Burkert's theory of religion is a social theory of religion is evident in the definitions of both ritual and myth: the myth/ritual complex, the very core of religion for Burkert, is an authoritative, memory-based, repetitive system of interrelated signs that communicate and thereby teach socially relevant categories, values, and information; it is a form of "indelible transmission" made possible through contexts of heightened anxiety, fear, and even terror. For, "as civilization became too precious and too complicated to leave its preservation to individual choice or chance, new institutions had to arise to guarantee social cohesion across long spans of time. . . . The permanent authority of ancestors or the immortal gods provides the needed stability" for such communication across distances of space and time (1996: 15). Through song and dance in the midst of the seriousness afforded by the setting and the formalization, the key components of collective identities are taught and reinforced. Religion, for Burkert, is therefore a long-lasting form of social replication and social regulation.

The crucial point that must not be lost in all this is that the notions of myth, ritual, and even religion do not refer to real things in the human environment; they are, instead, comparative categories of our making, categories that serve just our purposes—as the constitution of this "our" changes, so too do the purposes for which these categories are wielded. Despite how our informants might use these same terms, religion, myth, and ritual are part of our scholarly toolbox and, therefore, ought to be part of a theoretically based vocabulary used to describe what the researcher sees as uniformities in observable, human behaviors—in Burkert's case, the common means by which the evolutionary fitness of social formations has been enhanced.

After recognizing that our descriptive and comparative vocabularies are involved in the necessary creative activities of simplification by means of abstraction, generalization, reduction, and classification—meaning that, despite realist misconceptions, "every decoding is another encoding" (for Burkert on a related topic see 1996: 165ff.)—we must further recognize that such phenomenological categories as sacrifice, veneration, gift, worship, and even religion, lack explanatory value. This point was lost, however, on some our predecessors, for they seem to have thought that scholarship had accomplished its task once the diversity of human religiosity had been classified in extensive handbooks with chapters devoted to such apparently real things as sacred stones, sacred water, sacred fires, sacred trees, and sacred mountains. Regardless of its utility in classifying, sorting, and organizing certain sorts of human behaviors by means of the adjective *sacred*, once one moves to the level of analysis, the very practices so termed "religious" or "sacred" are in need of explanation. In other words, at the level of analysis, the descriptively useful adjectives *sacred* and *religious* are expendable, for at that level we pose such questions as Why is it that these, and only these, stones rank? What purpose can this, rather than that, tree serve? To appeal once more to the remarkably fertile writings of Jonathan Smith, for our work to qualify as scholarship the behaviors or sites commonly described as religious (e.g., sacrifice, worship, pilgrimage, etc.) need to be redescribed in terms of a scholarly, third-order language, thereby necessitating what he has termed the "rectification" of the original descriptive category itself. We can appeal to Burkert for a practical example: what on the descriptive level is usefully termed "religious" (e.g., sacrifice made to the gods) turns out, on the level of redescriptive analysis, to be a biologically driven, socially efficacious mechanism (e.g., a part stands in for the whole—whether that part be a finger, a tithe, or a member of the herd).

Redescriptive scholarship presupposes that accurate description and nuanced comparison are crucial yet hardly ends in themselves; instead, they are governed by theories that are preparatory to the task of analysis and explanation. You would think that this would be obvious since it is only in light of such theories that this or that description can count as accurate in the first place. Moreover, as Lawson and McCauley have asked, without prior theories, how would we ever know what to describe or when to stop describing it (McCauley and Lawson 1996: 182)? Our work as scholars is therefore only half done once we have described, for example, various sacrificial rites and found similarities and differences across times and places; there remains the crucial job of making our theory explicit in the act of explaining both the results of the comparison (Why this or that similarity/difference in the first place?) and the very existence of blood-letting institutions to begin with. By adding explanatory analysis to their toolbox, theoreticians of religion, such as Burkert, are not suggesting that description and comparison are somehow secondary intellectual procedures, for they are the very foundation upon which all subsequent analyses rest.

Therefore, we must not forget that the descriptive and comparative vocabularies we employ operate in the context of larger explanatory theories. Unfortunately, not all of our colleagues agree, and a number of scholars continue to employ categories that have questionable analytic use and little or no defensible theoretical backing. What fuels this continued use of troublesome categories is—as I've already suggested—the general confusion of phenomenological *description* with social scientific *analysis*, for, whatever descriptive value our categories may have, they generally originate from, and continue to be inscribed within, the vocabularies and belief systems of the groups we study *rather than* the analytic vocabularies of the academy. This suggests that there is an often-undetected self-interest at work insomuch as scholars are often participants in the very communities they study, employing indigenous vocabularies as if the local values inevitably encoded within such terminology were nonexistent. Conflating these two domains of inquiry amounts to failing to redescribe our emic descriptions by means of etic categories. To appeal once again to Marvin Harris, writing nearly twenty years ago, "[r]ather than employ concepts that are . . . appropriate from the native point of view, the observer is free to use alien categories and rules derived from the language of science" (1979: 32). To paraphrase the last of the Bruce Lincoln's thirteen theses on method, whereas faithful reporting, even advocacy and color commentary are descriptively based, scholarship is fundamentally analytic and therefore redescriptive (Lincoln 1996a). That this point is not widely accepted by late-twentieth-century scholars is troubling.

To help illustrate this point, I went looking for an instance of contemporary scholarship on comparative religion that confused description with analysis. Sadly, I didn't have to look far, for, at the same time, my colleague Jack Llewellyn was reading what he found to be a rather problematic book entitled *Pilgrimage: Past and Present in the World Religions* (Coleman and Elsner 1995). That the very category of pilgrimage is not a natural kind but is, instead, a cross-cultural, comparative category requiring theoretical backing is, unfortunately, lost on the readers of this book. Furthermore, that the book's authors are not scholars of religion (one is an anthropologist and the other an art historian) suggests our own failure to make it clear to our colleagues that our vocabularies are not in a one-to-one fit with reality but are, instead, extensions of the models we use to talk about the complexities of human beliefs, behaviors, and institutions.[3]

For example, instead of seeing pilgrimage as a fundamentally human institution caught up in acts of social formation (i.e., the ongoing activity whereby social identities are constructed and contested), the authors portray it as, to borrow some of their very own terminology, a sacred journey across a sacred landscape and sacred geographies to sacred architectures and holy objects located at a sacred center. That their excessively used and overly vague technical term *sacred* is never defined should hardly be surprising since it is a term that functions rhetorically and not substantively.[4] In fact, it is only after they have used this category repeatedly, along with its equally undefined synonyms *holy* and *spiritual* (all three are used fourteen times in a two and a half page introduction!), that they offer their readers an endnote that simply says, "For a discussion of what is meant by the 'sacred,' see individual chapters and particularly the Epilogue" (1995: 221 n. 1). Despite this note, nowhere is this category defined. Instead, the authors resort to definition by example, the strategy of inductivists the world over: "You'll know what I'm talking about when you see it." So, the reader comes away with an understanding of pilgrimage as "a quest for a transcendent goal," which often entails the pilgrim obtaining a token or relic that acts as a "physical manifestation of the charisma of a sacred centre" (1995: 1). Finding "charisma" still used as a technical, explanatory category, not to mention such ill-considered concepts as 'manifestation' and 'sacred centre', suggests that for all those who protest that Eliade's ghost has left the building, this book alone constitutes sufficient evidence that he yet haunts the field.

As an aside, I should say that such scholarship likes to haunt our lecture halls most of all, places that I am convinced are some of the most important sites for renewing the field. Although I hardly wish to paint all class resources with the same brush, I must, nonetheless, say that, sadly, the classroom happens to be the site of some of the most unsophisticated scholarship we collectively produce. It is the place where we often fail to live up to our responsibility of educating critical thinkers and future scholars and, instead, where we often act as trustees concerned for the general well-being of religion. Couple this sympathy for our subject matter with the contemporary demands of the "customer service" model adopted by many universities, and you end up with a class that reproduces "common sense," designed to make students feel good about themselves.

Like many of our colleagues, the authors of *Pilgrimage: Past and Present in the World Religions* fail to recognize that human beings involved in routine, mass, or coordinated movements from place to place are not inherently "pilgrims"—they're just people on the move. After all, both the Middle English word *pelegrim* and the Old French equivalent *pelegrin* are derived from the Latin *peregrinus*, which simply means a foreigner or one who travels abroad. Such travelers are only pilgrims, involved in making a pilgrimage, once we as observers come on the scene armed with certain descriptive and comparative tools intent on generalizing and systematizing their behavior in light of an overall hunch we have as to why people periodically move as a group from this place to that place according to a generally accepted schedule. People on the move become "pilgrims" rather than, say, "political delegates," "travelers," "wanderers," or "tourists" only because of certain interests we the observers have, because of certain theories we come up with.

Change the viewpoint of the observer, and what was once a pilgrim becomes a tourist snapping pictures at Niagara Falls.

No doubt some will say that because *pilgrim* is itself a term of self-description for many of the people we study, it is a worthwhile term for the scholar. First off, it should come as little surprise to us that some participants in these mass movements might wish to distinguish themselves as pilgrims, given the essentially spiritual, privileged, and noncritiquable connotations of this category. Were not the organizers of the Million Man March on Washington D.C. and the various mass gathering of the Promise Keepers in football stadiums, both of whom have clearly political agendas, at great pains to portray their gatherings as spiritual rather than political? For such groups, the rhetoric of apoliticism is a powerful force, and 'pilgrimage' is a key part of this rhetoric. Therefore, we must not overlook the fact that the context in which such terms as *pilgrimage* generally derive meaning is one that is often limited to elaborating on some idealized, abstract, and universalized religious devotee's own rhetoric. Second, using 'pilgrimage' as an explanatory (rather than just a descriptive) category fails to satisfy the scholarly requirements of explicitly redescribing participant claims and behaviors in light of our own theories and interests. In fact, we can go so far as to say that whenever we see 'pilgrimage' understood as the result of a sacred center's mysterious, magnetic pull, we should immediately suspect that some sort of mischief and mystification is afoot in such scholarship, for there is always something at stake in spiritualizing the otherwise complex tug-and-pull of the material, historical world.

To reproduce such a rhetoric in our scholarship is none other than to engage in a kind of anti-intellectualism that merely reproduces the obscurantist claims of apoliticism or spiritualism embedded within such talk of the sacred, the holy, spirits, impulses, charisma, and indescribable essences. Instead of understanding pilgrims, like all human beings involved in coordinated mass movement, as engaged in acts of social formation and identity construction and contestation, our colleagues often join such widely acknowledged experts as Edith Turner who, writing on 'pilgrimage' in the *Encyclopedia of Religion*, essentialized and privatized this social behavior by noting that pilgrims "feel the call of some distant holy place," something caused by what she terms "the spiritual magnetism of the pilgrimage center" (1987: 329). This purely descriptivist, individualizing, and depoliticizing approach is repeated in a second article from the *Encyclopedia of Religion*, this time on Roman Catholic pilgrimage in Europe:

> Pilgrimage, making one's way to holy places, is above all an ascetic practice that lets the Christian find salvation through the difficulties

and dangers of a temporary exile. It is also a means of coming into contact with that which is divine and thereby obtaining grace because of
the accumulation of supernatural power in the pilgrimage site. (Sigal
1987: 330–31)[5]

Only because we generally presume that pilgrimage is essentially concerned with an individual's private perception of essentially other-
worldly affairs, inner calls, impulses, and salvation (making it an obviously ascetic practice), all of which is realized or manifested within a
temporarily idyllic zone of exile from the stresses of everyday life, an
exile where social equality reigns and all normal rules and roles are suspended (i.e., the state of *communitas*), are writers such as Turner perplexed by the apparent paradox of so-called spiritual or sacred pilgrimages also being sites for national independence movements where the
rhetoric, symbolism, and politics of exclusion dominate (1987: 328–29).
"How odd," we can almost hear such commentators remark, "that religion, which is personal, inclusive, and other-worldly should coincide
with nationalism, which is political, exclusive, and worldly." Were we
to start with a theory of religion as but one component in the larger,
ongoing process of social formation and identity construction, rather
than a theory of religion as a private impulse, then we would immediately have recognized coordinated mass movements of people to be intimately connected with modern, nationalist discourses. Their coinci-
dence would hardly have surprised us at all.

In fact, redescribing our vocabulary within a thoroughly social theory of religion would also allow us to understand that so-called zones of
communitas are none other than a conservative (in the sense of con-
serving) mechanism for supporting social orders of various types. As
Burkert phrases it: "'Rites of passage' allow for recruitment while stabi-
lizing cultural meanings and values even through the change of generations" (1996: 167). In making what Burkert calls the "crisis of transition [more] manageable," we must not forget that social zones described
by means of Victor Turner's notion of *communitas* do not exist in a vacuum but are temporary, fleeting, and preparatory to reentering a fixed
social location within a complex hierarchy, suggesting that sites of *communitas* are as fixed and structured as any social locale.

The notion of pilgrimage, then, can be effectively redescribesd as none
other than one among many strategies human beings use to accomplish,
reinforce, and at times contest social identities that span time and place.
Fortunately, I'm hardly the only one to have arrived at this conclusion.
Surpassing the *Encyclopedia of Religion*, the detailed entry in the *Harper-
Collins Dictionary of Religion* places emphasis on studying the value judgments made by the participant we study (rather than the so-called

charisma of a place) when it defines pilgrimage as "a round-trip journey undertaken by a person or persons who consider their destination sacred (Smith 1995b: 841—where 'sacred' simply refers to 'things set apart'). In their 1991 volume on Christian pilgrimage, entitled *Contesting the Sacred*, John Eade and the late Michael Sallow conclude that the complexity of the social processes usually termed "pilgrimage" has largely been lost by treating them as essentially homogenous instances of self-evidently sacred quests. The heterogeneity of the human interactions so termed, which was "marginalized or suppressed in the earlier deterministic models of . . . those who adopted a Turnerian paradigm, is here [i.e., in their volume] pushed centre-stage, [and thereby] rendered problematic" (1991: 2–3). In other words, only by means of a new theory of social formation is the old category seen to be problematic; accordingly, a redescribed category assists scholars to get at some of the messy parts of human behavior where power and identity cross paths. Instead of treating pilgrimage as a pristine site of sacred magnetism, charisma, and purely religious expression or devotion, we must reconceive of coordinated, ritualized mass movements as sites of cognitive classification, social control, competing discourses, and contested identities. The very category of pilgrimage must therefore be redescribed (or, as Eade and Sallnow term it, "deconstructed") within a coherent and thoroughly social theory of religion.

What all this suggests is that despite the theoretical emptiness of many of the comparative terms we currently use in the field, we can effectively redescribe our vocabulary and make some traditional, phenomenological categories part of a more sophisticated, theoretically productive vocabulary, informed and fueled by a social theory of religion as a natural human construct. Such a redescription will not be easy, for at every turn we will be called upon to justify our terminology and to lay bare not only its theoretical underpinnings but also the costs and benefits of retaining it. We will also have to deal with the complaints of those who claim to exercise a territorial prerogative over such terminology.

This is precisely where I return to Burkert. Whether or not one agrees with his quest for evolutionary origins and contemporary social functions, the fact that his definitions and theory are explicit, and his vocabulary theoretically based, makes his work a fitting example of what scholars can contribute to the analysis of religion as an aspect of human behavior. Furthermore, it is the creative nature of his application of a theory derived from one field to another that suggests Burkert's work as an example of the multidisciplinary study of religion. Because it is in part a speculative theory of origins that clearly cannot be tested—an acknowledgment that he makes up front (Burkert 1996: 20, 23)—the success of his work will be seen in the more controlled projects that it prompts and inspires.

By way of a conclusion, let me suggest that such attempts to make the implicit explicit are generally limited to oppositional and emergent scholarships, when writers know all too well that their presumptions are not widely shared and that their readers will immediately question the authority they have to say what they say and write what they write. An unarticulated consensus within the academy breeds a culture of sound bite scholarship where truisms are easily packaged and repeated to a nodding audience; the obvious is thereby reinforced and never contested. Even panels at professional meetings predetermine our inability to engage in a serious reconsideration of our assumptions, for the often invisible but no less real demands of concision are all too obvious. If not for an unarticulated consensus that we study a self-evidently meaningful ahistorical reality, manifested in the historical realm, more colleagues would likely agree that there is a fundamental need to start their work by defining and theorizing their object of study. An academic enterprise grounded by an unarticulated scholarly consensus, where socially constructed categories are continually mistaken for realities, and where the datum of study is presumed to comprise private, other-worldly emotions and impulses, is the sign of intellectual and institutional zombification (to borrow an apt term from the National Public Radio commentator Adrei Codrescu [1994]); instead, creativity, opposition, and ongoing debate will keep us alive and healthy. And in the midst of the current consensus on exclusively culturalist or local approaches to the study of human institutions, Burkert has graciously provided us with a healthy dose of all three.

To dislodge the lethargy that dominates our field, to inject the creativity and irony fundamental to the activities of historically and socially grounded model building, redescription, critique, provocation, and opposition, is to challenge our peers to acknowledge that none of us actually studies pilgrimages or religion; instead, we all employ constructed categories such as "pilgrim" or "religion," as rubrics, as tools to study the various ways in which human beings name and rename who they are. To convince our peers to acknowledge this will indeed be a challenge, for, to borrow the liberal theologian Margaret Miles's apt comments regarding American moviegoers, scholars too "prefer familiar scenarios overlaid with a thin veneer of novelty" (1996: 30).

Having tested the limits of concision, I now close in the same manner in which I opened, by quoting the fitting words of Burkert, this time from the end of his book:

> [W]ithin a world dominated by self-created technology [such as concepts and terminology], humans . . . will not easily accept that constructs of sense reaching out for the nonobvious are nothing but self-created projections, and that no other signs from the universe around are there to be perceived except for the irregularities resounding from the first big bang. (1996: 179)

NOTES

1. An earlier version of this paper was presented to the Comparative Studies in Religion Section of the American Academy of Religion, San Francisco, 23 November 1997.

2. See *Method & Theory in the Study of Religion* 10/1 (1998) for a review symposium on *The Creation of the Sacred*; the reviewers include Pascal Boyer, Willi Braun, Daniel Dennett, Tomoko Masuzawa, C. Robert Phillips, with a response by Burkert.

3. See Juschka 1998 and Llewellyn 1998 and forthcoming for examples of writers taking theory seriously when studying pilgrimage.

4. I think here of the 2000 presidential race in the United States. When asked to name the political philosopher who most influenced him, Republican candidate George W. Bush simply answered, "Christ"; at a different public meeting, Democratic candidate Al Gore pulled out the old nugget, "WWJD: What Would Jesus Do" as his answer to a question about how he makes policy decisions. This is politics practiced as a high art; both answers are purely empty, rhetorical devices, plastic enough to be filled by any listener's presumption about who Jesus or Christ was and what "he" represented. That both politicians' discourses clearly exclude non-Christian citizens of the United States simply demonstrates how thoroughly dominant the Christian "we" is in the United States.

5. As might be expected, the *Encyclopedia of Religion* has several purely descriptivist articles on pilgrimage (e.g., under Roman Catholicism, the Holy Land, Islam, Hindusim, Tibetan Buddhism, etc.). None, however, offers an actual theory of pilgrimage; instead, they all reproduce folk understandings. This is lamentable, if for no other reason than students will generally go to resources such as this for information. Sadly, apart from learning the names of this or that group of people, city, or river, they will leave knowing what they already knew when they first set foot in the library's reference section.

CHAPTER 5

"We're All Stuck Somewhere": Taming Ethnocentrism and Transcultural Understandings

While a number of contemporary scholars of religion continue to refrain from—or have actually expressed what amounts to a disdain for—discussing theoretical issues, and instead go about what they say is the business of "taking religion seriously" (whatever that may actually mean), yet another anthropologist has stepped into this void and made a significant contribution to theorizing in the academic study of religion.[1] One of the more notable aspects of Benson Saler's work, *Conceptualizing Religion* (1993), is his effort to, in his words, "tame" the inevitable ethnocentrism that comes along with attempts to speak about the other by examining its foundations in the very concepts and assumptions operative in the Euro-American study of *religion*. He acknowledges that, from the outset, both the observer and the observed—the outsider and the insider—are entrenched in their own specific cultural, and hence conceptual, contexts and that, in his words, "some amount of ethnocentrism is probably unavoidable as a cognitive starting point in the search for trans-cultural understanding" (1993: 9). Thus, from the start at least, both observers and informants—the latter of which is a better term than Saler's choice of the dated term *natives*—are separated by a gulf, each inside their own cultural and historical context making neither position ultimately authoritative nor normative.

Regardless of the gap in respective starting points, it is clear from Saler's work that this initial gulf *ought* to be bridged and that some convergence of understanding is desirable; for developing transcultural understanding is the goal of his anthropology. Although it is uncertain whether this gulf will ever be completely overcome, Saler's effort to diminish *our* and *their* situatedness comprises a three-fold task: (i) it is incumbent on scholars to acknowledge the culturally entrenched, and hence partial and limited, nature of their own observational starting point, that is, recognizing the entrenched nature of our idealized, prototypical notions of just what constitutes religion—and for that matter, what constitutes and counts as race, kinship, nation, gender, society, and all other folk categories that we as scholars translate into analytical, comparative categories; (ii) due to this perspective-bound nature of our starting prototypes, we must always hold them tentatively, as exemplars instead of norms. Accordingly, we must be thoroughly familiar with their history, implications, limitations, and various uses. This is accomplished through conceiving of them as "unbounded categories," which are to be distinguished in terms of loose sets of family resemblances that are always open to being revised; (iii) and last, due to the variety of not only behaviors and beliefs but also the variety of both folk and scholarly categories that overlap and can be grouped together and compared through one or more shared family traits, Saler calls for scholars to explore the use of other people's folk categories as possible scholarly, analytical categories. While the other may know us through what we can only hope are equally openended folk categories, we can venture to explore using their categories as our own starting points—hence, a dialogue takes place. Regardless of where or when—if ever—such dialogue ends, Saler maintains that "religion," conceptualized as just such an unbounded category, serves as a possible cultural bridge; for, from the outset, such an unbounded category excludes no one from gaining entrance to the dialogue and the bridge-building game. In other words, since religion is best conceived polythetically rather than monothetically, as an issue of more-or-less rather than yes-or-no, we never know where the comparative enterprise will lead us nor who will join in the conversation.

Right off, let me say that I welcome Saler's efforts to demonstrate the contextual nature of not just the subject under study but observing outsiders complete with their categories as well, a demonstration that is all the stronger since I read his recognition of cultural and contextual relativity as not necessarily implying that there is no difference or no point of demarcation between the insiders and outsiders. Postmodern critiques of authority are often appropriated by scholars of religion acting as caretakers and used to legitimize and relativize all contexts; in other words, because we are all contextually bound, or so the argument goes, then all viewpoints deserve equal time in any one given discourse. Surely, Saler's work will help us in the effort to incorporate the best aspects of the postmodernist challenge and construct an academic discourse on culture in general, and religion in particular, that can maintain the analytically productive demarcation between subject and object without the ontological, essentialist, and normative loadings of former efforts at demarcation.

With this notable contribution in mind, however, we must have a closer look at the last of the three previously mentioned strategies that

Saler recommends: namely, that scholars should experiment with non-Western folk categories in the study of Euro-American settings as one way to redress past conceptual and sociocultural imperialism by bringing about some convergence of understanding.[2] A somewhat similar critique of scholarly and conceptual imperialism in the study of religion has recently been made by Ninian Smart, and a brief look at Smart's recommendation may shed some light on some of the theoretical issues at stake for the academic study of religion if we accept Saler's own recommendation for taming ethnocentrism.[3]

In his paper, "Retrospect and Prospect: The History of Religions," which was delivered at the closing session of the 1990 Rome Congress of the International Association for the History of Religions (IAHR), Smart observed that scholars of religion have made little progress "in absorbing values from East and South to compliment the terminology of our profession, which is so largely drawn from Northern, that is to say Western cultures" (Smart 1994: 902). (Note the very different values that are expressed in Smart's use of East-West *as well as* North-South.) Much like Saler, then, Smart criticizes the fact that the categories of research in our field continue to reflect not simply its European but also its Christian origins. As part of his discourse on "absorbing values," which I read as related to Saler's goal of generating transcultural understandings, dialogue, and a multicultural anthropology, Smart argues that our scholarly vocabulary must become more international: "*bhakti* and *li* as well as *devotion* and *ritual*," Smart writes, ought to be equally useful scholarly tools. Because our scholarly vocabularies and categories are not theoretically autonomous but are products of our research methodologies and theories, Smart's recommendations are implicitly a critique of the insular nature of our theories as well.

It is true that the field has not rushed to rid itself of localized folk categories that are entrenched within not just a nineteenth-century European but also a Christian and philosophically idealist context. To substantiate Saler's timely criticisms of the sometimes unsophisticated use of such folk categories as religion and faith, one need only think of the number of comparative religion textbooks and monographs that continue to employ such categories as sin, savior, prayer, God, and even spirituality as if they were self-evidently useful analytic and therefore comparative categories. For example, the problems of employing the term *God*, as opposed to *gods, deities, superhuman agents*, Burkert's *nonobvious beings*, or even Smart's own term *focus*, as a cross-cultural comparative category should strike us all immediately, given the clearly English and Christian context in which the folk term *God* is most often imbued with patriarchal, monotheistic, and moralistic meanings. Although on one descriptive level it may make sense to observe, as we have seen done by Karen Armstrong, that "Muslims worship God," given the important distinctions between a Muslim and Christian, not to mention a Jewish, conception of a monotheistic deity, it would be more accurate to employ a multiplicity of such indigenous terms (ranging from *Allah* to *God the Father*, as required by each individual context) *at the descriptive level of our research.*[4]

But the academic study of religion is not simply about accurate description and faithful understandings: It is also about developing cross-cultural generalizations about certain types of human behavior and beliefs. Although we may be able to purge our terminologies of some of their earlier baggage (e.g., one no longer refers to Islam as "Mohammadism"), we will not be able to purge them totally of their intellectual and cultural contexts, *for the very effort to develop cross-cultural generalizations of human behavior is a specifically scholarly endeavor alien to many of the people whose behaviors we study.*

To return to the above example, although talk of all human beings "worshiping God" is part of the discourse of religious (and often Christian) pluralism, the effort first to describe, then compare, and finally account for *why* human communities often posit and subsequently interact with immaterial beings is part of the discourse of the academy. Although Saler is correct to point out that both efforts are equally entrenched in cultural contexts, what is far more interesting to me is that they are entrenched in *distinguishable* discourses. For example, the discourses differ precisely in terms of their theoretical commitments as represented in their vocabularies: *worship* as opposed to *posit* and *interact*; *God* as opposed to *nonobvious being*. So, given that all discourses are sociohistorically entrenched, it should not be a matter of taming ethnocentrism, as suggested by Saler, but instead, a matter of distinguishing which types are part of which discourses and which institutional settings. If discourses are concerned with dividing up, classifying, and organizing what might otherwise be a complex continuum of human perceptions, the question should not be whether we can minimalize or eliminate situatedness but, instead, which vocabularies and assumptions are appropriate to which context. Both Saler and Smart, then, may be wrong to talk of diminishing and taming ethnocentrism by degrees; perhaps it is instead a question of which type or degree of "ethnocentrism" we as scholars use.

But first we need to introduce a clarification: when we talk of ethnocentrism, it is important that we make an explicit distinction that Saler only sometimes makes. For although he recognizes that ethnocentrism involves not simply *describing* but also *judging* others in terms of our local categories (Saler 1993: 8), at times he appears to confuse this sense of the term with what I would refer to simply as the inevitable "situatedness" of our scholarly prototypes, models, and interests. A defense of this latter sense of the term is unnecessary since it simply describes the inevitable situatedness of all human attempts to know.

For example, at the outset he writes, "the practitioners of a mostly Western profession (anthropology) employ a Western category (religion), conceptualized as a component of a larger category (culture), to achieve their professional goal of coming to understand what is meaningful and important for non-Western peoples. This privileging of Western categories, it might seem, constitutes, or betokens ethnocentrism" (1993: 8). Toward the end of the book, where Saler returns to this topic, he observes that in "pursuing their ethnographic research, anthropologists must also work out from their conventions, discourses, and language-games. What they do cannot be entirely 'open-textured,' and in significant measure it can be accounted 'ethnocentric'" (1993: 260). Having conventions, using theories-as-models (i.e., redescriptions), pursuing goals relevant to these theoretical perspectives, and operating from within discourses, much like having a culture and a sociohistorical context, are not in and of themselves conditions of culpability.

However, mistaking such tactical, relative, and contingent contexts for necessary and normative centers, and then moving from these centers to form judgements, is indeed such a condition. And it is precisely this that makes much scholarship on religion ethnocentric. Or, to put it another way, failing to recognize the theoretical basis of one's efforts to describe, understand, or explain is in part at least what constitutes scholarly ethnocentrism. It is precisely in this manner that Saler's following statement may, ironically, qualify as being ethnocentric: "Whether they have a word for it or not," he writes, "many peoples have ideas about *transcendence* in [the sense of a hope of changing one's human condition]" (1993: 61; italics added). I say that it may be ethnocentric precisely because this seemingly neutral, unobtrusive, and quite possibly accurate observation may in fact be a projection on the part of scholars based on what may turn out to be their own highly localized, liberal humanist notions of individuality, progress, hope, and betterment. Simply put, as a theoretically defensible generalization, it surely is not ethnocentric, it is just in need of testing and application; but, as a seemingly transparent and self-evident description of a basic and universal human hope for the future, one of the supposed aspirations of the Human Spirit or that which characterizes the Human Condition, it may very well be ethnocentric.

Demonstrating the culturally specific nature of our endeavors and tools and arguing that these tools and goals should not be taken as essentially normative (thereby, I would say, avoiding the traps of ethnocentrism) are indeed worthwhile contributions. But attempting to limit, correct, or compensate for that same culture specificity on route to transcultural understandings by means of employing insider categories seems to me to miss the point that we are inextricably stuck with asking just our questions and using just our tools in posing those questions. As my doctoral supervisor at the University of Toronto, Neil McMullin, would say, "We're all stuck somewhere." And this is where I see some difficulties for Saler's approach, a difficulty that results from confusing the two senses of ethnocentrism and thereby seeing scholars as culpable simply for carrying out culturally entrenched scholarship.

For example, later in his book Saler asks: "Are there human universals on which we can base analytical categories that might be defensively used across ethnographies? Or should each ethnography be constructed largely by employing native categories?" (1993: 147). Given Saler's arguments for the contextual and discursive nature of our knowledge, the first option is ruled out, for our analytic categories cannot be based on human universals simply because those very universals are themselves the constructs of our theories. Regardless of whether such universals are really out there, all we know for sure is that we think them up for specific reasons and purposes. I am thinking here of such theoretically driven universals as class, religion, society, gender, politics, and so on. If we acknowledge that humans deploy theoretically generated analytical constructs in specific contexts for specific reasons, then we are left with only the second option, that of employing insider categories. To this point I have no disagreement with Saler. We as scholars in the European tradition have specific questions (that produce our own insider categories and jargon) that make sense given our specific theoretical, political, and social contexts and histories. *They are ours and may very well be no one else's.* (Note the difference between making this observation, on the one hand, and the normative and undefensible statement that they *are* in fact no one else's, on the other.) Hence, the ethnographies we construct are, in the very least, specifically our own creations. What I see as troubling, however, is the way in which Saler attempts to address what some would point out as the extreme relativity and solipsism of this option.

His argument, as I read it, goes something like this: If each ethnography is constructed solely by employing insider categories, then how are we to gain transcultural understandings across those categorial, and hence cultural, divides? To gain such understanding there must be a way to transcend, to translate back and forth so as to bring about some convergence of understanding. His recommendation? We should begin to cross the bridge by experimenting with other people's categories.

For a number of reasons I am not convinced that this solution really works, for it is not immediately clear that a scholar who employs "native categories" is open to recognizing the implicitly theory-based position of such terms. If anything, in our field such insider categories are often privileged in our research and held somehow to transcend theory. However, such categories are no less problematic, no less theory-based, than our own scholarly categories, and our use of them brings with it just as many predicaments as those that many scholars try to avoid by using them in the first place. For example, it seems certain that the insiders who use these categories do not necessarily use them in a uniform or flawless fashion. So, we must ask, which informant do we trust? Which insiders are we to take as the *real, normative,* or *prototypical* insiders? To his credit, Saler anticipates this problem, for he recommends that we begin by trusting the word of the sociopolitical and doctrinal elites within a group, or at least that is who I take to be the usual informants for the world religion textbooks that Saler recommends as a source for these insider terminologies. The problems with this recommendation should be evident. It overlooks the following: the majority of the world's so-called religious people are not to be found among the doctrinal elites; elite doctrinal claims are tied up with economic, social, and political issues when seen on the redescriptive level; and, finally, all insider terms are themselves highly theoretical and contextual in nature, as are our terms—the main difference being, however, that only in the latter context do we have the responsibility to make our theoretical commitments explicit and rationally defensible.

Although religious claims may be employed by some people as if they perfectly represent Reality, in a one-to-one fit shall we say, scholarly insights into the constructedness of all human discourses should prevent us from placing much more trust in them than in our own theoretical vocabularies. Even if we assume that we can somehow access some insider terminologies and categories, we are left with the gaps between the theoretical contexts of their terms and the very different theoretical goals of our research. In other words, no matter how empathic one attempts to be, no ethnographer can let the people "speak for themselves," for, if left to their own devices, would the people we study even be interested in systematizing, describing, categorizing, and representing (or possibly defending) their case to a larger, reading audience? Simply put, as soon as *bhakti* and *puja* come from *our* mouths and pens, they become something entirely different than what they once might have been—for they are now part of *an analytic, comparative vocabulary*—whether used to understand or explain—rather than *a way of life.* Therefore, to presume that what for us becomes an analytical, comparative category used to understand the other was for the other him- or herself such a category as well is perhaps the most problematic issue of all. It is based on the assumption that all humans are equally concerned with developing a convergence of transcultural understandings. As David Hoy has phrased it: "the difficulty with ethnocentrism is not so much that we see the world through our own self-understanding, but instead that we expect every other self-understanding to converge with ours" (1991: 78; see also 1978).[5]

Consider, for example, a recent book by the well-known feminst theologian Rita M. Gross. Right off the bat her introduction to *Feminism and Religion* draws the reader's attention to the thorny problem of enthnocentrism and puts Gross's cards on the table: "[C]hief among my methodological biases is the conviction that relevant thinking can no longer afford the luxury of Ethnocentrism" (1996: 3). Interestingly enough, she immediately goes on to write: "In keeping with the cross-cultural nature of the discipline of religious studies, I will always discuss at least one major Western religion and one other major religion in each of the four central chapters." Although Gross's emphasis on cross-cultural comparison is certainly laudable, the ease with which she banishes the specter of ethnocentrism from any form of "relevant thinking" while simultaneously using such terms as the Euro-Latin *religion* and the all too troubling classification *Western* deserves our attention. Based on Gross's writing, it appears that everyone in the world naturally has a religion and that it is profitable to divide the world between the East and the West—a designation based on the presumably spiritual differences between the "Western and the Eastern mind" as opposed to the way in which the North-South designation is based on the material difference, that is, who owes International Monetary Fund debt to whom.

As insightful as Saler's analysis of the culture-bound nature of all human discourse is—and, indeed, I do not mean to diminish his timely contributions, for especially when compared to most scholars of religion, Saler's contributions have injected much-needed theory into the field—I am not entirely sure that this goal of cultural dialogue, convergence, and translation helps the situation that we find ourselves in as scholars. As important as such a goal may or may not be for the good of the human species, I am not convinced that it is our specific goal as culture critics. For to think that we can somehow understand the *other*, and that they are equally interested in understanding *us* strikes me as rather modernist and just a little bit ethnocentric; it overlooks the many ways in which imperial powers are the ones who are most often interested in doing the understanding and, more important, in doing the conceptual and material appropriating that seems to come along with such efforts to understand (for example, see Chidester 1996c). The appropriation and subsequent domestication of *their* means (in our case, intellectual categories) for *our* ends (in our case, increased cross-cultural understanding) may bear intriguing and possibly disturbing resemblances to earlier instances of economic colonialism where the colonies' natural resources became the colonizer's finished products, profits, and, eventually, meanings.

As I argued in *Manufacturing Religion* (1997c), in the recent history of the study of religion there may be no more explicit example of such domination by appropriation and domestication than the numerous works of Mircea Eliade, where the supposedly ahistorical and purely religious myths, rituals, and symbols of the other—known as the politically autonomous *Homo religiosus*—were to be interpreted and appropriated by Western, secular people in order to revitalize Western culture. This is none other than what Eliade called the "new humanism." Although I most certainly do not mean to suggest that Saler's proposals are part and parcel of such ethnocentric domestication—indeed, Saler is rightfully critical of Eliade's scholarship (e.g., 1993: 102)—I do find his recommendation that *their* means will be useful in serving *our* ends problematic. What may be most troublesome is equating our specific ends with everyone's. As already stated, ethnocentrism is not the fact of having a culture but the assumption that one's own culture—as well as the goals relevant to one's own culture—is by definition everyone's goal. This extends to developing a convergence of transcultural understandings as well. Reading Saler's book, I kept wondering just who is interested in the goal of cross-cultural understanding? The answer, of course, is that *we*, as inheritors of the European tradition of scholarship, have this particular goal—others may or may not share it. This does not make it an illegitimate goal, but it does suggest that it may not be everyone's, meaning that no matter which categories we use (*ritual* or *bhakti*), they are always serving just our purposes, making them inescapably just our categories. For, as Roy Wagner has noted, "the study of culture is in fact *our* culture" (1981: 16). To build on the image used by William Paden in his address to the XVII Congress of the IAHR in Mexico City, although many of us eat apples, oranges, pears, and grapes, it may well only be a relatively small group of us who wish to develop and use the higher order, analytical category "fruit" as a means for organizing all of these various foods under one classification.[6] To recognize the relativity of such analytical interests means that we must ask: Is the intellectual capital of the other worthwhile in its own theoretical and historical contexts, working toward its own goals, or must it continually find its place and define its worth only in terms of being translated and domesticated by our own epistemological and sociocultural goals?

Although Saler's efforts seem eminently concerned with the welfare of the other, I fear that his recommendation of categorial translation and appropriation, motivated by the goal of transcultural understanding, brings with it a number of troubling implications. With this in mind, it is to our own detriment that we often forget that earlier efforts on the part of Christians to convert and missionize, on the one hand, and the more contemporary and largely Christian-initiated efforts at dialogue, on the other, may be intimately related in terms of the shared strategies and technologies that function to translate, manage, and domesticate the other.

Would it not be better simply to acknowledge that we base our observations on culturally determined values and theories that are not Reality (the natural world) but rather models for that reality (social 'worlds')? Because, as Saler himself suggests, theories ground descriptions, definitions, and explanations, none of which will ever fit perfectly with what is or is not really out there, our goal should not be for our experiences to overlap with those of the other, but, rather, to explain, from our admittedly entrenched point of view, what we perceive to be going on out there and, given our own theoretical interests, why it is going on. What I am suggesting is that a return to explanatory efforts, this time understood not as ontologically based (such as the ultimately reductive explanations of early social scientific theorizing) but instead as theoretically and taxonomically grounded, rather than Saler's goal of transcultural understanding, may be one of the more productive ways to address scholarly, as well as sociocultural, ethnocentrism. In other words, if one's goal is to understand meaning, which amounts to an effort to access privileged, insider data, then the inevitably situated nature of human cognition becomes a stumbling block. For in such a case our contextually bound categories impede accurate, empathic, intuitively grounded descriptions and understandings. If, on the other hand, our efforts are to redescribe and explain insider behaviors based on clearly articulated and defensible theories of human culture and belief systems, then our categories are hardly to be critiqued for their lack of overlap with the self-perceptions of the insider. In fact, the recognition of this inevitable gap is what makes some aspects of human behavior data for other humans to study.

So I am suggesting that Saler's first two recommendations (first, to recognize that our research is based on preconceived and culturally bound prototypes, and second, that we must endeavor to learn the histories and implications of our own categories and hold them open to testing and change) should, as he persuasively argues, capture our attention, but that his last recommendation (that we must develop a plurality of folk categories) is based on a somewhat problematic assumption that context and ethnocentrism might be overcome, or at least tamed and minimalized, through an apparently shared interest in developing cross-cultural translation and understanding. Ironically, these efforts at developing such universal convergence of human meaning might more properly be conceived not as part of the solution but as part of the problem of ethnocentrism.[7]

NOTES

1. For a survey of the rich history of anthropological theorizing on religion, see E. E. Evans-Pritchard's classic *Theories of Primitive Religion* (1992 [1965]). Most recently, the work of Stewart Guthrie in *Faces in the Clouds* (1993; see also 1996, 1999) comes to mind as another example of an anthropologist making a significant and sustained contribution to theorizing about religion.

2. It should be noted that I take Saler to be using the term *understanding* in a sense similar to the widespread notion of *Verstehen*, implying that to understand the experiences and cultures of an informant means appreciating, re-experiencing, empathically participating in, and virtually reproducing those same experiences in the observer. In other words, despite his claim concerning the virtually indistinguishable natures of interpretation and explanation (1993: 4), I read his thoughts on understanding as being very different from efforts to generate historically grounded causal analysis.

3. For my analysis of Smart I rely, in part, on work published in McCutcheon 1995, 1997c.

4. For a more detailed examination of the issue of how scholars treat religious insiders' folk names for deities, see McCutcheon 1990.

5. I must thank Tim Murphy for bringing Hoy's insightful work to my attention.

6. Having said this, it should be clear that the old saying, "like apples and oranges"—a saying that implies that two things are incomparable—is actually a good example of Smith's point that a comparison of any two items—for example, apples and oranges—always implies an unstated third used to juxtapose the two items under consideration—in this case, the unstated third is "fruit." Despite the old saying, apples and oranges are indeed comparable, insomuch as we label them both as fruits.

7. An earlier version of this essay, which was presented at the 1995 Mexico City congress of the International Association for the History of Religion (IAHR), was published in *Method and Theory in the Study of Religion* 12/1–2 (2000). For their thoughts on Saler's work, along with Saler's own reply, see the review essays of William Paden, Donald Wiebe, and Gary Lease in the same special issue of the journal.

CHAPTER 6

The Economics of Spiritual Luxury: The Glittering Lobby and the World's Parliament of Religions

INTRODUCTION

Richard H. Roberts's recent article on the theoretical setting of the 1993 Parliament of Religions (1995) provides some examples of the thorny problems scholars of religion encounter when they presume from the outset that their datum is distinct, autonomous, or, simply put, *sui generis*. By conceiving of religion, or, more accurately, so-called religious experiences and spiritual consciousness as independent variables that have sociopolitical implications, but *not* causes, such scholarship romanticizes and thereby depoliticizes historical, human interactions and institutions.

Despite what may be the best intentions of such authors, this romanticization promotes the efficient incorporation of certain human behaviors within totalized, hegemonic discourses. Simply put, in his efforts to identify "religion as global resource," Roberts has, perhaps unknowingly, entrenched one of the most powerful hegemonic discourses of the postindustrial revolution era—the liberal commodification of human beings as sociopolitically autonomous individuals. It is precisely because his article argues that "global religion," as exemplified in the World's Parliament, *resists* such hegemonies that the contradictions of Roberts' article—indeed, the contradictions of research that posits the sociopolitical autonomy of religion—deserves to be brought to light.

FROM DESCRIPTION TO REDESCRIPTION

As should by now be clear, the critique that I have been developing throughout these opening chapters is based on three related presuppositions, the first two of which develop directly from the previous chapter: (i) there is no part of social life that can be protected from cultural and historical pressures; (ii) all so-called facts are already part of elaborate frameworks that often remain unacknowledged; and therefore (iii) we as scholars of religion can do more than just describe and then interpret the essentially free-floating meaning of the various claims made by the people we study.

In stating these three presuppositions—and as the book's opening epigraph from Joe Queenan makes evident—I fully realize that much of the current scholarship on religion deviates dramatically from my position, for it presumes that religious experiences, myths, rituals, spirituality, and so on, are somehow privileged and either originate from, or gain meaning by reference to, something that lies outside historical change (whether it is called the "sacred," the "*mysterium*," "ultimacy," "Meaning," or so on). Accordingly, so-called religious facts are treated as if they were self-evidently meaningful realities that exist outside the scholar, much as ripe fruit sits on the tree waiting to be picked.[1] Because they are thought to originate from, or refer to, some external referent, these religious realities are said to share deep and abiding value—hence the overused categories of essence and manifestation in the history of comparative religion and phenomenology of religion. The reasoning? Though the fruits and branches may differ, they all share the same unseen (i.e., nonempirical) roots. The dominant position in the field argues that the inductivist historian of religion arrives on the scene free of predetermined theories and definitions, assesses the factual data (e.g., religions in the plural), and describes it faithfully, picks out the appropriate methods to ascertain their shared, deep essence, and only then draws conclusions about religion in the singular. It is precisely this position that I am contesting in these chapters.

Instead, others have suggested that we as scholars are, from the outset, involved in the act of *re*description based on assorted frameworks and theories of human minds, behaviors, and social institutions—theories and definitions of our own makings. Accordingly, the act of scholarship is deductive and involves the redescription of emic claims in terms of inevitably and unapologetically reductive, etic categories and theories that we as scholars devise and bring with us to the scene. If our work is understood in this manner, it is the act of scholarship itself that concocts and applies such categories as religion, myth, ritual, sacrifice, pilgrimage, and so on, uses the human data they help to organize to test theoretical models of how minds or institutions work—such categories allow us to map these models onto what might otherwise simply be termed "diverse, observable" human behaviors. It is important to note that such a position is not antirealist; it does not argue that the world is all in our heads and that there is no such thing as a historical event. Instead, it argues that the *meanings* of the world and the emplotment of just this or that chronologically past event as worthy of attention and memory (making otherwise discrete events into historical narratives) are the products of contestable human choices and interests (see Trouillot 1995; Connerton 1998; and Braun 1999a).

Because a number of our colleagues have traditionally identified themselves as religious people involved either in practicing missionary work or promoting religious pluralism, uncritical insider categories and claims have generally passed unnoticed into the vocabulary of analytic scholarship. Accordingly, the distinction between emic and etic scholarship, or what are simply descriptions faithful to the reporter's vocabulary and belief system, on the one hand, and theoretically based redescription, on the other, has largely been blurred. However, for those of our colleagues who study non-European- or non-Mediterranean-based social systems, the degree to which many of our commonly used categories do not fit the data has long been apparent. As suggested in the introduction, if one studies peoples not sharing Latin-based languages or a history of European contact, then the very use of 'religion' in naming a specific subset of their reported perceptions (religious experiences), observable behaviors (religious acts), and institutions (religious associations) is hardly a faithful act of empathetic description; instead, it amounts to a redescriptive act based on a certain way *we*, and not *they*, have of carving up the world (our taxonomy). Therefore, any so-called inductivist who employs such categories as religion or myth in their descriptions is by definition already involved in using taxonomic frameworks foreign to the so-called factual data; they are unknowingly working in the realm of theoretical redescription. Deductivists in the field make the conscious, redescriptive step primary to all research. After all, none of us is identical with what we study, and no facts are self-evident.

Scholarship therefore begins with the act of creating taxonomies and models for redescribing the behaviors that we witness around us (they have to be observable, no?) and that we find intriguing. It then moves on to classifying, organizing, and comparing the data created by our taxonomies and models. I take it that this is precisely what Jonathan Z. Smith meant when he reminded us that maps are not to be confused with actual territory. Having come this far in our studies, we may attempt to explain the similarities and differences that become apparent in our taxonomically based comparative efforts. And, if we are lucky, we may be able to organize all these scholarly acts by identifying the wider sets of concerns and values that suggested to us in the first place just what type of taxonomy to build, let alone why we were curious about this or that behavior in the first place. Simply put, the world around us does not jump up and tell us what is important and interesting; these are socially based judgments we make.

THE POLITICS OF MYTHMAKING

By failing to live up to the requirements of theoretically based redescriptive scholarship, scholars of religion engage in mythmaking and mystification; they depoliticize their data and, in the process, depoliticize both their motives and the implications of studying the data in just this fashion. This is a fourth presupposition to my general critique.

As already suggested, the very methods used by scholars of religion most often presuppose that an essential, spiritual essence or core lies at the heart of diverse historically conditioned human belief systems and behaviors. In an earlier chapter, Karen Armstrong—much like the late Wilfrid Cantwell Smith before her—simply called it "transcendence"; Eliade referred to it as "the sacred"; van der Leeuw named it "power." However, taking the emic claims regarding autonomous and culturally free-floating spirits, souls, jivas, atmans, essences, and transcendent values as the basis for etic redescriptions sadly confuses the practice with the study of religion. It confuses the act of historicizing our data with its mythmaking. Mythmaking is one strategy whereby social formations abstract their beginnings from history, thereby privileging one particular view of the present by linking it to a mythic, originary moment (see Mack 2000, McCutcheon 2000 on mythmaking and social formation).

But this is not simply a theoretical or intellectual issue (as it is for those who most often engage in the reductionism debate); it is a political issue as well. What I mean is that if we understand religious discourses not to be about the hereafter, as the people we study maintain, but instead take such dehistoricizing claims as the object of study, we will contextualize and historicize them and see them as being about the here and now. In this way, claims of ahistoricity and autonomy can be understood as powerful rhetorical and ideological vehicles that authorize and normativize certain systematic distributions of power and privilege in a social group. Despite the fact that the people we may study profess to be talking about other-worldly concerns, we as scholars have nothing to study but what we can observe in this world and what we can organize theoretically; therefore, what we observe and study are socially and materially entrenched human beings engaging in certain behaviors, maintaining specific social institutions, and deploying artful rhetorics for this or that material or social end. As suggested in the first chapter, to fail to historicize the mythic claims made by the people we study risks reproducing the politics, even the economics, embedded within their discourses. I believe that this is precisely what we find happening in Richard Roberts's 1995 essay.

EMANCIPATION FROM THE GLOBALIZING HEGEMONY

Roberts argues that the 1993 World's Parliament of Religions was an example of postmodern, global religion insomuch as this event admitted "a truly extreme heterogeneity and complexity of space and signs" while "assimilat[ing] them, albeit proleptically, under a single global agenda" (1995: 132). The agenda of this event was "not characterized by regressive pre-modern traditionalism, but a dynamic, emancipatory post-modern-tending discourse in which a variety of 'genres' (in the Bakhtinian sense) were dialectically combined" (132). In spanning barriers and bridging gaps, this postmodern "tending" global religion is then able, "in special ways," to challenge the alienation produced by "globalising hegemony" (129). Therefore, global religion functions as a "globally well-dispersed resource to be drawn upon when confronting the absence of an adequate immanent critique of the modern world system." Simply put, by addressing and enacting what Roberts presents as self-evident human universals (e.g., religious discourses, the need to address the ecological crisis, mediation and prayer, the need to follow one's bliss and attain self-realization), global religion combats "hegemonic ideologies" and "the seamless consumerism of late capitalism" (129). Roberts concludes that the parliament "was a remarkable expression of global spirituality which embodied and enacted forms of reflexive consciousness with important emancipatory potential" (134).

One of the central difficulties with Roberts's "optimistic interpretation" (121, 123) of this event is the manner in which his conception of what he simply terms the "modern world system," "globalising hegemony," and "hegemonic ideologies" forces him to obscure and overlook the surprising ways in which the 1993 World's Parliament of Religions is not, as he suggests, necessarily a challenge to the "seamless consumerism of late capitalism" but, rather, could very well turn out to be one of its primary instances and products. However, because of his efforts to protect religion as somehow distinct and removed from this ill-defined consumer ideology—the rhetoric of 'religious experience' comes into sight once again—Roberts fails to identify just how intimately his experience of *emancipation* was ironically the result of virtually complete *incorporation*. In other words, by uncritically reproducing the rhetoric of autonomy (the explicit capitalist analogy would be the rhetoric of free markets), his description of the event fails as a scholarly redescription and *actually reproduces the very system he proclaims to critique.*

If one were to sum up his thesis, Roberts advocates gathering together into one global religion the many separate world religions, something that would serve as an effective countermeasure against rampant consumerism. Consumerism, of course, is associated with the capitalist economic system and its notion of exchanging private property; consumerism is predicated on the assumption that physical and intellectual goods can be privately owned and exchanged for a value higher than the cost of their production (surplus value), this profit thereby being accumulated in a never-ending growth economy. However, it has been long known that there are explicit contradictions embedded within this system. Not only is the so-called level playing field of the free market continually undermined by the lopsided accumulation of capital and access to the halls of decision making, but the notion of continual economic growth contradicts the relative stasis of populations and their material needs. As identified long ago, ideologies function to gloss over these explicit contradictions and gaps. Historically, beliefs in afterlives and homogenous national or even world unity have been among the most effective of such ideologies. By the inclusion of such fields as feminist, race, class, and postmodern studies in the university curriculum—fields that focus on disjunctions and rifts rather than glossing over them—an explicit challenge has been leveled at the dominant ideology. The tremendous degree of conservative backlash against such fields of study suggests just what is at stake in this debate.

The result of the consumer system, then, seems to be that human beings who might be considered valuable in any number of ways become packaged goods valued exclusively in terms of their exchange value as determined by a competitive, so-called free market of labor or ideas. For instance, despite the fact that people generally think that they are the buyers when it comes to print media such as newspapers, in actuality they are the prepackaged goods being sold by the newspaper to its advertisers. Under capitalism, then, we become the ultimate consumers; we not only consume but are consumed ourselves; it is indeed a "dog eat dog world out there."

SPIRITUALITY IN THE GLITTERING LOBBY

Given his criticism of such a model, I find it puzzling that Roberts's paper is filled with the kind of economic or exchange metaphors reserved usually for rational choice theorizing: religion is understood as a "global resource" that, much like a bank account, can be "drawn upon"; one can shop, it would seem, in the "religious market" or "religious bazaar" where one will find Neo-Pagans, Catholics, Buddhists, and so on, all of whom have made or can make a contribution to (or investment in?) "a dynamic form of cultural capital." Moreover, the very approach of the paper suggests not simply economic images but the kind of idealist privatization so important to capitalist ideologies; after all, the paper is situated in terms of Roberts's own personal experiences at the parliament. From there it goes on to discuss private religious experiences, spirituality, and consciousness and throughout draws upon a participant-observer methodology whereby the private experiences of others are entertained and made one's own (and thereby consumed). Instead of considering 'religion' to be a rubric whereby we as scholars organize specific public, observable social data produced through certain historical, cultural, political, and economic relations, Roberts conceives of it as an essentially irreducible private experience or consciousness. This understanding relies on the rhetoric of autonomy and is but one of the many instances of the private affair tradition in our field.

If his paper's overall thesis were not so concerned with critiquing consumerism and commodification, the reproduction of this rhetoric would possibly not be all that important. However, this implicit rhetoric of autonomy flies in the face of the paper's explicit thesis. Perhaps we can explain all this simply by acknowledging that Roberts attended the parliament "as a member of a team of ethicists (mainly employed in business and management schools) who met with business leaders at an adjunct meeting about half a mile from the Palmer House Hilton where the Parliament itself took place" (123). Given his professional focus and role it might be only natural that such metaphors and presuppositions find their way into his writing. I find this answer not to be all that compelling, however, for the manner in which his commodification of so-called spirituality blatantly contradicts his emancipatory thesis suggests that there are deeper issues present. And it is precisely in his use of the capitalism/religion dichotomy that I think we find the root of the problem.

As may already be clear, early in his essay Roberts sets up a profoundly important distinction between capitalism and religion. On the one hand, there is the hotel in which he is staying while in Chicago for the parliament, the "fortress-like and forbidding half-light of the Midland Hotel with its grey-suited businessmen and anonymity." On the other, we see the "golden-tiled glowing lobby of the Palmer House Hilton" (123), where the parliament is being held. Moreover, moving from the business meetings at the former to the parliament at the latter "obliged a participant to make the transition between *two very different centres of power* (those of the capitalist world system, and global religion, respectively)" (123; emphasis added). In making this rite of passage, the ritual participant must cross a liminal space or no place by "passing through the canyon-like streets of Chicago, there encountering the human dereliction of junkies and crazies—besides an ordinary humanity going about its daily business." The initiate is "overwhelmed by the grid-iron plan of the city . . . thus imposing a brutal, rational logic upon the traverse Indian trails that had preceded the arrival of the white man."

After successfully passing through the liminal phase, populated by dangerous people of no status (derelicts and junkies), one arrives at the Palmer House only to find an entirely different world and, as we were told at the outset, a very different center of power:

> The ambience of the Palmer House Hilton was significant. A magnificent and grandiose hotel, the lobby of the Palmer House was both simultaneously like a gilded sarcophagous and a womb-like, fecund beehive of religious activity. Here, in an enclosed, windowless and secure environment what took place could perhaps best be described as a global religious 'happening', a temporary suspension of physical distance as many life-worlds converged in the ultimate post-modern religious bazaar. In the temporary sacred space of the Palmer House it was possible to observe many intimate human encounters taking place across many a cultural abyss. (123)

This is one of the many intriguing descriptions that focus explicitly on the "Palmer House Hilton Hotel." The hotel is mentioned by name in the very first line of the paper, and, before the third page is over, its name (along with literally glowing descriptions) appears seven more times. At the close of the paper we again return explicitly to the Palmer House Hilton; building on Ninian Smart's comments on a future global civilization where the "great traditions are woven together in a glittering net . . . like the jewel net of Indra" (134),[2] Roberts concludes that in the

> glittering lobby of the Palmer Hilton many jewels in the net of Indra reflected and refracted each other's light. World religion drew together for a moment; much of what it saw was good, not least in the experience of the multitude of 'Others' who experienced each other both as difference and likeness—but also as complementarities within the greater community of religions and of humankind itself. (134)

Given that the paper is explicitly concerned with the *theoretical* setting of the parliament, we are forced to question why its *physical* setting in the Palmer House Hilton is so important. For, upon first reading the essay, I was taken by how closely it resembles an explicit advertisement for what is admittedly a beautiful hotel. But the hotel's surprisingly prominent role in the essay is indicative of the paper's troubling contradictions mentioned above. Reading the first few pages of the essay critically enables the reader to see a number of dichotomies or binary oppositions that float throughout the text, oppositions that construct 'global religion' as beneficial, distinct from, and therefore a challenge to, the ill-defined yet implicitly evil 'globalizing hegemony'. For instance, we see the following interrelated oppositions (note that all terms on the left are associated with each other, as are all on the right):

capitalism	religion
secular	sacred
inhuman	human
modern	postmodern
anonymous	intimate
permanent	temporary
Midland Hotel	Palmer House Hilton
fortress	beehive
male	female
rational	spiritual
grid-iron	golden-tiled
Whites	Indigenous peoples
roads	trails

For example, to paraphrase Roberts, whereas the business*men* operate in the invasive, rational, gray, half-lit, anonymous, and inhuman world of the Midland Hotel's capitalist context, spiritual specialists have intimate encounters in a sacred, golden, fertile, indigenous womb of religious activity. Moreover, the ritual, sacred space of the latter is made possible by the ambience and secure environment of the windowless and cavernous Palmer House Hilton, where one sits amidst religious luminaries, far removed from those at the margins who have been alienated by capitalism.

If postmodern criticism has taught us anything, it has taught us that the authority afforded one binary pole over another is highly tentative and tactical; its seemingly self-evident authority is the result of a number of ideological and rhetorical mechanisms that, in the midst of ranking what are essentially paired binaries, often pass unnoticed. These mechanisms effectively disguise the manner in which the two poles are actually hardly different at all. However, if one is able to call into question these mechanisms and problematize the manner in which unquestioned norms are authorized, then such self-evident equations as

capitalism = anonymous = iron = male = invasive = rational = inhuman

let alone their apparent inferior status to

religion = intimate = gold = female = indigenous = spiritual = human

can be deauthorized and shown to be stereotypes constructed for specific material and discursive ends, thereby establishing that the "experience of the Parliament" is only possible at a specific institutional site. In other words, the authority of Roberts's entire argument rests on its rhetorical ability to maintain the tactical advantage that supposedly socially, politically, and economically autonomous global religion has over the alienating forces of capitalism. This advantage is bought at the price of proclaiming such a global spirituality to be socially and historically autonomous and free floating. If this tactical advantage were to be lost, if his descriptions were shown simply to be a repetition of the claims of religious people, and if the religious marketplace were understood as but an aspect of social, political, racial, gendered, and, yes, even economic forces, then his critique would ironically be understood to entrench the very systems it sets out to undermine. Global religion, like capitalism, would then be but one more site where a totalizing discourse—the discourse on Universal Human Nature—effectively reproduces itself; the gold facade would crumble, and the luxury of 'religious virtuosity' would turn out to have much in common with the mundane business of derelict and ordinary humanity.[3]

THE ECONOMICS OF SPIRITUAL LUXURY

Such a critical reading of Roberts's article can easily begin with more specific information on the highly romanticized—mythified—Palmer House Hilton; after all, it is the romanticization of this specific site that simultaneously frames and best represents the mythification responsible for the creation of the binary oppositions in the first place.

Far from being a virtual ahistorical cathedral or womb of spiritual consciousness—in other words, far from Roberts's idea of the Palmer House Hilton—lies a very real, material item of discourse, culture, and history. It is a deluxe hotel with 1,639 rooms, five restaurants, three bars, and meeting rooms that can accommodate thousands. Regular nightly rates for single occupancy range from $165 to $240 (U.S.), while double occupancy varies from $190 to $265 (U.S.).[4] It is owned and operated by the seventh largest U.S. hotel and casino chain: the Hilton Hotel Corporation. Shares in this public corporation are bought and sold on the New York Stock Exchange; the corporation has two divisions, four subsidiaries, and one affiliate company. It has between 40,000 and 44,000 employees; in 1995 and 1996, its revenues totaled over $1.5 billion (U.S.), and its earnings topped $121.7 million (U.S.).[5] The corporation earns profits for its shareholders by selling rooms for travelers to sleep in, food for them to eat, and dreams of material wealth for gamblers to bet on. Note: this is *not* a critique but merely an accurate description; the Hilton Hotel Corporation, like any other corporate venture in a capitalist economic system, has a product that it packages and sells, for surplus value, to an international market of buyers. Those buyers are travelers looking for a night's rest, gamblers dreaming of the big payday, and investors looking for a good return on their buck. Given that I do not hold an M.B.A., I presume that an overall 12.4 percent return on total revenues makes the Hilton Hotel Corporation a relatively good buy.

Only if Roberts obscures or ignores this explicitly materialist reading can he sell to his readers the picture of the Palmer House as a disembodied, gilded womb of spiritual value. Much like the hotel lobby, his rhetoric of autonomy is windowless and therefore blind to context; it effectively obscures the concrete relations between the supposedly spiritual and the material. Far from being the autonomous, sacred space Roberts thinks it is, the venue for the parliament is one of the very pinnacles of the capitalist system of which he is so critical. To put it another way, glittering hotel lobbies are not lowered from the heavens. It turns out, then, that the walk down the canyonlike streets from the Midland to the Palmer House is not, as Roberts portrays it, a rite of passage from secular to sacred or from anonymous to intimately personal. Instead, it is a brief departure from one site of capital investment and profit motive to another, a departure that requires that for a time one bump up against the derelicts, crazies, junkies, and ordinary humanity who live in the margins of private property and wealth. Moreover, this brief excursion is not a climb up Jacob's ladder but a climb up the corporate, class ladder, a move from the mundane surroundings of a middle-class hotel to the downright glittering lobby of a hotel that caters to economically elite customers. Just as it takes tremendous amounts of money and planning to create the physical and mental illusions that guests purchase when they enter hotels such as the Palmer House Hilton, it takes tremendous material and rhetorical effort to create the romantic, mythic image of the hotel as a spiritual oasis amidst the gritty world of buyers and sellers.

A powerful example is found in the case of the Coca-Cola Company, whose highly successful marketing campaigns continually manufacture an idealized world of no racial, national, or social boundaries. Who can forget the nationless and classless singers on that mountain side in their 1970s television ad campaign: "I'd like to teach the world to sing, in perfect harmony." According to the company's mission statement, however, all this simply serves their "ultimate commitment": "We exist to create value for our share owners on a long-term basis by building a business that enhances The Coca-Cola Company's trademarks" (*The Coca-Cola Company: Our Mission and Our Commitment*, 1994). Although there is no need for a capitalist company to apologize for having such a goal, there is indeed something highly problematic when consumers fail to recognize this goal for what it is. Note: the mission statement does not make reference to their carbonated beverage but to the company's trademark; it makes no reference to consumers and buyers of the beverage but to the company's share owners. Capitalism "works" by camouflaging such contradictions as the fact that the company's annual profits are linked to the consumers' inability to recognize that they are themselves the product, not the beverage, and that their consumption is being bought and sold for profit. There is an irony that in capitalism the product that seems to be the focus of all this consumption (e.g., a carbonated beverage) is rather irrelevant to the entire process. In other words, if it makes a profit, no doubt the Coca-Cola Company would sell something as seemingly benign as patriotism—as in their sponsorship of the 1996 U.S. Olympic Torch relay.

And this is precisely the irony of Roberts's emancipatory critique: the experience of emancipation afforded by global religion is made possible, is framed, manifested, and embodied in the hallowed but hollow halls of international, corporate commodified culture. Indeed, religion and spirituality turn out to be just another global commodity, in this case participants are buying and selling a romanticized view of the world along with a block of conference-rate hotel rooms. The participants are afforded the illusion of nonattachment and autonomy only because they (or their benefactors and sponsors) have the finances to afford not only plane tickets around the country and across the globe but the price of food and lodging in a luxury hotel, the costs of which preclude most Chicagoans from ever dining, let alone sleeping, in the Palmer House. Somehow to think that this privileged spirituality allows one to challenge and critique this system only betrays a naive understanding of the benefits that the system offers those attempting to combat it. Simply put, the "temporary," artificial, and romanticized view of reality experienced by Roberts at the parliament is made possible only by the generous support of corporations such as the Hilton Hotel Corporation! As Joan Wallach Scott, Robert Sharf, and Tim Fitzgerald were quoted as saying in the introduction to this collection, "experience" is from the outset a social product; to take "experience-talk" at face value necessarily reproduces a specific sociopolitical world that made such a discourse possible in the first place.

Much like a butler in a mansion, a chauffeur in a limousine, a waiter in a restaurant, or rules of formation in a discourse, the Palmer House Hilton supplies the unspoken and invisible context for both Roberts's essay and his experience of the parliament. In fact, the "success" of butlers, chauffeurs, waiters, discursive rules, *and* hotels—not to mention ideologies that go by the name of *common sense*—relies on their silent, invisible, unquestioned operations. From the outset, then, Roberts's critique is framed and completely submerged within the smoothly functioning hegemony he thinks he is combating; the luxury of the Palmer House floats silently throughout his essay, setting the stage for his critique, uniting the first sentence with the last paragraph; he unknowingly buys the capitalist project hook, line, and lobby.[6]

THE AUTONOMY OF RELIGION AND THE IDEOLOGY OF GLOBAL CONSUMERISM

All of which brings us back to the first presupposition identified at the outset of this paper: that there is no part of social life that can be protected from cultural and historical pressures. It is precisely this presupposition that distinguishes public scholarship on religion from the practice of religion. Despite the fact that he shies away from John Cumpsty's explicit articulation of *sui generis* religion (1995: 132–33),[7] Roberts repeatedly presumes that religion, especially when seen as global religion, is a distinctive and special case and, therefore, somehow separate from the tug and pull or socioeconomic life in general, and the global hegemony of capitalism in general. The fact that he routinely employs economic metaphors when discussing religion; conceives of religion as an essentially privatized feeling, experience, or consciousness; and fails to see the explicit economic conditions that make such feelings as awe and wonderment possible in the first place, suggests that the notion of religion as private and distinct is so filled with internal contradictions that it cannot stand under its own weight.

To prop it up we need the romanticized and idealized support of windowless walls where the world of economic activity, of buying and selling products, people, and ideas, is "temporarily" hidden from view. The nameless derelicts, crazies, and businessmen are obscured, while, within the artificial and temporary confines of the glittering lobby, elite practitioners can find their bliss and revel in disembodied insights of self-realization. That the glittering lobby in which they meet and meditate is the direct result of an economic process that equally produces the gray-suited businessmen and the junkies is completely obscured. In fact, the gray-suited businessmen *own* the lobby! In a way, they equally own, market, and sell for profit this very bliss that fills its lobby. In failing to recognize that the very discursive and physical context in which this bliss is experienced is made possible by a complex network of social, political, and economic forces, we have in Roberts's essay an example of Marx's notion of false consciousness.[8]

Ultimately, spirituality, much like humanist talk of universal values, is a commodity that has a specific manufacturing history and is bought and sold daily. In 1993, the Palmer House Hilton provided the perfect wrapping for this supposedly global product, for without windows one cannot see the seams that stitch together the highly constructed consumer ideology of late capitalism. Like his description of the Palmer House, Roberts's romanticized and autonomous global religion effectively entrenches this very consumer ideology.

This all brings to mind two recent marketing campaigns in the United States. First, the Hanes underwear company, which notes in its television ads that instead of seeing people in terms of their national identities (which, given the images shown on the screen, by definition implies their skin color), it understands them simply as small, medium, or large. To redescribe this, all people are simply part of a global market of underwear consumers. Second, IBM's highly effective "Solutions for a Small Planet" television campaign, in which people from around the globe, speaking in their own languages, discuss computing problems, communicate on email, and enhance their colorful "ethnic" lives through computer technology, all of which is communicated to the television viewer by clever on-screen English vernacular subtitles. In the case of both of these ad campaigns, the mere facade of ethnic, gendered, linguistic, cultural, material, and geographic diversity—in a word, history—is cast off by portraying people simply as consumers submerged within a global shopping mall. That the majority of the world's population does not have sufficient disposable income to spend on underwear (nor does it necessarily wear underwear) is not considered of relevance, for obviously the commercial is simply aimed at selling the product to Americans. That Americans are in reality highly divided along class, gender, and race lines (take, for example, the dramatic difference of opinion among many Whites and Blacks over whether justice was served in the two trials of O. J. Simpson) is equally irrelevant. In fact, such disjunction is precisely what mythmaking camouflages and thereby overcomes. And that two out of three human beings currently alive have never made a phone call, let alone used a computer or the Internet, is completely irrelevant to IBM's campaign to celebrate how global technology supposedly unites all peoples.[9] After all, their advertising campaign is simply designed to reflect back on American viewers an idealized image of themselves as cosmopolitan buyers and sellers whose language and culture transcends all other merely quaint, local languages and cultures. All that is needed in the case of any multinational corporation is the myth of homogeneity and unity, a myth that is painstakingly constructed through the adept manipulation of desires, symbols, and rhetorics, but that is quickly dispelled when race, gender, or class—in a word, history—is brought into the debate. Of course this is missed by those who refuse to view rhetorical flourishes on anything but the most idealized, apolitical, *sui generis* levels—by those who fail to problematize and redescribe them.[10]

Such an oversight is also found in many uses of the very term *globalizing*, for they often fail to take account of the military-industrial origins and uses for the communications technology that has afforded the supposedly new global unity. In this light, the global whole is simply an ideological, technological construct that bears little resemblance to whatever the whole may actually be—if in fact there is such a thing as the whole. By likewise failing to understand the Palmer House or the parliament on any scale other than the *sui generis* (or, in Roberts's words, taking the parliament "on its own terms as a global religious event" [1995: 127]), its highly elite, local, and socioeconomic aspects are overshadowed and obscured.

CONCLUSION

The contradictions embedded within Roberts's representation of the Palmer House are indicative of larger contradictions embedded within both his emancipatory critique and capitalism as a whole. But these contradictions are disguised and glossed over by means of homogenizing strategies and tropes. Just as his opening paragraph's incredible leap from the original 1893 parliament to the "Beatles' association with Maharishi" is facilitated, so too Roberts's liberal ideology of global unity compresses social, economic, racial, and political complexity into an individualized quest for privatized bliss. Ahistorical self-realization and enlightenment, then, end up being perhaps the most sought after and privatized resources exchanged in deluxe hotel lobbies—they are games for international elites (material *and* intellectual) but not for so-called ordinary humanity who live in the canyons, on the margins of power and property. Globalized religion, then, turns out to be yet another transnational commodity. There is an economics to the spiritual luxury afforded by the glittering lobby, an economics effectively obscured by the totalizing and inductivist discourse on *sui generis* religion. Naming and challenging precisely this ideology comprises a better instance of a postmodern, oppositional discourse than the merely "postmodern-tending" example offered by Roberts.

It should now be clear that what we find in this essay I have examined is but one more example of the manner in which phenomenologically based caretakers simply describe and report on spiritual self-evidencies and fail to accept the challenge of developing redescriptive theories of religion. Such a failure makes scholars of religion complicit in the political obscurantism that I have labeled as "mythification." Accordingly, without recognizing the full import of his words, Roberts was cor-rect when he concluded that at the 1993 World's Parliament of Religion heterogeneity and complexity were temporarily subsumed under a single global agenda. However, that global agenda was the commodification of heterogeneous historical human beings, packaged as "spiritual," "busi-nessmen," "junkie," "crazy," and "ordinary." Ultimately, this process entails the production of elite consumers ready to pay for the luxury of momentarily and artificially suspending divisions of class, race, gender, and nation by means of manufactured, ritualized places with cavernous ceilings, glittering walls, no windows, and silent multinational owner-ship—whether this is Disney World or the windowless Palmer House Hilton. However, there is much at stake in forgetting that within Indra's glittering, jeweled net one only sees one's own reflection.

NOTES

1. As should be clear from the preceding chapter, the comparison of the terms *religion* and *fruit* is particularly apt since each is a higher order concept used to classify and organize aspects of the observable world that strike the observer as having significant similarities. Clearly, trees do not have fruit on their branches; they only have things we call apples or oranges or pears or cher-ries, etc. It is the same with religion.

2. Roberts is quoting Smart from his textbook, *The World's Religions: Oral Traditions and Modern Transformations* (1989: 561).

3. I have elaborated on the effectiveness of such a critical reading strategy when analyzing the claims made by Huston Smith in his popular world religions textbook—claims concerning the irrational, unthinking basis of "tradition" ver-sus the supposed rationality and individuality of modern societies (1997c).

4. These rate estimates are for the fall of 1996.

5. The information comes from *Ward's Business Directory of U.S. Private and Public Companies*, New York: Gale Research Inc., 1996, vol. 2, 1887, and *Directory of Corporate Affiliation*, New Providence, NJ: National Register Pub-lishing, 1995, vol. 3, 867. Although these two resources agree on such things as operating revenues and profits, they diverge on the total number of employees.

6. My critique shares certain characteristics with the critique made in an article by Marsha A. Hewitt; she finds ironically oppressive aspects to the so-called emancipatory feminist theorizing. See Hewitt (1993).

7. He is referring to Cumpsty's *Religion as Belonging: A General Theory of Religion* (1991). For a highly critical assessment of Cumpsty's Tillichian approach to interpreting religion, see Lawson (1994).

8. It is all the more significant, then, that Joseph Campbell's troublesome notion of individual bliss is brought up twice in Roberts's paper (see in particu-lar 124). Roberts's emphasis on the utter difference between the Midland and the Palmer House bring to mind Campbell's own thoughts on the meditative and purely aesthetic atmosphere created by cathedrals (see in particular his com-

ments in "The Hero's Adventure," the first of his several videotaped interviews with the journalist Bill Moyers). For a biting critique of the relations between Campbell's individualistic notion of "follow your bliss," his rise to popularity in America in the mid-1980s, as well as Reaganomics and rampant consumer individualism, see B. Gill (1989; as cited in chapter 3 of this collection).

9. This is a statistic of the U.S. Federal Communications Commission, cited in the weekly news magazine *Harper's Magazine*, May 1997: 15. The same issue of the magazine cites a report from the American Association for the Advancement of Science in Washington D.C./U.S. Bureau of the Census: the ratio of the number of telephones in sub-Saharan Africa to those in Manhattan, NY, is also 2:3. The contradictions embedded in free market rhetoric as well as the myth of equal global opportunity is all too apparent.

10. The 1996 summer broadcast of the centennial Olympic Games on NBC in the United States provides an even more explicit example of this ideology of homogeneity that supports global consumerism. While the rhetoric of world unity was thickly layered over almost every aspect of this event, based on the actual televised coverage, it was difficult to believe that countries other than the United States were competing and winning medals. In this case, the myth of global unity was completely in service of legitimizing a form of nationalism that in turn promoted consumer loyalty to corporations manufacturing and selling everything from carbonated beverages to rental cars—as it likely is for many countries that televise the games.

CHAPTER 7

"My Theory of the Brontosaurus . . .": Postmodernism and "Theory" of Religion

> The words of everyday language, like the concepts they express, are always susceptible of more than one meaning, and the scholar employing them in their accepted use without further definition would risk serious misunderstanding.
> —Emile Durkheim (1952: 41)

THE PROBLEM OF DEMARCATION

As suggested in earlier chapters, one of the more perplexing things about postmodernism is the manner in which this critical perspective is often called upon to relegitimize theological discourses in the academy. I say "re"-legitimize, for the history of the study of religion over the past one hundred years is generally conceived as a clash between naturalist approaches to the data over against overtly or implicitly theological approaches. As most everyone knows, theological discourses were, at least in publicly funded institutions, disallowed from participating in the effort to explain human religiosity, for they were generally considered to be not so much one among other explanatory options but, instead, to be one aspect of the data under study. As interesting as the work of theologians may be, such writers' sophisticated interpretations of religion's meaning and value—as opposed to its historical, economic, psychological, sociological causes—are but one more item in need of study and explanation.

Even though efforts to demarcate the practice of religion from its nonreligious study and analysis have been quite successful, with the rise of the postmodern perspective in such related areas as literary criticism and philosophy, the privilege naturalists have accorded their social scientific theories and methodologies has itself become the focus of much critique. More specifically, the rhetorical and even ideological strategies by which the social sciences have traditionally demarcated their domains and acquired their authority in the first place have become the target of some devastating, destabilizing, and long-needed criticisms. Indeed, the very possibility of a social science has become an item of debate. Given the questionable nature of the social sciences' authority for *definitively* studying human behavior and beliefs—an authority that was previously the main criterion for excluding the practice of theological discourses from the public university—the relativizing brought about by the postmodern turn has provided what some theologians see to be the means for reclaiming lost ground. We now find theologians arguing that they too, along with those who practice rationalist or naturalist discourses, have a place in the work of the public university (for example, see Marsden 1994, 1997).

In the past, arguments on the relations between (or lack of relations between) the academic study of religion and theology have rightly focused on this issue of demarcation—methodological, theoretical, and institutional.[1] However, in the postmodern university many of the rather successful arguments formerly used to distinguish what some conceived as the objectivist or value-neutral science of religion from confessional theology seem to have lost much of their punch. No longer can one so easily argue that science is neutral: as Darlene Juschka put it recently, "Marxist, feminist, and postmodern critiques of Western ideology have noted that an identity lays at the core of Science along with English, History, and Philosophy: male, white, western, and middle or upper class" (1997: 9). It is precisely this formerly undisclosed identity, this system of culturally entrenched values, to which some critics now appeal in their attempts to reauthorize theology in the university curriculum. Therefore, today the challenge is for those who maintain that there is a utility in demarcating the academic study of religion from religious practices and institutions to find a way to do so while acknowledging and even using the methods of postmodern critique. I for one believe that this is entirely possible: one *can be* a postmodern naturalist who studies human behavior in a way different from that of the theologian.

In an effort to critique the manner in which theology has been re-authorized in the postmodern university, in this chapter I would like to tackle issues of definition and discursive boundary maintenance by examining the use of the very terms *postmodern* and *theory*. Specifically, my critique focuses on Garrett Green's odd proposal that Karl Barth's 'theory' of religion ought to be included in the religious studies canon (1995). As I will demonstrate, as in the case of Roberts's essay on the World's Parliament of Religion, the reasoning behind Green's proposal is an example of the suspect nature of much scholarship on religion, scholarship that entails larger theoretical, discursive, and institutional implications. Green's misunderstanding of the technical use of 'theory' is reminiscent of a Monty Python routine concerning a scientist, Ann Elk, who is invited to a talk show to discuss her theory of the brontosaurus. In a nasal voice punctuated with equally nasal coughs, she proclaims: "My theory of the brontosaurus is that it is skinny on one end, fat in the middle, and skinny on the other end." Needless to say, the interviewer is not impressed, and we laugh—at least I did. But why? Although the folk (or, as Durkheim phrased it, the accepted) use of 'theory' is rather vague, the usually recognized scholarly use of this tool is rather precise; the humor of the Monty Python sketch—as is the case with many instances of humor in general—lies in the listener's ability to recognize a confusion of two semantic levels, a confusion that happens to deauthorize Ann Elk, whom we would expect to be schooled in the technical, rather than the vacuous, sense of the term. It is the same confusion that lies at the heart of much Python humor—recall the applicant looking for funding from the British Ministry of Silly Walks, the Twit of the Year competition, or the student looking for a lesson in logic who, instead, keeps getting uninvited lessons on receiving a bump on the head. The usually unquestioned gravity of government, sporting competitions, and university is thereby effectively harpooned; likewise, such a confusion deauthorizes Green's essay and his conception of the field.

What ought to attract our attention is the manner in which Green's perplexing use of postmodernism significantly challenges the very existence of the academic study of religion practiced as part of the human sciences rather than as part of an elite religious discourse. Just such a challenge lies implicit in Green's essay, where he argues that along with the work of such liberal theologians as Paul Tillich, the work of Karl Barth ought to be added to our syllabi in courses on theories of religion. Why? Green argues that, given that postmodernists accept that all data are theory laden, we have no right or defensible grounds unilaterally to exclude conservative theologians such as Barth simply because they do not fit the unarticulated consensus that only liberal theologians ought to be accepted into the ranks of scholars of religion. In Green's words, the "question that needs to be asked about this religious studies canon is why it includes some theologians while excluding others" (1995: 474). Green answers his own question by suggesting that the postmodern study of religion as it now exists is actually a bit of an embarrassment because it does not practice what it preaches: being biased in favor of liberal religious positions, it is not epistemologically relative. The problem is, in Green's opinion, that it does not go far enough in its efforts to relativize all discourses. This can only be corrected, he argues, by the inclusion of a host of more conservative theologies that will thereby balance the unarticulated liberal bias. The postmodern relativizing of discursive authority, therefore, opens the door for Green to include Barth's thoughts on the benefits of revelation and the evils of religion in his own undergraduate religious studies course on theories of religion.

JUST WHAT IS POSTMODERNISM?

But what do such writers accomplish when they invoke the slippery signifier *postmodernism*? Is postmodernism, as Terry Eagleton characterizes it, "a style of thought which is suspicious of classical notions of truth, reason, identity, and objectivity, of the idea of universal progress or emancipation . . . [and] Enlightenment norms" (1996: vi)? Does postmodernism imply the radical critique of aligning essences with historical origins, a historiography devoid of teleology, a self-consciously playful attitude toward the production of meaning, the death of metaphysics, a spirit of antirationalism, radical epistemological pluralism, the demise of transcendent signifieds? Or, along with Michael Ryan (1984), should we see in the eternal, postmodern play of signifiers the vindication of the materialist dialectic? Sadly, for many in the field, 'postmodern', a term often utilized as if it carries with it self-evident meaning (which is itself a modernist assumption!), signifies nothing other than "anything goes"—a usage of the term that stands as a poor testament to the critical potential of the postmodern turn.

Green's use of 'postmodernism' mainly emphasizes the destabilization of the privilege once afforded social scientific approaches. Given this critique, earlier totalizing theories that claimed to have reduced religion to one cause (think here of the grand narratives of a Marx or a Freud, let alone their equally modernist counterparts Weber and Jung) are seen to have been ontologically reductive, groundless, and therefore out of place in the postmodern study of religion. With this I can agree completely. As well, I applaud Green's effort to draw our attention to the entirely odd place that liberal theologians such as Tillich and Otto— not to mention Wach, Eliade, and Marty—have come to occupy in our so-called canon. The rather schizophrenic nature of the professional organizations to which many of us belong and the journals in which we publish are perhaps the best examples of this perplexing blend of approaches to the study of religion. Often we find books on improving one's preaching style reviewed alongside books on the history of Tibetan Buddhism.

Although I obviously agree with some aspects of Green's critique, we part ways in our understandings of the significance of 'postmodernism' for the study of religion and our view for the future of the field.

What he fails to recognize is that the very discourse that his postmodern turn has apparently revalorized is itself one of, if not *the*, primary instance of what Jacques Derrida early-on labeled as "logocentrism." As noted by the political scientist, Pauline Marie Rosenau:

> Postmodernism challenges global, all-encompassing world views, be they political, religious, or social. It reduces Marxism, Christianity, Fascism, Stalinism, capitalism, liberal democracy, secular humanism, feminism, Islam, and modern science to the same order and dismisses them all as logocentric, transcendental totalizing meta-narratives that anticipate all the questions and provide pre-determined answers. (1992: 6)

We are therefore forced to ask a rather simple question: How can Green's use of the postmodern turn away from grand narratives, teleology, essences, foundationalism, privilege, and monolithic identities be used to re-authorize theology (liberal or conservative) when theology is the very discourse that is most in need of the radically historicist, postmodern critique? One of the most intriguing aspects of the postmodern movement, then, is that in the study of religion this critical technique has thoroughly protected, rather than destabilized, discourses that claim as their basis of authority some kind of inspiration from beyond history. What should be of most interest is not that the epistemological relativism of the postmodern turn apparently provides an opening for Barth's "theory" to be taught alongside such other naturalist theories as those of, say, Rodney Stark and William Bainbridge (1987), Thomas Lawson and Robert McCauley (1990), Stewart Guthrie (1993, 1996), Pascal Boyer (1994), or, most recently, Walter Burkert (1996), but that by selectively applying postmodern criticism of discursive authority, one can so conveniently ignore an equally basic postmodern tenet: that discourses can be distinguished by their differing rules of formation, as well as their varying institutional settings. Although I agree that discursive relativism entails the loss of normative status for any one discourse—as Green has rightly said, all positions are implicated in "paradigmatic commitments to certain values, concepts, and methods"—this hardly does away with the ability to distinguish between discourses. Simply put, although we may all have prior commitments, not all our commitments are necessarily the same.

GAMES PEOPLE PLAY: TENNIS ANYONE?

We can appeal to the often-used example of games. I would presume that all but the most ardent fans and players of such social activities as hockey, football, volleyball, rugby, ping pong, cards, horseshoes, and golf, to only name a few, would acknowledge that no one game is any better than any other. Indeed, for whatever reason, one may have his or her preferences, but they are completely relative and possibly arbitrary preferences at best, no more or less authoritative than the preferences of anyone else. Although baseball is the national pastime, it is hardly the normative pastime.

My point is that the relativity of games does not mean that, when it comes to playing specific games, "anything goes" or that we cannot distinguish various games from each other—and along with this, the appropriate equipment by means of which, and venues (i.e., institutions) in which, they are played—by means of the rules that make of them a game in the first place. Singles tennis is no better or worse than doubles tennis. They are just different, a difference initially evident in two additional players and two different sets of white lines that demarcate 'court' from 'not court', 'in' from 'out', 'participant' from 'observer', and 'acceptable' from 'unacceptable'—not to mention that a considerably smaller check goes to the doubles winners. Without sets of rules that put into practice and at the same time comprise these intriguing dichotomies, how would we distinguish a good serve from a bad one, a fan or umpire for that matter, from a player, the start from the end, or a winner from a loser? In fact, the court itself is simply material evidence of these seemingly immaterial rules; without these unquestioned rules circulating in the minds of people, it would hardly be a game at all.

Much like games, postmodern criticism informs us that discourses and institutions are comprised of seemingly invisible yet socially reproduced sets of rules—in Michel Foucault's terminology we simply refer to them as "rules of formation"—which construct a series of polarities. That one discourse, one set of discursive rules, or one term in the polarity could, in the abstract, be any better than another is not a claim that postmodernists would entertain. Neither would they claim that discursive rules merely shaped or expressed some kind of preexistent raw matter. On this point Green is correct: the postmodern critique focuses on the modernist "assumption of a single universal order of truth. . . . Postmodern theories, whatever their differences, assume a relativity of perspectives that precludes any possibility of an epistemologically 'pure' or neutral access to truth" (1995: 473n. 2). Indeed, discourses and discursive rules, like the games under question, are themselves sociohistorically and politically embedded and constructed. In fact, the postmodern critic will study the ways in which such seemingly arbitrary discourses are authorized and perpetuated.

Using a form of ideology and rhetorical criticism, postmodern critics historicize the strategies that obscure discursive relativity and allow for authority and power to be naturalized, legitimized, and even mythi-fied. The kind of postmodern criticism open to the scholar of religion, then, is a form of demystification. But in identifying these often dis-guised rules of formation, the critic presumes that different discourses will have different sets of rules; hence the clash of discourses, much like Thomas Kuhn's conflicting paradigms, will provide a most intriguing case to study. Can one discourse replace another, and if so, how? Is such replacement gradual, or is it violent? Or can one discourse be completely subsumed within another, leaving the internalized discourse intact yet subjugated? How, precisely, can one oppose a dominant discourse? In the case of Barth's 'theory' of religion joining the religious studies canon, what we have is one instance of conflicting discourses.

APPROPRIATING POSTMODERNISM

By now it should be apparent that I consider Green's misuse of the post-modern turn to be found precisely in the assumption that discursive rel-ativity necessitates theology's reentry into the academic study of reli-gion. Such a grand reduction of all discourses to one is an ironically modernist move. Therefore, we need to investigate the way in which Green appropriates postmodern relativity to construe just about any-thing to be a 'theory', thereby making everything from conjectures, to assumptions, worldviews, ideologies, hunches, and guesses all instances of theory building at home in the university. For it is only by relativiz-ing the very category of "theory" that he can authorize Barth's work as a fitting example of academic scholarship on religion. Despite his appar-ent allegiance to the postmodern cause, Green's work is a useful exam-ple of the modernist backlash against postmodernism; for in smuggling grand narratives back into the study of religion, Green threatens the very discourse from which he claims his authority.[2]

After demonstrating his questionable use of 'theory'—and obscuring this questionable use is the *key* to the success of Green's overall argu-ment—I will suggest that, although one cannot prove either Barth's or anyone else's claims regarding religion's origin and function, one can at least identify a variety of discursive rules (most important being a spe-cific definition of 'theory') that distinguish the proper settings in which these various claims circulate. Distinguishing these various claims from each other allows us to describe some as theological, mythic, or simply ideological (those that presume essential, ontological status to their con-structs) and others to be naturalistic (those that acknowledge the con-stitutive role of the theorist and the theory). Given the discursive rules that contribute to the formation of, and ongoing justification for, the public institutions in which many of us carry out our research and teaching on religion, we can conclude that one can be a fully critical postmodern while excluding the practice of mythic discourses from the academic study of religion. To be postmodern does not mean "anything goes"; rather, it entails being critically aware of the inevitably social and political nature of the exclusions and rules that are the necessary conditions for any and all claims to knowledge.

The primary difference, then, between Green and myself is that I do not agree that inconsistencies in the application of the postmodern perspective, coupled with "implicit criteria of selection" in our field, have led to the inclusion of liberal and not conservative theologies. Instead, I am troubled that such a highly selective, and therefore suspect, understanding of the postmodern perspective has led to the inclusion of *any form of theology whatsoever* in the academic study of religion. Contrary to Green, the question that should be asked is whether the postmodern study of religion must be so relativized as to include any theology whatsoever.

Earlier I suggested that rules of formation, much like the white lines that demarcate 'court' from 'not court', are the means by which discourses are not only perpetuated but differentiated from one another as well. Tennis would hardly be worth watching, let alone playing, if there were no limits to the court; for, as already suggested, to limit a court is to construct and define it as a court. Without the white lines it would undoubtedly be something (either a lawn bowling green or an awfully well tended sod farm?), but it would hardly be a tennis court. Discourses, like definitions and white lines on the grass, are by their very nature tactical and exclusive, like the rules of grammar and syntax. So, despite the current political pressue for limitless inclusion, we see that any discourse, social group, or for that matter, any definition, is only as useful as the things that are excluded from being a member of a certain class or category.

One of the discursive rules by which the academic study of religion is constructed is in its particular definition of 'theory'. In conflating 'theory' with other sorts of social practices, Green has obscured the boundary between different discourses on religion—an important strategic move since his aim is to relegitimize the academic standing of theology in general or Barth's work in particular. Conversely, by defining 'theory' so that not everything counts as a theory (I have yet to hear a good argument as to why everything *should* count as a theory), we will not only reestablish one way to distinguish theological from naturalistic discourses but also deauthorize Green's primary strategy for the inclusion of Barth's work as one theoretical option—as opposed to an instance of data—for our field.

THEORY AS EXPLANATION

Although originally derived from the Greek term *theoria*, signifying "a visually determined contemplation of the world from afar" (Jay 1996: 171), as a folk term, 'theory' now denotes almost anything from a hypothesis to a conjecture. Influenced by nineteenth-century intellectualist scholarship, many people go so far as to conflate theories with myths, reasoning that, after all, both are simply attempts to explain natural phenomena. Even the *Oxford English Dictionary* lists a number of different, even conflicting, definitions (including such vague notions as a system of ideas, a conceptual or mental scheme), making 'theory', 'paradigm', 'worldview', 'philosophy', and, in some of its softer usages, 'ideology' virtually indistinguishable.[3] Green employs 'theory' in just this ambiguous manner, a use that corresponds to its nontechnical, folk usage. But, as the epigraph from Durkheim warned: "the words of everyday language, like the concepts they express, are always susceptible of more than one meaning, and the scholar employing them in their accepted use without further definition would risk serious misunderstanding."

To avoid such misunderstandings—and to avoid the institutional confusion that undoubtedly will result from such a misunderstanding—and for it to be of any analytical use in the study of religion, I agree with Stark and Bainbridge when they define 'theory' as "a set of statements about relationships among a set of abstract concepts. These statements say how and why the concepts are interrelated. Furthermore, these statements must give rise to implications that potentially are falsifiable empirically" (1987: 13). Accordingly, for 'theory' to be of any use to us, it must meet a minimum number of conditions: (i) a set of related propositions (ii) that possess predictive capability and can therefore be tested empirically (iii) that function to explain the causes of (iv) empirically observable events or processes. Although such theories can never be confirmed, based on their predictive capabilities, they can at least be tested, critiqued, and possibly discarded.[4]

One benefit of such an understanding of 'theory' is that it distinguishes among other sorts of cognitive processes. For example, while most everyone has assumptions, a system of ideas, or a worldview, not everyone's worldview entails the attempt to investigate whether there are any regularities in causal relations among observable events that the researcher finds interesting or curious. This attempt to *explain* that which the *researcher* finds *puzzling* is therefore fundamental to what constitutes theories. The article in the *HarperCollins Dictionary of Religion* makes this all quite clear in its opening lines:

> [T]heory, an explanatory account of some puzzling or intriguing phe-
> nomenon. . . . In order to count as a theory, the set of principles would
> attempt to . . . designate [religion's] causal origin, and describe its sys-
> tematic functions. A theory attempts to achieve its explanatory objec-
> tives by employing idealizations, that is, by abstracting away from
> irrelevant details in order to focus upon what was most significant
> about the phenomenon being accounted for by constructing a model.
> (Smith 1995b: 1068. See also the entry "religion, explanation of,"
> 894–96)

This definition also helps us to understand how theories can qualify as
postmodern: theories are understood as constructed *models* of reality
that are not to be mistaken for *reality itself*—whatever that may or may
not actually be. In fact, there are grave intellectual, institutional, and
even sociopolitical issues at stake when we overlook this seemingly subtle point. As Smith has time and again reminded us, there is a price to
mistaking our maps for the territory they re-present (1978).

Therefore, the postmodern use of the term—as opposed to the modernist usage of 'theory' characteristic of a former age of grand theorizing—is far from a "contemplation of the world from afar"; instead,
postmodern theories/theorists are actively constitutive of the world of
perception and experience. Although there are most definitely a number
of postmodernists who would critique the very effort to build theories
to begin with,[5] those postmodernists Rosenau labels as "affirmative,"
rather than skeptical, support theory construction by acknowledging
from the outset that we as humans are in the extremely odd predicament
of suspecting that we do not necessarily know for sure what is going on
around us—and that may be why we are so interested in trying to determine causal regularities around, and sometimes even in, us. Affirmative
postmodernists "argue that although they aim to end the intellectual
hegemony implicit in grand theory, this need not mean all theories are
equal" (Rosenau 1992: 83). Theories, then, are models that have yet to
be thrown away. Accordingly, theory building is *not* to be confused with
first-order experiences of the world—modernists might conflate the two,
but to their own peril. Theories are, instead, a meta-activity, a higher-
order cognitive map designed to provide a rational, explanatory account
for just this or that series of experiences, observations, and events *that
we as scholars deem important, puzzling, or curious.*

THEORY AS CRITIQUE

In such a postmodern context, critique is useful to identify how these
maps are often confused with the territory itself; re-presenting models as
reality can be of tremendous material benefit to an individual speaker,

economic class, gender, or entire society. Critique identifies just what is at stake for portraying or perceiving maps as territories, models as reality, etic as emic, and the local as universal. Critique is therefore of most use when modernist re-presentations masquerade as presentations. Or, as Catherine Bell notes, by means of such critique we begin "to understand better how we enter into such [theoretical] networks, how they also include who and what we study, and what study means in this context, and what type of explanatory authority resides in the constructions of such networks" (1996: 188).

Such critical practice is an even higher order cognitive activity and is therefore not to be confused with theory as defined above.[6] However, it is precisely this critical activity that constitutes 'theory' in some fields (e.g., literary theory or critical theory). In his survey of the many uses of 'theory', Martin Jay has delineated a number of cases that are concerned not with the term's ability to denote sets of propositions with predictive power, but rather, with the rejection of any "alleged God's eye view above the fray supposedly assumed by theorists" (Jay 1996: 171). It is just this sort of critical use of 'theory' that the Marxist literary critic Terry Eagleton has in mind when he writes: "Theory is just a practice forced into a new form of self-reflectiveness on account of certain grievous problems it has encountered. Like small lumps on the neck, it is a symptom that all is not well" (1992: 26). Theories, in both senses of the term, are therefore tactical in nature and engage things that we as scholars find curious (once again to borrow some choice phrasing from J. Z. Smith).

These two broad notions of theory differ in precisely the effort of the former to propose general regularities based on the analysis of particular cases, while the latter constitutes an even higher-order critique, based on such categories as class, race, and gender, of the universalizing assumptions and mechanisms of the former. To phrase it another way, one sense of theory (as critique) finds the activities of the other (as explanation) to be curious. For example, take the work of Tomoko Masuzawa in *In Search of Dreamtime: The Quest for the Origin of Religion* (1993).[7] Masuzawa's book does not constitute a new theory of the origin of religion. Instead, it is a metacritique of the very effort to construct such theories in the first place (specifically, the grand theories of origins found in Müller, Durkheim, and Freud). When compared with scholars who develop theories of religion's historical origins, her efforts are of a different intellectual order altogether.

It is important to keep these two technical understandings of 'theory' separate, for they are different yet equally necessary and interrelated enterprises.[8] Where one constructs models of reality, the other continually demonstrates the shortcomings of the model-builders as builders of realities—they are therefore dialectically related. The latter continually brings the supposed "God's eye view" of the former down to earth by making explicit the assumptions, internal logic, and sociopolitical preconditions of the theory in question.

Accordingly, a postmodern theorist can acknowledge (i) that theoretical models are only as good as the past instances in which they have stood the test; (ii) that predictions are a matter of more or less (statistically probable but hardly certain); and (iii) that theories are constructed, *ad hoc* models that can never be in a one-to-one fit with reality but that, instead, have a tactical utility in some given situation. Because of this we therefore understand (iv) that there is, by definition, no such beast as a final or grand theory of any- or everything. Postmodern theorists tip their hats to Kant: there are intellectual and social conditions for and limits to our knowledge. The promise of postmodern theorizing, therefore, is to be found in the continual, self-critical, or, as both Ryan and Eagleton noted, self-reflective movement between these two different levels of analysis. Recognizing the ironic, tactical nature of theory building may then open the theorist to critique and, quite possibly, theoretical refinement. Critique will hardly put an end to theory building, however, for we all move in complex worlds where we continually conjecture about what awaits us around the next corner. Instead, critique is a necessary part of the inevitable theory building we always do.

That many scholars of religion so easily gloss over the very important distinctions we generally employ in our academic categories suggests that the contributions of contemporary theorists have yet to make their way into the undergraduate and graduate classroom, let alone the readings of our colleagues throughout the field. Theory generally does not appear on our course syllabi, which suggests that there are indeed implicit and unstated criteria of exclusion operating in the field; however, these criteria have not so much to do with promoting liberal at the expense of orthodox theologies (as Green suggests), but with limiting efforts to study certain sorts of practices, beliefs, and institutions as dynamic historical, cultural, discursive artifacts instead of portraying them as manifestations of an ahistorical essence of mysterious derivation and meaning (i.e., *sui generis* religion). These are none other than modernist criteria that preempt the postmodern study of religion.

The embarrassment that Green speaks of, then, is not (as he suggests) that the postmodern study of religion has failed to include such writers as Barth, but, rather, that many scholars of religion have failed to understand just what it means to theorize and have most recently disguised this shortcoming through their conveniently selective appropriation of the postmodern turn. If, however, scholars of Barth, to take just one example, are willing to read his work on such topics as revelation,

Christ, sin, and so on, as historically grounded and rhetorical, metaphoric mechanisms whereby he constructed discursive authority, encoded/manufactured sociopolitical identity, and gained much needed cultural legitimacy—as opposed to seeing it as his ongoing exegetical struggle with the word of God as communicated through the historically free-floating meaning in the Bible—then his work might indeed have a place in the postmodern study of religion. However, this would entail the complete loss of Barth's so-called religious authority. Quite possibly, then, the postmodern study of religion will have nothing unique to study. For, as already noted by Rosenau, under postmodernism, 'theology' dissolves into but another historically constrained discourse working to authorize itself by appeals to a manufactured transcendent referent—be that the realm of the Spirit, God, Justice, Destiny, Human Nature, or even Objective Facts. The postmodern study of religion is therefore thoroughly playful and redescriptive (Gill 1998, 2000).

IN WHAT SENSE IS KARL BARTH A "THEORIST" OF RELIGION?

Because the technical, scholarly use of 'theory' that I am proposing presumes either the general components of explanatory hypotheses, prediction, testing, falsification, and model-building, on the one hand, or meta-critique, on the other, Barth's "theory" of religion will have to meet one of these two boundary conditions to gain admission into the academic discourse on religion. If it does not, then Green will have to persuade us of a new technical definition of 'theory' that simultaneously rules out certain sorts of cognitive activities (for if all cognitive practices can be theories, then, as the old argument goes, nothing is a theory) while dismantling the former definitional and discursive boundaries of the social sciences. For instance, Green might attempt to persuade us that Barth's work is a higher order critique of grand narratives. However, we can easily conclude that such a foundationalist myth as Barth's—who, after all continually addresses ahistorical realities and revelations in a cosmic framework—fails to qualify as critical theory in any technical sense of the term.

If these alternatives cannot be argued, then Green and others will have to abandon the pursuit to have such scholars as Barth included in the "religious studies canon." As for Green's claim that there are no "cogent academic grounds" for excluding such religious scholarship from the canons of the field, I would hope that my discussion of the two dominant meanings of 'theory' has drawn attention to a rich tradition that has quite effectively elaborated a number of credible grounds for demarcating what is, from what is not, a theory—a demarcation that not only affects Barth's role in our classrooms but the dubious place of such others as Schleiermacher, Otto, Tillich, Buber, Wach, and Eliade, to only name a few who, until now, have enjoyed prominent places in our field's pantheon.

Having already ruled out understanding Barth's work as that of critical theory, we must determine whether Barth's theory of religion can make predictions, if it can be tested or critiqued, and if it is geared toward explaining the causes of religion. If it is not, then (i) it is questionable at best whether it can meaningfully be understood in any sense as a theory, which in turns means that (ii) it should not be taught in our classrooms as one among other approaches available to the student of religion. While this does not mean that Barth is "wrong," or that those who develop testable theories are "right," it does mean that only the latter group are playing a game suited to the requirements of the public study of religion, and that is my only concern at this point: to develop a manner in which these different approaches to "talk about religion" can be usefully distinguished from one another.

Although Green refers to Barth's thoughts on religion as a theory, and even though he notes that teaching Barth's approach is an important aspect of his own advanced undergraduate course on theories of religion, he fails to provide his readers with a succinct statement of Barth's actual theory. Although this shortcoming may be nothing more than an unfortunate oversight, it is actually the first piece of evidence that, instead of a theory of religion, Barth has an intuition concerning what religion *ought* to be. As far as I can tell, the following statements comprise those claims quoted or paraphrased by Green that constitute the basis for Barth's theory:

Religion is the limit or frontier (*die Grenze*) of human existence.

Religion *is* the *adversary*, the *adversary* of man, of the Greek and the barbarian, disguised as the truest friend; it is the *krisis* of civilization and uncivilization. It is the *most dangerous* adversary that man has this side of death (apart from God).

Religion is God's revelation in the outpouring of the Holy Spirit [which] is the judging but also reconciling presence of God in the world of human religion, that is, in the realm of attempts by man to justify and sanctify himself before a willfully and arbitrarily constructed image of God. The church, insofar as it lives by grace through grace, is the locus of true religion.

The Christian religion is the true religion.

Religion is . . . *the* concern . . . of the *Godless* human being.

The true religion, like the justified human being, is a creature of *grace*. (Green 1995: 476, 477, 480, 482)

Apart from the fact that all of these statements presume from the outset, rather than attempt to theorize about, such things as the opposition of 'revelation' and 'religion', or the meaning and function of such terms as *grace*, *God*, *Holy Spirit*, and *church*, it should be clear that these statements hardly constitute a theory of religion in any meaningful sense of the term. I see no way to find in them any predictive, testable, or explanatory capacity whatsoever. Instead, they comprise bold rhetorical, metaphoric, and totalized claims that are firmly based on a specific type of Christian perspective intent on demarcating 'true' from 'false' and 'revelation' from 'religion'. As much as these polarities may assist in constructing the authority of Barth's rhetoric over other rhetorics, they hardly have any relevance for the academic study of religion conceived as culture critique. Simply put, Barth is no theorist of religion; instead, his work offers one piece of *data* for the development of a theory of religion, a theory that would have to account for the authority generated and legitimized by religious discourses such as his. To refer once again to Smith's fertile suggestions: "In the same spirit in which I welcome the study of the totalizing mythic endeavors, the *univers imaginaires*, of an Ogotemmêle . . . or an Antonio Guzmàn . . . I would hope, some day, to read a consonant treatment of the analogous enterprise of Karl Barth's *Church Dogmatics*" (Smith 1997: 61). Such would be the act of redescription that Green fails to accomplish.

In fact, Green already suggests that Barth is not a theorist of religion by means of his own confusion of three otherwise distinct characterizations of Barth's statements. Apart from the claim that Barth simply has a "theory of religion," Green also refers to the above-cited claims as, on the one hand, a "theological theory of religion," and, on the other, as a "theological interpretation of religion." If I had to pick, I would choose the latter characterization, for, much like the work of John Hick (and I have in mind his Gifford Lectures [Hick 1989]), Barth is involved in religious hermeneutics; that is, his massive *Church Dogmatics* employs numerous exegetical techniques to identify and subsequently translate the supposedly ahistorical meaning of a text's claims. Furthermore, Barth's preoccupation with the rhetoric of "true" religion and his use of the category "unbelief" (*Unglaube*) presume a normative standard that is not available to the scholar, implying—even necessitating—that Barth's interest is not so much in theorizing on religion as in judging its various manifestations (a word I have purposely selected) in light of the apparently self-evident measure of the revelation in Jesus Christ as communicated through the Bible. If Barth is half the postmodernist Green claims him to be, he would hardly navigate the treacherous waters of truth.[9]

What we really must press is precisely how and why Barth's rhetorical claims could ever be considered to constitute a theory of religion, for the success of Green's argument depends upon his ability to persuade us (i) that Barth indeed has a theory and (ii) that students of religion ought to study his writings as an example of theorizing in the field. If anything, what we have here is certainly an example of one type of Christian theological judgment as to what religion ought to be. But this by no means implies that it ought to be studied alongside the work of Durkheim or Freud, let alone Stark and Bainbridge, Lawson and McCauley, Guthrie, Boyer, and Burkert. Only when one disregards Barth's *a priori* commitment to the veracity and validity of biblical revelation can one, even for a moment, begin to compare him profitably to someone like Durkheim who is not trying to distinguish true religion from the many apparently arbitrary religious constructions of human beings but, instead, is trying to explain the fact of certain human beliefs and practices in the first place. In order for the comparison to work, one must conveniently forget that neither Durkheim nor even Freud made claims concerning the way religion really ought to be practiced or believed. Although Freud, for example, was clearly very critical of the function of religious practices, his effort was to account for their existence, not to conjecture on true versus false and how best to interpret what are taken to be the words of a deity. Despite their limitations, neither Durkheim nor Freud was hiding in his back pocket the privileged type of religion—termed "revelation" by Barth—that was not open to his critical methodologies. It should be clear, then, just how much depends on the reader's blind acceptance of the unsubstantiated claim that is made in the title to Green's article: that Barth *actually has* a theory of religion.

CONCLUSION: CONFUSING THEORIES WITH DATA

Throughout history scholars have been interested in taking the data derived from descriptive exercises and developing theoretical, redescriptive analyses that question the discursive, historical, and material causes and functions of the claims people make concerning how things really are, where they came from, and what will happen after their deaths. For these scholars—who number far more than Green might be willing to admit—there is indeed a distinction between studying religion (a field comprised of theories and methods) and promoting it (the data of the field). Failing to make this distinction risks confusing theories with data. In one's work the critic who theorizes on religion must be willing to entertain that indeed the insider might not have the "big picture" entirely correct; for "in the imperfect world we inhabit, indeed in virtually any world constructed by fallible humans, no possibility of self-sufficient immanence exists on the level of practice, experience, hermeneutic interpretation, narrative intelligibility, or empirical facticity" (Jay 1996: 178).

In recognizing, along with the postmodernists, this inherent limit both to redescriptions and theoretical work, postmodern theorists also recognize that the models they construct to help them negotiate and compare what they find to be the curious claims and behaviors of their fellows might themselves be misguided and in need of critique. Accordingly, they will work not only to make their theoretical assumptions as explicit as possible, but they will do so in the hope that colleagues will critique their claims, explanations, and unstated assumptions. For scholars of religion also have an inside to the religious devotee's outside: it is simply the rules of discourse in the public university where our claims must be open to public criticism and debate. Because we can describe, compare, and analyze these discursive rules, we can engage in the ongoing metatheoretical critique of scholarship itself.

In many areas of the study of religion, founded as it was on intuitivist methods limited only to description and interpretation of supposed meaningful self-evidencies—as if meaning was not itself a social effect—and where religious insider perspectives are privileged, scholars do not have the benefit of their colleagues in such fields as linguistics, sociology, psychology, anthropology, of knowing precisely what constitutes their field. Because many scholars of religion yet maintain that religion and religious experiences somehow transcend the rational categories of academic scrutiny (much as, for Barth, true religion transcends human constructions of mere images of God), their theories are not explicitly articulated, making their work exempt both from testing *and* critique. The modernist study of religion, then, is bereft of defensible theories of religion precisely because the identity of the field, as well as its datum, is presumed by many of its practitioners to arise not from theories about human behavior and cognition but spontaneously from the scholar's apparently direct experience—or empathetic reexperience—of some sort of an ineffable element either "in here" or "out there" that somehow eludes the hands of "reductionists." However, much like the impossibility of having a tennis game where there are no white lines, with no definition and theory of religion that we can articulate, apply, and critique publicly, "the data pursued by critical inquiry have no frame of reference to give them any significance. The results of [such] . . . critical inquiry seem to be free floating in the archives of a guild that has no log or registry to keep track of the knowledge it produces" (Mack 1996: 248). It is therefore little wonder that, in many institutions, the intuitively based study of religion is aimlessly adrift.

Although I have no interest in debating whether Barth's attempt to explain human religiosity is correct or not, it is in our best interest to distinguish his efforts from the naturalist tradition in our field—a tradition that, despite Green's misgivings, offers much for the future of the field. What is at stake in this effort to demarcate—or, conversely, what is at stake in disregarding the issue of demarcation—is the current self-definition and the very future of the academic study of religion as an institutionally viable practice. In our postmodern world there are indeed multiple, decentered explanations and assorted scales of analysis, but only some of these can be considered to be part of the work of the public study of religion; after all, not all athletes play hockey. Using the multiplicity of the postmodern world as a means for smuggling a foundationalist perspective back within the academy strikes me as a giant step backward.

Much like Ann Elk's interviewer, then, we must seriously question whether the theories our peers produce actually count as theories and whether they tell us anything interesting about the behaviors and events under investigation or whether they are simply telling us about the brontosaurus being skinny on one end, fat in the middle, and skinny on the other end. Despite his efforts to relegitimize one particular brand of theology's place in this intellectual pursuit, as well as in our classrooms, Green's article is but one instance of a wide misunderstanding of what it means to theorize; moreover, it is also evidence of caretakers' general failure to entertain the full implications of postmodernism in the study of religion. Indeed, as Green notes from the outset, "all data are theory laden," but there are ways of distinguishing explicit theories from unarticulated hunches. As I have noted elsewhere, "as much as we are all immersed within a framework, we are not all swimming in the same conceptual [and institutional] pond" (1991: 256). To misunderstand this simple point risks many of the advances made over the past 150 years in the study of religion. To ignore it invites ideology critique.[10]

NOTES

1. Donald Wiebe is perhaps one of the better known participants in these debates, either in North America or Europe. For example see Wiebe 1983 and 1989. Although I understand some of the issues differently from Wiebe, I am nonetheless deeply indebted to his work on the topic of demarcation.

2. One could also take issue with the fact that Green critiques social scientific studies at their weakest: as they were practiced more than two generations ago. Although some could say that to critique Barth is equally unfair, I am instead critiquing the argument of a contemporary scholar of religion who advocates using Barth's work as an example of the work of the theorist of religion.

3. For example, only because he fails to distinguish between 'theory' and 'philosophy' (on this, see Campany 1996: n. 4), is Robert Campany able to compare the ritual theories of the third century B.C.E. Confucian Xunzi to that of Emile Durkheim. They both have theories primarily because Campany under-

stands 'theory' in its classical sense as being the view of the self-reflective spectator (89, and n. 6).

4. If this were not the case, if theories were not testable, then we would hardly know that Marx's, Frazer's, Müller's, Lang's, Tylor's, Freud's, and even Durkheim's theories were inadequate for the task of explaining religion. But this hardly means that the very act of explanatory theorizing is not worthwhile or has no place in the field.

5. For instance, the literary critic Paul de Man argued that theories resist the multiple interpretations favored by many postmodernists (1986).

6. For an attempt to distinguish clearly the different logical levels involved in explanation and description, see Jeffrey Carter (1998).

7. For a review symposium on this book, including a response from the author, see *Method & Theory in the Study of Religion* 8/3 (1996): 291–325.

8. In the last chapter of *Manufacturing Religion* (1997c), I failed explicitly to distinguish between these two distinct yet interrelated notions of theory.

9. I am reminded here of Alan Wolfe's incisive comment on George Marsden's claim to be a postmodernist: "As a believer, after all, Marsden cannot really be a postmodernist" (Wolfe 1996).

10. See Arnal 1998b and MacKendrick 1999 for published responses to this essay.

PART III

Culture Critics
and Caretakers

The truth of the matter is that not only religious traditions
but Religious Studies itself furthers certain views and values
that are in fact indissociable from certain ideological/politi-
cal ones. The idea that there are nonpolitical forms of
inquiry is simply a myth (in the ordinary sense) that furthers
certain political agendas all the more effectively.

—Neil McMullin (1989:20)

CHAPTER 8

A Default of Critical Intelligence?
The Scholar of Religion
as Public Intellectual

The moment you publish essays in a society you have entered
political life; so if you want not to be political do not write essays
or speak out.
                                                —Edward Said (1996: 110)

To exist socially is to be rhetorically aligned. It is the function of
the intellectual as critical rhetor to uncover, bring to light, and
probe all such alignments. This is part of the work of ideological
analysis.
                                          —Frank Lentricchia (1985: 149)

The historian of religion cannot suspend his critical faculties, his
capacity for disbelief, simply because the materials are "primitive"
or religious.
                                          —Jonathan Z. Smith (1982: 60)

What is the role of religion in public life? This is the common question
asked in a number of books that have recently appeared (see, among
others, Cady [1993], Carter [1993], Dean [1994], and Marsden [1994,
1997]). Virtually all of their answers involve an increased role for 'faith'
and even theology in the intellectual, social, economic, and political
affairs of the state. As suggested in the previous chapter, the destabiliza-
tions of objectivity and science brought about by postmodern critiques
are the means by which these writers return this religious commitment
to public life. As George Marsden argues, given that "many of the original reasons" for excluding religious faith from the academy and matters
of public concern have, along with other Enlightenment notions,
recently come under severe critique, "is it now time to reconsider the
rules that shape the most respected academic communities?" (1994:
8–9). Because the question of religion's role in matters of public concern

125

is clearly of relevance to such theologically inclined commentators on civil life, some readers may wonder precisely why such books ought to attract the attention of the scholar of religion. In other words, what does this recent spate of books have to do with redescribing the public study of religion?

Books on the resurgent role of religious commitment in public life ought to attract the interest of the scholar of religion precisely because they are evidence of our failure as public intellectuals. Outside of a small number of readers and writers, few members of our own society—and few members of the academy—know what we do or know who we are, let alone are influenced in their public decisions by our scholarship. When one examines the books written by those who advocate an increased role for religious commitment in the affairs of a nation (most often this turns out to be a particular type of liberal Protestant Christian commitment), it is as if the academic study of religion—even its earlier incarnation as comparative religion—had never existed nor made any significant contribution to the human sciences. It is as if we had nothing to add to public affairs whatsoever and that theologians are the only commentators on 'religion' who have a role to play in helping to decide issues of law, justice, and social welfare.

Given the tools that scholars of religion routinely employ in their wide-ranging studies, I believe that we have a vital role to play in public affairs, but, as may be gathered from preceding chapters, it is a role that is rather different from the one championed by many current writers. This chapter is therefore an attempt to outline some of the reasons for our failure as public intellectuals and to argue for a different role for the scholar of religion as public intellectual.

A PROBLEM OF OUR OWN MAKING

In my reading, the very question, What is the role of religion in public life? has so far been the almost exclusive territory of self-identified religious people staking out claims on how their insights into the ways in which nations ought to work can be put into practice. What we should note from the outset is that the very phrasing of the question already presumes that the issue of what exactly religion is has already been settled; for virtually no one in this debate presumes that religion is the result of alienation from socioeconomic relations (Marx and Engels), that religion is an illusory practice of wish fulfillment (Freud), that religious practices and stories symbolically deny the contingency and transience of life and human institutions (Bloch 1994), that religion is but one species of anthropomorphism (Guthrie 1993, 1996), or that religion is but an evolutionarily developed mechanism (Burkert 1996). If any of these alternative options were seriously entertained, then undoubtedly many people would argue that religion must be kept far from the mechanisms whereby decisions in a culturally, economically, and technologically diverse/complex nation are made. It should be apparent, then, that this unarticulated consensus concerning the self-evidently positive and enriching role that religious commitment can play in political affairs betrays the silence of scholars of religion—a silence that I believe is self-inflicted. So, the question posed at the outset of this chapter, What is the role of religion in public life? might better be phrased, What is, or can be, the role of the scholar of religion in public life?

What I am suggesting is that unlike Stephen Carter's (1993) thesis that so-called elite, liberal, and secular society has actively trivialized and marginalized those with a religiously inspired viewpoint, it is actually scholars of religion, in their very conception of both their datum and themselves, who have trivialized and marginalized both themselves and their own social contributions. The methods most widely used in our field, phenomenology and hermeneutics, both of which happen to be the primary means by which our field was established as institutionally autonomous in the first place, are directly implicated in the absence of critical intelligence in the field. In their insistence that religion is comprised of *sui generis*, nonfalsifiable meaning derived from a private experience of mystery, awe, power, or the sacred that can only be described, intuited, felt, and understood by the outsider, scholars of religion have, to borrow Jonathan Z. Smith's words cited at the outset of this essay, suspended their own critical faculties. By so doing, they have created sufficient conditions for their own political malignment and cultural silence in contemporary public debates.

Ironically, perhaps, our almost exclusive reliance on the phenomenological and hermeneutical methods as the means for securing our intellectual and institutional turf has ensured that scholars of religion have little or no voice in either the university or other public forums. This is the very conclusion reached by Cristiano Grottanelli and Bruce Lincoln over a decade ago:

> There can be no shrinking away from the painful fact: the establishment of an autonomous field has, paradoxically, damaged the study of religion (and of religions) immensely. . . . The consequences of this situation may be summed up by stating that the discipline of "History of Religions" managed to marginalize itself in the name of autonomy. Its connections with history, anthropology, sociology, political science, and other relevant fields are scarce, while its ties with theology—however much they are denied—remain strong, if implicit, covert, and distorted. (1985: 8)

It falls to us to elaborate on this insight by identifying how this self-marginalization brings with it political and not just intellectual and institutional implications.

In constructing a field solely concerned with getting to the deep core, the kernel, or the ahistorical essence, we may have argued ourselves out of business when it comes to developing critical commentary on the mechanisms whereby privileges are bestowed, revoked, and contested in our own society. Although we may have gained personal enlightenment through the use of our hermeneutical skills, as Joseph Campbell and Mircea Eliade advocated,[1] we end up like the solitary renunciant; we have forgone our name and identity, we do not really have a way of putting it all into words or of communicating anything to our fellows; we have taken refuge from the society in which we live. As Catherine Albanese has rightly—though perhaps unwittingly—observed, "scholars of religion . . . find in the mental worlds they create and construct a *refuge* and *safe haven* from the general assaults of change that come with time's passing" (1995: 222; emphasis added). It is in constructing just such a "safe haven" that we find evidence of our complicity with power.

THE ESSENTIAL MAKEUP OF THINGS
AND THE SCHOLAR OF RELIGION

My claim concerning the self-inflicted default of critical intelligence may remind some of Carl Raschke's own criticism of the field (1986). Employing crisis rhetoric, Raschke argues that the spirit of relativism that he claims dominates the field has led to a "fanatical pluralism" where the scholar of religion "fosters a rabid preoccupation with the pluralistic display of religious givens and psycho-subjective ephemera at the cost of more profound ontological probing and analysis" (135). Instead of simply describing a diversity of religious manifestations, he argues that we as scholars of religion "should be able to make certain normative distinctions that reflect our commitment to discriminating analysis and critical intelligence" (136). Our default of critical intelligence, then, is a refusal to accept the role of providing "normative guidance" (137), a guidance that is fueled by on our "ontological probing" and "normative distinctions," both of which are specifically concerned with identifying such self-evident "aberrations of religious thinking and behavior" (136) as, for example, Jim Jones and the Jonestown deaths or the rise of various religious cults. According to Raschke, then, our failure as public intellectuals is in not distinguishing good from bad or normal from abnormal religion (recall Barth's preoccupation with making such normative judgments).

Although I agree with Raschke that critical intelligence, in part, constitutes "the ability and drive to penetrate beneath the mere surface of things," and, moreover, that our current institutional woes are of our own making, I cannot support his insistence that the scholar of religion can "apperceive [the] . . . essential make-up" of things, nor that our task is to differentiate "the valuable and enduring from the pernicious or inconsequential, the veracious from the merely specious" (136). Accordingly, Raschke and I differ dramatically in our conception of the discursive limits in which scholarship on religion takes place. It is in light of this longstanding but misguided assumption that studying religion provides deep, essential, absolute, or otherworldly insights into the very nature of things that scholars such as Raschke can argue that their scholarship provides normative guidance for a society—this is the same claim made by Eliade's reactionary political program, which goes by the name of the *new humanism*. If anything, and this is indeed the ironic part, the undefended *and* indefensible assumption that there is in fact a real nature to things that lurks beneath the surface (i.e., metaphysical reduction) is for me the primary instance of our default of critical intelligence. Our ability "to penetrate beneath the mere surface of things" is nothing more than the ability to historicize all ahistorical claims. For the scholar of religion as public intellectual, what is most intriguing is that many of our colleagues think there is such a thing as good or healthy religion, as opposed to aberrations of religious thinking and behavior. Contrary to this position, I would build on a Durkheimian tradition in arguing that religious discourses, which are neither good nor bad, are simply a brute fact of social ideologies and rhetorics. Contrary to Raschke's recommendation, then, I see the default in critical intelligence as being the unquestioned acceptance of deep, essential truths.

These may seem to be rather harsh words for a field that recently has experienced actual or at least threatened department closings. Given the current budgetary issues facing administrations, both university and government, it would seem that the last thing on a scholar of religion's mind would be to implicate his or her own field as being responsible, at least in part, for the current problems. After all, "he that troubleth his own house shall inherit the wind, and the fool shall be servant to the wise of heart" (Proverbs 11:29). For yet others, this may all sound like I am unjustly blaming the victim. Indeed, this would seem to be the ideal time to circle the wagons, proclaim the important place—even ontological loadings—our work has in the modern university's humanities curriculum, and, like many of our predecessors, leave it up to the sheer self-evidency of our claims to sway our audience. Such a phenomenon has been observed by Warren Frisina: "Committed to the intrinsic value of our work, especially our research, we continue to be 'productive' and hope that this intrinsic value will sustain us through difficult times. . . . I am concerned when I see this option taken by my colleagues" (1997: 30). By presuming both their datum and their work to have self-evident authority, relevance, and value, scholars of religion have evaded their social responsibility by side-stepping rational argumentation and persuasion; they may have thereby paved the way to their own institutional decline. Sadly, we cannot have it both ways: the study of self-evidencies and intuitions need not be termed "scholarship" and need not be funded by financially troubled governments.

SCHOLARS OF RELIGION AS TRANSLATORS: OUR FAILURE OF CRITICAL NERVE

The absence of the scholar of religion from the ranks of public intellectual is, at least in part, the result of what Donald Wiebe (1984b) aptly described as a "failure of nerve." As I understand this classic article on the field's history, Wiebe was referring to the failure of scholars to carry through with critical, explanatory studies of religion conceived as but one aspect of human cognitive, biological, cultural, and historical practices. Instead, Wiebe saw the field's turn from the late-nineteenth-century attempts to found an explanatory science of religion based on theories of religion (exemplified in the work of such scholars as F. Max Müller and Cornelius P. Tiele) and toward the phenomenologically and hermeneutically based approaches so dominant today, as a failure of scholarly nerve. (For some of Wiebe's more recent views on this problem, see 1994a and 1994c, 1999.)

One of the implications of this failure of critical nerve is that scholars of religion find themselves all but speechless when it comes to debating the so-called religious contributions to be made to making decisions of relevance to the public concern. To be sure, we can describe assorted claims, translate back and forth between sides, try to interpret the sometimes obscure claims made by one or another side in any given debate or controversey, and provide interesting historical and doctrinal background for understanding this or that insider viewpoint. But such is the job of a translator or color commentator, a role that many in the field think should occupy a greater amount of our time (e.g., see Judith Berling's [1993], Martin Marty's [1989], and Robert Wilken's [1989] presidential addresses to the AAR[2]). Conceived essentially as an exercise either in nuanced descriptions or reflexive autobiography, the study of religion has rarely amounted to more than a reporter repeating the insider's unsubstantiated claims, all the while invoking methodological agnosticism as their justification for doing so. Sadly, such scholars must inevitably remain silent when it comes to matters of explanation and analysis. When it comes to deciding whether and to what extent religious positions that claim ahistorical authority, wisdom, and direction are useful in charting the course of a public school curriculum, a welfare agency, or even a policy for war, translators have no voice and little, if anything, to add.

POLITICAL MARGINALIZATION
AND THE AUTONOMY OF RELIGION

It is not just that our almost sole reliance on the *method* of description rules out our public involvement; as already suggested, the very manner in which religion is conceived already rules out our critical contributions. This is a matter of *theory*. From the outset, religion is presumed to be diametrically opposed to, and is in fact the victim of, so-called secular issues such as politics and economics. In other words, our use of the sacred/profane rhetoric, which is itself one of the primary tools used by communities to maintain themselves (recall Richard Roberts's use of such binaries in a previous chapter), is part of the problem that deserves attention. Take, for example, how religion is conceived by one prominent contributor to these debates, Stephen Carter: it is self-evidently personalistic, moralistic, and experiential, and most definitely of the monotheistic variety (rarely do social systems outside of Judaism, Christianity, and Islam figure in these debates). "What does it mean," he asks, "to say that religious groups should be autonomous? It means, foremost, that they should not be beholden to the secular world, that they should exist neither by the forbearance of, nor to do the bidding of, the society outside of themselves" (1993: 34–35). Or, as Carter asserts a little later: "Religions are in effect independent centers of power"; religion is an "independent moral force" and, "at its heart, a way of denying the authority of the rest of the world; it is a way of saying to fellow human beings and to the state those fellow human beings have erected, 'No, I will *not* accede to your will'" (35, 39, 41). It is on the basis of such a suspect understanding of religion that Carter argues for the legal, institutional, and social autonomy—and therefore public authority—of organized religion in America. It is little wonder, then, that Carter's book has been so well received.

Based on such a use of the religious/secular distinction, a distinction that fuels the exceedingly misleading notion of the "separation of church and state," 'religion' is construed as an independent variable occupying the untainted realm of pure and private moral insight that is opposed to, and the salvation of, the messy public worlds of politics and economics. However, Burton Mack has rightly described the dilemma faced by scholars who employ this rhetorical move:

> [T]he usual approach to the definition of religious phenomena is . . . limited to what moderns have imagined as the "sacred," or as reference to discrete "subcultural" systems of religion that take separate institutional forms. This way of defining religion leaves out of account the arenas of discourse, practice, and display where a society's values and attitudes are regularly cultivated in the "secular" realm. (1989: 30)

Much as an earlier generation of North American historians of religions argued that because religion is *sui generis*, sociologists and anthropologists cannot adequately study it, so too many writers stake out their institutional turf through the deployment of strategies of containment and privilege. However, such privilege, generated largely through the presumption that religion is *sui generis* automatically isolates and excludes the scholar of religion from making a contribution to larger issues of public concern, a point nicely articulated by Mack. If we follow Terry Eagleton and, at least in part, define the intellectual as "somebody who trades in ideas by transgressing discursive frontiers" (1992: 83), then such definitional and methodological autonomy—let alone the institutional autonomy scholars of religion require to survive in the university—effectively rules out all forms of transgression and intellectual provocation, for the boundaries of just what is and what is not within the reach of the scholar of *sui generis* religion are quite clear (i.e., if there are no gods, no myths, no rituals, and no hierophanies, then it is hardly something about which the scholar of religion can have an informed opinion).[3] As we all know, "the economics department is interested only in abstract models of a pure free enterprise economy; the political science department is concentrating on voting patterns and electoral statistics; the anthropologists are studying hill tribesmen in New Guinea; and the sociologists are studying crime in the ghetto" (Rai 1995: 138). And scholars of religion study and comment on the free-floating, *sui generis*, and supposedly sacred quality of private human experiences.

The effect of such a rigid compartmentalization, characteristic of the disciplinary, administrative, and funding structures of the modern university, is that certain questions, by definition, cannot be asked. This in turn prevents creative and oppositional forms of scholarship; for moving across, between, and around disciplines means calling into question the rules by which we normally divide up, study, and understand 'reality'. Institutional as well as methodological containment and isolation make it all but impossible to assess the relations between these assorted pieces of the pie we call "reality," let alone assess the very conditions (both intellectual *and* material) that are prerequisite for just these pie pieces and just this pie in the first place. This is surely one of the reasons why cross-disciplinary scholarship is met with suspicion in many sectors of the university—not least by scholars of *sui generis* religions. This is precisely why the work of a scholar such as Edward Said, whose *Orientalism* (1978) transgressed so many traditional intellectual boundaries, can offer us one model for our role as transgressive public intellectuals.[4]

TO REPRODUCE OR CONTEST AUTHORITY?
NOW THAT IS THE QUESTION?

It seems sensible that religious devotees make claims regarding the autonomy of their experiences and actions. After all, 'religion' is easily understood as a powerful and pervasive means by which human communities authorize their claims of historic and practical import by, in Roland Barthes's words, dressing up their own creations in "decorative displays" to make them pass for "what-goes-without-saying" (1973: 11). Raschke's assertion that it is sensible to talk of religious aberrations relies on just such unquestioned and undefensible decorative displays. Through their use of the tools of nuanced description, their effort to recover authentic meaning, and their disdain for transgressive questions, scholars of religion risk uncritically reproducing their subjects' claims of autonomy and authority—whether that authority sanctions politically liberal or conservative actions. Where they could instead be involved in studying the mechanisms that make cultures possible, thereby uncloaking the ahistoric rhetoric that makes its appearance in all debates, scholars of religion *qua* translators have instead opted for the highly conservative practice of entrenching ideologies and rhetorics—a point convincingly argued by Graeme MacQueen in his critical study of scholarship on myth. MacQueen argues that by creating of 'myth' a seemingly uniform set of existentially meaningful narratives, largely concerned with ahistorical origins, scholars have ignored the relations between sociopolitical and gendered dominance and subordination in the societies they study. This "leaves students of myth in the dangerous position of lending unconscious support and legitimacy to structures of authority in societies that they study" (1988: 144). In the words of Karl Mannheim, the scholar as translator is little more than one who "takes refuge in the past and attempts to find there an epoch or society in which an extinct form of reality-transcendence dominated the world, and through this romantic reconstruction [they] . . . seek to spiritualize the present" (1985: 259). They are precisely the people involved in what

Jeppe Sinding Jensen and Armin Geertz have aptly labeled the "politics of nostalgia" (1991; see McCutcheon 1997c).

If, instead, religion is conceived as but one aspect of human practices, if "religion" itself is understood to be a second-order category of description (where the first order constitutes the behavior or claims being redescribed by scholars) and not a third-order category of redescription, then scholars of religion will have a significantly different role to play in both the reproduction of authority and in public debates where such authority is legitimized and contested. What I mean by this is that for scholars of religion, the behaviors we name "religion" ought to be the subject of theorizing not appreciation or translation. Our involvement in the public debate is, then, on the higher level of critical, comparative, redescriptive analysis and critique. Whatever else religion may or may not be, it is at least a potent manner by which humans construct "worlds" by which they negotiate not simply their way around the natural world but through which they defend and contest issues of social power and privilege in the here and now (Paden 2000). Religious language, therefore, is a terribly efficient and often uncontested means for abstracting issues, claims, and institutions from the tug-and-pull of historical existence, thereby privileging them, their participants, and one particular view of how reality ought to be constructed. Scholars of religion come upon the scene with sophisticated tools for comparing, analyzing, and critiquing the strategies by which communities decontextualize and marginalize, mythify and deify one side in what is more than likely a complex situation. We call into question the "aestheticization of the political" (Carroll 1995: 15) and the "authority of detachment" (Merod 1987: xi) in the very act of contextualizing and historicizing our data.

As opposed to being what Jerome Karabel labels a "moralist" (intellectuals making normative claims on how the world really ought to work), scholars of religion are in the position of "identifying the conditions and processes that shape the actual political consciousness and actions of different groups"—including members of their own group (1996: 206).[5] Differing somewhat from the moralist stands of such intellectuals as Noam Chomsky and Edward Said, who see the role of the public intellectual as being proactive, of speaking 'truth' to power, exposing lies, and making normative claims (Chomsky 1987: 60; Said 1996: xvi, 85–102), the scholar of religion as critical rhetor instead exposes the mechanisms whereby these very truths and norms are constructed in the first place, demonstrating the contingency of seemingly necessary conditions and the historical character of ahistorical claims.

However, we can at least in part follow Chomsky's lead by consistently exposing the intellectual and material conditions of thoughts and actions in any given society (1991). When compared to the moralist intellectual, however, the scholar of religion as public intellectual—and as publicly accountable intellectual—is more timid about making pronouncements on what these conditions really should be. Clearly we come equipped with our own assumptions—assumptions that are themselves deserving of scrutiny and analysis—but we have little interest in making normative claims concerning the need for all scholars to do as we do or for all citizens to engage in the never-ending practice of critique. The particular game we play, however, does presume that there are intellectual, social, and material motivations and implications to *all* human behaviors, beliefs, and institutions. To presume otherwise, to presume that mysterious, divine, or other-worldly forces of unknown origin and design routinely come into play when human beings interact, is to play a significantly different game within an institutional context far removed from the public university. Given our presumption that all human actions are historically constrained, such claims to mysterious forces will themselves attract our critical attention.

Perhaps it is the realization of just this potential role for scholars of religion as public intellectuals that explains our absence from the citations of those writers who advocate an increased role for religious faith in the affairs of the state. For, as argued in the introduction, the scholar of religion as critical rhetor comes not to inform the world of how it *ought* to work, but explains how and why it *happens to* work as it does, making such critical scholarship a convenient resource to avoid when making pronouncements on the future of human meaning, the nation, or the world—claims that are either politically conservative *or* liberal, in support of dominant *or* oppositional regimes.

THE SCHOLAR OF RELIGION AS CRITIC

It is in his or her analysis of so-called religious institutions, traditions, myths, and rituals that the scholar of religion can contribute most to uncloaking and laying bare the conditions and strategies by which their fellow citizens authorize the local as universal and the contingent as necessary. We can find in seemingly insignificant gestures and rhetorical flourishes the makings of larger issues in the practice and reproduction of power and authority. In our analysis of the manner in which humans represent the world and their place in it—let alone our analysis of the representations of our colleagues in the university!—we are equipped to scrutinize the ideological sleight of hand that leads to a seemingly perfect fit between the model constructed and sanctioned by the society or group in question, on the one hand, and reality, on the other—whatever that reality may in fact turn out to be. It is this very sleight of hand, the "institutional imperative," or the refraction of the seeming facts of the case through "the prism of Western ideology" that has attracted the attention of Noam Chomsky's own analysis of mass media (Rai 1995: 28); for what type of reality do we expect to find represented in, for instance, elite media other than the reality tailored to suit the interests of elite producers/manufacturers who finance the media as an avenue for selling products to upper-class consumers? It is through the comparison and analysis of competing representations that the public intellectual juxtaposes competing models of the world and attempts to explain why it is that such-and-such an institution or story accompanies this or that model.[6] Therefore, we are justified to inquire into just what we are selling our readers and students when we uncritically reproduce authoritative accounts in our merely descriptive scholarship.

Accordingly, for the scholar of religion as public intellectual, "religion" is a category that holds little analytical value. As both Pascal Boyer[7] and Jonathan Z. Smith,[8] have suggested, it is a second-order category, and part of the problem to be studied, not a higher-order category that is part of the analysis: it is part of the data to be explained because as they are commonly defined religious discourses remove something (a claim, an institution, a practice) from history, thereby privileging it over all other historically embedded claims and knowledges. What else can it mean to encourage public debates to be settled by "discerning and then enacting the will of God" (Carter 1993: 77)?[9] Such rhetoric is presumed by many in the field to be beyond naturalist or material analysis and reproach. But we must inquire into just what other part of our public debate would sanction a position that is based upon such ahistorical certainty, such undefended and indefensible self-evidency. Even the phrase *We hold these truths to be self-evident* has received its share of critical attention; for it is abundantly clear that only land-owning, free white males benefited from the privileges accorded by those so-called self-evidencies concerning the fact that *all men are created equal.*

Therefore, the scholar of religion as critical rhetor has a crucial role to play in matters of public concern, for who else will question just what sense it makes to talk, as William Dean does, of such abstractions as "a sense of the whole," "transcendence," "religious identity," "ultimate importance," "ultimate meanings," and "implicit religious values." Take for instance Dean's reference to a former U.S. National Security Advisor: "In *Out of Control* [1993], Zbigniew Brzezinski attributed the forthcoming collapse of America's world leadership, not to politics, economics, or the rise of rivals, but to the growing spiritual illness of the whole American culture" (Dean 1994: xiv). That contemporary writers can so easily talk of such things as the crisis of "American spiritual emptiness," its "spiritual illness," and its "pervasive spiritual impoverishment" as if these were all causal agents (I recall here Martin Marty attributing causality to "religious impulses") attests to the dire need for scholars of religion to enter this public debate. The point is that despite the fact that *empty spirits* is a wonderful metaphor, it is hardly a useful explanatory category; moreover, by marginalizing the explanatory power of political and economic analysis, by presuming that there is such a thing as a "whole" to culture in the United States, not to mention the problematic assumption that indeed the United States *ought* to be an unrivaled leader in world politics, economics, and the military, both Dean and Brzezinski betray their own uncritical acceptance of a rather narrow party line. Simply put, we must question what is implied in reducing empty *stomachs* to empty *spirits* and why it is construed as a crisis if others do not sanction such a spiritualization. The scholar of religion as public intellectual is the one who is capable of identifying the ideological mechanisms working in such efforts to, in Mannheim's words, "spiritualize the present."

Instead of being a translator, or, in his estimation, a caretaker for religion (*caretaker* nicely communicates the role advocated by many AAR presidents), Burton Mack has recommended that we become culture critics. "Culture" is, for Mack, the larger category into which religious practices and beliefs fall when they are correctly understood as being no different in origin or implication from other social authorizing practices. "Since modern societies in the western tradition make such a fuss about keeping religion separate from society," Mack writes, "we need the term culture to cover the phenomenon of values and attitudes cultivated within a society apart from overtly religious inculcation" (1989: 30).[10] Scholars of religion as culture critics agree that religion, religious discourses, and religious practices are part of the descriptive, historical data that requires theoretical study. We find no more succinct statement of the problems that arise when we are anything other than scholars and critics than in the last of Bruce Lincoln's thirteen "Theses on Method." He writes:

> When one permits those whom one studies to define the terms in which they will be understood, suspends one's interest in the temporal and contingent, or fails to distinguish between "truths," "truth-claims," and "regimes of truth," one has ceased to function as historian or scholar. In that moment, a variety of roles are available: some perfectly respectable (amanuensis, collector, friend and advocate), and some less appealing (cheerleader, voyeur, retailer of import goods). None, however, should be confused with scholarship. (1996a: 227)

The only role possible for scholars who see religion as a powerful means whereby human communities construct and authorize their practices and institutions (i.e., their "regimes of truth") is that of the critic.

As already noted, and this bears repeating, for scholars *qua* critics, religion is not itself part of the explanation or solution (as it is for translators and caretakers) but is, instead, part of the data to be explained (as it is for virtually all who develop theories of religion). That human beings who normally construct their lives based on often mundane experiences of the material, physical world sometimes invoke immaterial, nonempirical causes and explanations should itself attract our attention as scholars. How is it that they distinguish between when it is, and when it is not, appropriate to invoke such devices as gods, spirits, or fate as part of their understanding of the world at large? It has always struck me as intriguing that readers of "Scriptures" somehow are able to decide, seemingly without any articulated or identifiable criteria, when to read a text as metaphoric or symbolic and when to read it as literal. What varying criteria are being employed, and how do they develop? If scholars of religion wish to make a contribution to the public debate, then perhaps this is one place to begin: developing theories of decision making and the means by which humans represent/manipulate the world at large. For when it comes to public decisions on who should or should not receive welfare, when it is or is not allowable to have an abortion, whether and where the budget should be cut, or when to go to war, then implicit, intuitive, and nonfalsifiable criteria are hardly desirable. In fact, if democracy is desirable at all, it is precisely because the decision-making process must ideally answer in public to the demands of a diverse citizenry. Our critical contributions comprise one component of that citizenry.

Be clear: I am not advocating that the scholar of religion become a politician, nor that she or he is the only critic capable of calling long-established certainties into question. To advance the former thesis would confuse the public role of intellectuals with the possible contributions they may or may not make as private citizens participating in other aspects of a representative democracy. To advance the latter would lead to yet a new turf war and further dangers of compartmentalized professionals. Moreover, I would hope that readers recognize that I am hardly advocating the onetime popular notion of the intellectual as dispassionate, objective observer. Further, I am not claiming that most of the population should abandon their own normative convictions—in fact, given the centrality of using rhetorical, ideological, and normative claims and strategies in constructing and sanctioning the social and political models we live by and within, it would be naive to think that these sorts of claims would ever disappear—hence the epigraph from David Lodge that opens this book. Instead, I am recommending that scholars of religion as public intellectuals should not simply repeat or merely translate uncritically religious claims; instead, they are the ones who accept the challenge of generating critical, scholarly theories *about* normative discourses; they recognize the critical potential of the tools at their disposal. Accordingly, normative reflection is not inherently problematic—one could go so far as to argue that it may actually be inevitable; it just happens to be a type of discourse that we have tools to study. Our scholarship is not constrained by whether or not devotees recognize its value; it is not intended to celebrate or enhance normative, dehistoricized discourses but, rather, to contextualize and redescribe them as human constructs.

MODELS FOR CRITIQUING AUTHORIZING STRATEGIES

I can think of no better example of the critical potential for our field than Bruce Lincoln's *Authority: Construction and Corrosion* (1994), especially his analysis of the 1992 attempt of the environmental activist, Rick Springer, to interrupt an National Association of Broadcasters award ceremony in honor of former U.S. President Ronald Reagan. Lincoln's creative and nuanced analysis of the strategies and mechanisms whereby seemingly self-evident authority was contested and reasserted demonstrates that the scholar of religion's tools apply to events and institutions not deemed religion by traditional, essentialist definitions. In fact, the development of Lincoln's work over the years seems to suggest the clear movement away from studying distinct religion (a static noun) to studying the complex relations among authorizing practices (active processes or verbs) that appear in any number of social and historical settings. In other words, his scholarship exemplifies the transgressive role available to the scholar of social authorizing practices.

A second useful example of the kind of work in which we can engage as public intellectuals can be found in Marc Manganaro's own study of authority (1992), a study that examines the particular rhetorical moves that allow scholars of myth to slide so easily from description to sociopolitical prescription (a topic at the very core of Ivan Strenski's well-known critique of myth theorists [1987]). Using Northrop Frye's book, *The Critical Path: An Essay on the Social Context of Literary Criticism*, Manganaro identifies how Frye's specific reading of the anti-Vietnam War protestors, as well as the counterculture of the 1960s in general, contains and constrains these events by decontextualizing and representing them simply as repetitions and manifestations of primordial human desires. According to Manganaro, from the outset such an interpretation effectively minimalizes and marginalizes the very social movement Frye is studying. Whether or not he intended it, by understanding the particular event as but one instance of a timeless universal theme, Frye dehistoricizes and marginalizes the actual event by elevating it (or, should we say, demoting it) to the level of the abstract universal.

Borrowing from the work of the literary critic Fredric Jameson, Manganaro identifies a variety of these "strategies of containment" operating in Frye's text, rhetorical strategies that enable Frye to depict the energy, novelty, and potential for concrete sociopolitical change found in the 1960s counterculture as but eternal returns of the same. Unable to entertain that the protestors may have had a significant, novel, and concrete role to play in contemporary social change, Frye's mythification flattens them and takes off their edge. In the hands of Frye's highly speculative comparative method, "[e]xtremist movements . . . are characterized structurally according to their off-centeredness" and are therefore bracketed within a universal, uninterrupted great tradition (Manganaro 1992: 145). An essentialist method that posits a transcendent manifested in certain discrete historical occasions inevitably reduces particularity to sameness.

As scholars of social authorizing practices, we fail to fulfill our role as public intellectuals when we decline to demonstrate consistently that such a thing as society, text, nation, ethnicity, tradition, intuition, gender, myth, or even religion, is "not a natural or god-given entity, but is a constructed, manufactured, even in some cases invented object, with a history of struggle and conquest behind it" (Said 1996: 33). We are trained to examine the specific sites where human communities construct their enduring representations, representations that function to make it self-evident "that the values one holds are grounded in the inherent structure of reality, that between the way one ought to live and the way things really are there is an unbreakable inner connection" (Geertz 1968: 97). Although some would argue that Geertz's definition of religion is far too wide to be of any analytical use (Asad 1993: 27–54), its benefit lies precisely in the assumption that religion is but one species of the human penchant for universalizing and spiritualizing the local and the particular. As noted by the literary critic Frank Lentricchia at the outset of this chapter, "it is the function of the intellectual as critical rhetor to uncover, bring to light, and probe" all such mechanisms. To uncover—and thereby challenge—the often occluded and disguised mechanisms that carry out these universalizations is nothing other than the *consistent* analysis of ideologies: the means by which slippage from *is* to *ought* routinely takes place.

CONCLUSION: A PERIOD OF SOME SIGNIFICANCE
FOR THE STUDY OF RELIGION

Whether we like it or not, then, as scholars we are public intellectuals already, for we teach, and our work is judged within public institutions. The question is whether we will accept this role or, through our efforts to spiritualize and dehistoricize the people and practices we study—and the students we regularly teach each semester—via such suspect conceptual devices as *sui generis* religion, we will continue to obscure both our data and our social role, thereby contributing to the very authorizing practices we could instead be identifying and questioning. To me, the choice is rather straightforward: whether to reproduce or name the ideological mechanisms and alignments whereby description becomes prescription and the local is represented as universal.

However, there exists a default of critical intelligence among many scholars of religion, scholars who proclaim their apoliticism and, in the very same breath, descriptively reproduce authorized "sacred histories." Through our insistent preoccupation with issues of intellectual, methodological, professional, and institutional turf—in a word, our autonomy—we tie our own hands and gag our own mouths, forcing ourselves to act as if the world passes us by alone, unaffected, and safe. As I have argued elsewhere: "To fail to make explicit the social and political motivations/benefits behind what the apparent majority of 'religionists' yet think to be the *sui generis* quality of religion, its texts, and its language . . . is to fall considerably short of what the academic study of religion could be" (1991: 256).

To accept the role of public intellectual requires us consistently to lay bare these mechanisms of power and control. Our role is not to act as caretakers for religion, trying, along with Raschke, to save "the vitality, as well as the moral and cultural influence, of religion in the world" (1986: 135), but rather our role is unfailingly to probe beneath the rhetorical window dressings that authorize conceptual and social constructions of our own making. To join with the many scholars in our field intent on protecting and caring for religion is implicitly to acknowledge that we have no critical contribution to make to the study of human behavior and institutions and are, instead, simply reporters and legitimizers of essential self-evidencies. As already suggested, however, reporting self-evidencies is hardly deserving of public support. But, given the alternative, even oppositional, role of uncovering, and teaching others to uncover, rhetorical and ideological window dressings—wherever and whenever we may find them—we must be prepared for an adverse reaction from both our colleagues and the wider public: one does not win a popularity contest by pointing out the emperor's general state of undress. Given our role as critics, we may very well have to come to terms with the fact that questioning self-evidencies might also hardly be deserving of public support. After all, few institutions have built-in self-destruct mechanisms. But given the general intellectual freedom that comes with operating within a cross-disciplinary setting in the public university, some of us will be able to make tactical and local contributions to the analysis of authorizing practices in a surprising number of sites.

It is with deep irony, then, that I now find myself seemingly in agreement with Mircea Eliade when he suggested, in his essay "A New Humanism," that the scholar of religion "is destined to play an important role in contemporary cultural life" (1984: 3). Eliade, however, saw this role as the therapeutic recovery of archaic meanings housed in supposedly timeless myths and rituals. This is nothing other than the regressive—and not transgressive—politics of nostalgia. Instead, I side with Mack and Lincoln in recommending for scholars of religion the role of critic, rather than Eliade's role of savior, for our work is carried out within the material contestations of history rather than in the mists of primordial time. Moreover, far from being "destined" for such a role, we are continually tempted to forsake critical thinking and, instead, to enjoy the spoils and privileges that are routinely awarded to those who accept the less controversial role of reporter, translator, and caretaker—all of which amount simply to being ideological managers. Instead, the scholar of religion as public intellectual and critic of authorizing practices comes equipped with methodologies and theories to identify those homogenizing, ideological strategies so necessary for the manufacture *and* management of human communities—scholarly communities included. For these very strategies are responsible for portraying that which is different as the same, the many as one, the fragmented as whole, the other as aberrant, and, perhaps most important, the religious as sociopolitically autonomous.

With such critical tools at our disposal, how can we *not* have something important to say on the public stage about such issues as the place of religious intuition, insight, and commitment in the academy and the public policy domain? Who, if not the scholar of social authorizing practices and mythmaking, will come forward to identify the slippery logic, rhetorical flourishes, and ideological strategies that, together, drive intellectual, social, and political practice in all its varied guises? Such cultural criticism is slowly taking hold at a number of sites throughout the late-twentieth-century discourse on religion, precisely when the previous rationale for our field is coming under well-deserved criticism; it seems, then, that John F.

Wilson's words ring as true now as they did over thirty years ago: "[W]e seem about to enter a period of some significance for the study of religion" (1964: 252).

NOTES

1. For, according to Campbell, our studies comprise an individual quest for personhood; according to Eliade, the history of religions is a spiritual technique meant to recover long-camouflaged and archaic cultural values.

2. The role of translator and mediator is advocated in a surprising number of presidential addresses to the AAR—most recently in Margaret Miles's 1999 presidential address, where it was stated quite openly that the age is over when theology and the study of religion were considered mutually exclusive exercises. For a critical survey of the history of the AAR and its presidential addresses, see Wiebe's *Politics of Religious Studies* (1999), in particular the chapters entitled, "Against Science in the Academic Study of Religion" (1999: 235–53) and "A Religious Agenda Continued" (1997; reprinted in 1999: 255–75).

3. I will return to Eagleton's notion of the intellectual as transgressor in a later chapter.

4. For a useful assessment of the reception of Said's work over the past two decades, see Prakash (1995).

5. Karabel's article is written from this alternative—or what he terms the "realist"—position and is concerned with identifying eight conditions that contribute to the political radicalization of intellectuals. Accordingly, Karabel is in a long line of sociologists of intellectuals dating back to Mannheim.

6. Chomsky's own work in comparing U.S. media coverage of Cambodian (official enemy) and Indonesian (official friend) atrocities in the 1970s is startlingly frank evidence of the way in which representations vary with socioeconomic and geopolitical interests. In *Manufacturing Religion* (1997c) I have used a similar comparative method to examine the differing scholarly and media representations of the so-called self-immolations of Vietnamese Buddhist monks in the early 1960s (chapter 6).

7. "The study of religion is an 'impure' subject [in the chemical rather than the moral sense], that is, a subject where the central or official topic is not a scientific object" (1996: 212).

8. "[T]he term 'religion' is not an empirical category. It is a second order abstraction" (1988: 233).

9. At this point in his argument, Carter tries to reduce (obscure?) the debate on whether or not women ought to be ordained to an essentially religious issue. The full quotation reads: "The answer [to the issue of whether women ought to be ordained] has everything to do with discerning and then enacting the will of God, and nothing to do with the rights of women." What ought to attract our critical attention is not whether a deity desires women to be ordained but how easily writers like Carter abstract this debate from issues of history, power, and gender—and then get away with it!

10. Needless to say, Mack immediately goes on to argue that such a change in datum would require us to reconceive and reorganize departments of religion that are still largely the product of a seminary model. An example of how the study of religion might be effectively reorganized as the comparative study of culture is provided by Tim Fitzgerald (1995, 1997, 1999). For an extremely helpful survey of some of the anthropological arguments concerning the questionable analytical usefulness of the category "culture" itself, see Brightman (1995); see also Eagleton 2000; Lincoln 2000a, Masuzawa 1998, and McCauley and Lawson 1996.

CHAPTER 9

Talking Past Each Other: The Issue of Public Intellectuals Revisited

In 1998, the editor of the *Journal of the American Academy of Religion* kindly invited me to reply to the unsolicited comments that an earlier version of the previous chapter prompted from Paul Griffiths at the University of Chicago (1998b) and June O'Connor at the University of California, Riverside (1998). Given the amount of material that crosses our desks and our computers every day, it is flattering to find that one's writing has not only been read by one's peers but has prompted them to take the time to compose and submit a reply for publication.[1]

MAN BITES DOG

I find Paul Griffiths's reply troubling because it sidesteps argumentation and is instead based on assertions that simply dismiss my essay as, in his words, naive and deeply confused. Griffiths waxes paternalistic in likening me to a "dog wagging his tail after having learned a new trick," confessing that he found himself "wanting to pat McCutcheon on the head for being so eagerly pleased with himself." This rather biting tone, which is pretty much repeated in his review of my book (1998)[2] *Manufacturing Religion*, can also be found in an unsigned review of my book that ran in *The Christian Century*, where the writer not only misrepresents my thesis but also expresses incredulity that I could even hold such a position.[3] After reading these two reviews and Griffiths's reply to my essay, I tried to envision what would have happened to my own essay had I engaged in such emotional rhetoric and simply dismissed positions with which I disagreed. I presume that my submission would not even have made it to the stage of anonymous review, much less be published in the academy's journal. In fact, were I to dismiss opinions different from mine as nothing but mere silliness, I do not think I would ever have been motivated to reply to Griffiths in print.

Taking such criticisms seriously, however, presents a challenge: how can one reply to this sort of *ad hominem* attack without either sanctioning it or, even worse, simply reproducing it? Engaging such critics on their own rhetorical level serves no purpose that I can see to be of any benefit either to me or the reader. Therefore, I would rather reply by making the style of the critique itself my datum, since his critique itself has little or no actual substance.

Given that my brand of scholarship on religion, at least in the AAR, certainly does not represent the vast majority of people (*if only* my position was as "sadly common" as Griffiths claims it to be!), it is surprising that my publications inspire such emotion. Come to think of it, though, such reactions are quite predictable. In fact, had my writing *not* prompted such a reaction, I might have feared that I was doing something wrong. After all, my critique concerns the manner in which the field, as well as its datum, is conceptualized, institutionalized, and, by extension, the social role and privilege of scholars working within just these institutions with just these conceptual tools and categories. I therefore welcome such absurd overreactions because they provide better confirmation for my critique than any of the data I could ever come up with on my own; as Chomsky wrote, "[t]he system protects itself with indignation against a challenge to deceit in the service of power, and the very idea of subjecting the ideological system to rational inquiry elicits incomprehension or outrage, though it is often masked in other terms" (1991: 9).

Apart from his paternalism and outright sarcasm, readers should notice a crucial rhetorical move Griffiths makes: he transfers my original sociopolitical argument to the realm of disembodied ideas and beliefs (i.e., metaphysics), a place of no place, where scholars of religion usually feel quite at home. Although it is implicit in his reply, his review of my book states quite explicitly that "everything is in the end and in the beginning, theology" (1998a: 48). His argument, then, seems to be that since we all have pretheoretical commitments, interests, and values, we are all religious, and therefore we are all doing theology. I would hope that the futility of this sort of reasoning is clear to readers: (i) as the old saying goes, if everything is theology, then 'theology' is an utterly useless and meaningless signifier; and (ii) despite all of us having all sorts of pretheoretical commitments, aims, and motives, the truth of which can neither be verified nor falsified, they do not all have something to do with intentional, invisible agents (whether personal or not) controlling the course of cosmic history (on this see Alton's very useful article [1989]).

It strikes me that transferring the argument to the level of metaphysics is obfuscating and regressive; it is another instance of the politically conservative, regnant idealist discourse that I have tried to identify and critique throughout these chapters. The prime example of this in our field is the manner in which many scholars study texts and doctrine as ahistoric self-evidencies in need of exegesis rather than studying them as the material products of particular genders, classes, eras, regions, and so on—products that both presuppose and legitimize a particular social world. Actually, this very topic was discussed in a recent issue of *JAAR*; Jamie Hubbard cited Neil McMullin's previous critique of the manner in which Hubbard's own study of doctrine "privileges the written expressions of elites, usually male, and thereby eliminates from consideration the vast majority of what religious people actually do. . . . [Thereby, such scholarship] replicates the vested interests of elites" (as phrased by Hubbard 1998: 60; see also McMullin 1989; Hubbard 1992; McMullin 1992). This earlier critique notwithstanding, Hubbard goes on to define doctrine as "those expressions about the nature of the world and the value of actions that are accepted by a community as authoritative (i.e., believed to be true) and relevant to their religious well-being" (61–62).

Apart from not knowing precisely what constitutes "religious well-being," such an understanding of doctrine leaves untheorized just *how* and *why* "a community" accepts (or is forced to accept) something as authoritative. Under this model of scholarship, both the homogeneity of the community and the self-evidency of the authority are seen as phenomenologically given rather than as the products of history; this is precisely the problem of reification. In outlining my model for scholars of religion as engaged intellectuals, I suggested that we can do much better than this; along with Bruce Lincoln, I think that there are a whole series of interesting questions that we can pose: "Who is able to speak with authority? Where and how can one produce authoritative speech? What effect does such speech have on those to whom it is addressed? What response does such speech anticipate? What responses does it allow? And what consequences can unanticipated and disallowed responses have for the construction, exercise, and maintenance of authority?" (1994: 2).[4]

Taking for granted that idealism ought to constitute the bottom line for the field is, to me, a bit like the tail wagging the dog. And that is precisely the critique of the field that I offered in my essay. Had I been so inclined, I might very well have used Griffiths's own work as an instance of this troublesome discourse, for in a previous book he criticized recent scholarly trends that contextualize religious doctrine instead of studying it on its own terms, that is, what he refers to as the "properly doctrinal study of doctrine" (1994: 2). As might be anticipated, his most recent book is significantly entitled *Religious Reading* (1999), a book that employs a phenomenological analysis to examine, in the words of the press's blurb, "the kind of reading in which a religious believer allows his mind to be furnished and his heart instructed by a sacred text." To be quite honest, I neither know what it means to have one's heart instructed nor to study such things as "doctrine-expressing sentences considered as expressive of doctrine, not as epiphenomena of social settings or institutional arrangements of any kind" (Griffiths 1994: 4)— this is quite possibly one of the best examples of Eliade's call for treating religious things on their own plane of reference that I have seen, something I argue against quite strongly. Little wonder that Griffiths and I have significant disagreements.

Despite his best attempts to study merely the "conceptual relations among ordered sets of sentences," I simply suggested that one cannot actually study disembodied ideas without overlooking the concrete historical agents and social structures that made these and just these sentences possible. Focusing simply on the study of ideas and/or studying these ideas exclusively within the rubrics established by the elite members of the communities we study (i.e., studying what counts as doctrine) amounts to overlooking human experience and action as the product of wider, often unseen, social structures. For, as McMullin argued,

> it is not primarily ideas but structures—economic, political, social, and so forth—that form the foundation on which any society is built and that determine to a great degree the shape of that society's religious discourse, and those structures must be taken into account if any particular aspect of a given society is to be explained with accuracy. (1989: 27)

Scholarship that avoids the structural, historical dimension, I argued in the previous chapter, is complicit with authority insomuch as it not only obscures all issues of power and privilege, but it also uncritically reproduces idealist rhetorics of social autonomy.

Before moving on, I should say that Griffiths is correct on one point: I do treat all claims as historical, meaning they arise from and are in support of social, economic, political, and so on, situations. As a scholar working in the human sciences, I have little choice but to presume this; Griffiths's identification of this presumption is hardly a criticism but an accurate description of my work. In fact, the objects of study that catch my attention are the creative ways (i.e., the sociorhetorics) employed by such real, historical people as Griffiths to portray just the opposite case.

MAKING A LIST, BUT CHECKING IT TWICE

Unlike Paul Griffiths, June O'Connor has done us the kind service of systematically outlining seven common ways of conceiving of religion (i.e., seven lenses), noting that my neo-Durkheimian definition is just one among the others. "Beware of mono-causal theories" I tell my students;

accordingly, O'Connor is entirely correct to point out that there are many ways in which these collections of human behaviors and social institutions we call "religion" can be defined and studied—at least there are many ways of conceiving of religion in a field that also inquires into the *why* of religion and not just one that documents and sorts the various whos, hows, wheres, and whens. Therefore, I agree with her completely; after all, my previous chapter simply said, "*Whatever else religion may or may not be . . .*" (italics added), suggesting that I am neither the arch metaphysical reductionist Griffiths makes me out to be nor the despiser of religion as O'Connor and Ivan Strenski as well seem to suggest. It has always struck me as utterly fascinating how quickly such criticisms fly when one *dares* to study religion as a thoroughly human enterprise. Because I happen to think that sociopolitical motivations and implications attend our theoretical choices, and because I am curious as to the manner in which communities negotiate social and material privilege, I select a particular lens through which I see anew what many in our field understand to be essentially idealist/belief/doctrinal systems of salvation, morality, or transcendence. I am not apologetic for the fact that my theoretical interests guide my selection of methods and choice of data; that my theories and methods hardly exhaust the data goes without saying.[5] However, because O'Connor's lenses 5, 6, and 7 (religion as beauty and hope; religion as truth; and religion as complex symbol system) have more than their share of advocates in the academy, they need no further help from me.

My reason for supporting naturalist (or, more specifically, social) theories of religion is not simply because they are underrepresented within the academy (i.e., not simply because, growing up as a Toronto Maple Leafs fan, I like pulling for the perpetual underdog) but because, as suggested above, the dominant approaches are philosophically idealist and presumed to be apolitical. This presumption carries some very real difficulties that need to be addressed. Although this may be old hat to many, these difficulties are numerous; I can do no better than refer to Bill Arnal's succinct contribution to UCSB's Andere-L listserve as a summary of these difficulties:

> Speaking only for myself, my objections to idealism are several. First, from the perspective of academics—and especially the study of religion—it is tendentious. We are individuals who, professionally, do mental work for a living. It strikes me as somewhat suspicious and self-serving, from our occupational perspective, that we tend to regard mental products as wholly distinctive from material products, and attribute to them causal force and causal independence in their own right.
>
> Second, idealism tends toward social conservatism, or so it seems to me. . . . Focus[ing] on ideas as causal tends to restrict social projects to the class of people who—as a result of prevailing social conditions—

are capable of excusing themselves from physical labor and devoting themselves to mental work.

Third, in the case of religion, idealism is circular and non-reductive. That is, since what we study has tended to be conceptualized and defined in terms of ideational content (not that I necessarily agree that this is the best way to approach it), understanding it within the framework of idealism does not permit us to retranslate it into a different set of terms. I assume (perhaps incorrectly?) that such translation is what ultimately fosters understanding.

I don't expect that these points—or others that might be raised—will actually convince anyone who is committed to idealism, but it should at least offer some sense of why one might find it problematic. (1998a)[6]

Arnal's thoughts on the requirement of scholars to redescribe observable, documentable claims and behaviors by means of a higher-order language of scholarship are pertinent to O'Connor's list of lenses, for, in constructing her list, I fear that she has grouped together what in fact can more properly be seen as two separate lists, one entailing second-order redescriptions of religion as a human institution (e.g., religion as social control, social change, illusion, and cultural critique), with first-order descriptions of religion as a source of empowerment, beauty, hope, and truth. Given the theoretical (generally sociological) context of the first list, the second set comprises raw, untheorized (untranslated if you will) descriptions in need of analysis—just as Griffiths's claims concerning contextless, necessary truths and universal moral claims are badly in need of contextualization and theorization. Combining these lists without subordinating the latter to the former (i.e., without seeing the former as attempts to explain the latter) entails confusing the work of theoretically based redescription with initial description. My essay argued that there is a sociopolitical implication to seeing these two sorts of scholarship on a par with each other. So, instead of disdaining reportage, as O'Connor suggests I do, I argued that, although nuanced emic reports are crucial, the field is unnecessarily truncated when phenomenological description and classification are understood to be sufficient goals of scholarship. After all, "[k]nowledge of any set of phenomena, whether natural or cultural, comes about not primarily from the application and development of taxonomies, but from explanatory theorizing" (Smith 1995b: 1102).

THEOLOGIANS, HUMANISTS, AND SOCIAL SCIENCTISTS

This leads to a final point about this debate: attentive readers will already have seen that this conversation is among a theologian, a humanist, and myself, a scholar who draws on social science research.[7]

The whole spectrum of the AAR is represented in these three positions, providing a perfect case study in how we are all talking past each other. While one argues for the inclusion of normative evaluations of competing truth claims within our field, and the other suggests that the systems we study must also be considered as sources of beauty, truth, and hope, I argue that the behaviors and institutions we study are sociorhetorical systems that establish, legitimize, and sometimes contest the very parameters for what gets to count as meaning, beauty, truth, and hope in the first place! In other words, I am concerned with studying the very manner in which certain behaviors and institutions are authorized as either morally creative or conformative; to say, as O'Connor does, that religions have ethical force is therefore to beg the question I believe to be of interest. To argue for the possibility, as O'Connor does, that a scholar of religion might "discover in religious rituals, myths, ideas, and values something insightful, beautiful, morally compelling or simply wise" is therefore to limit the scope of scholarship to the parameters of the religions themselves. To talk of such things as religious experiences, religious leaders, religious symbols, religious motivations, religious visions, religious values, religious ideals, religious narratives, religious perspectives, religious claims, and religious outlooks without theorizing the adjective *religious* is to fall considerably short of the contribution that the culture critic can make to the study of religion.

Two final questions: Are these sociorhetorical systems anything more than what the culture critic makes of them (and, as I've already stated in the first chapter, for the life of me I cannot conceive of a way of talking rationally about what this "more" could even be)? I leave answering this question to theologians and the devout, for it is, after all, their question not mine. And finally, am I free of the very structural constraints I see operating in the work of others? Certainly not! I'm a Maple Leafs fan, remember? Contextualist critiques are self-referential—how could it be any other other way? But since one can only accomplish so much in a chapter, I leave it to other enterprising scholars to contextualize (rather than idealize) my contributions to the public discourse on the study of religion. But please, leave the scoldings and head patting paternalism to the dog owners.

NOTES

1. Due to limitations on space in the journal, I provide here the text of my longer reply, all of which did not appear in print.

2. His review (1998a), which ran in *First Things*, ends by saying that either my book can be read as a prolegomena to theology (insomuch as I have undefended metaphysical commitments), or "[t]he only other way to read it—proba-

bly too uncharitable—is as a tissue of self-aggrandizing confusions." Apart from this condescension, the review misrepresents my book and its thesis significantly—so much so that he actually faults me several times for not holding the very position for which I argue in the book and elsewhere in print as well. Recently, Tim Fitzgerald's and Donald Wiebe's work has caught Griffiths's eye (Griffiths 2000).

3. The rhetoric of incredulity is apparent in the following: "McCutcheon belongs to a company of scholars who argue—get this! one is tempted to say—that the majority of religious studies scholars are too devoted to the truth claims of religion." The review closes by saying that "he has loaded his analysis with ideology and he writes mean-spiritedly" (187). Publishing such a comment as this suggests that my work has struck just the right nerve at this periodical.

4. For other models of the scholar of religion as an engaged, public intellectual, see Cady 1998 and Jensen 1998.

5. I detect the old inductivist tendency in O'Connor's lament that my proposal is limited because it "suggests that what religion is has been decided in advance. . . . This sounds too much like a recipe to be followed, a formula to be activated." I would have thought that this is precisely what made my proposal useful, for without a pre-observational definition (call it a model, a recipe, or formula if you will), I have no idea whatsoever how anything simply stands out as essentially religious.

6. Quoted with the permission of the author.

7. In terming Griffiths a "theologian" I believe I am simply describing his work accurately; there is not criticism implied whatsoever. Insomuch as musicians who thank God while accepting their Grammy awards can be considered religious, and part of the data in need of analysis, scholars such as Griffiths who thank God in their prefaces and term their work "an act of service to the Church" (1999: xii) are properly understood as theologians who thereby comprise the scholar of religion's data. It is to our detriment to confuse these two.

PART IV

Going Public: Teaching Theory

What we seek to train in college are individuals who know not only that the world is more complex than it first appears, but also that, therefore, interpretive decisions must be made, decisions of judgment which entail real consequences for which one must take responsibility, from which one may not flee by the dodge of disclaiming expertise.

—Jonathan Z. Smith (1991: 188)

CHAPTER 10

Our *"Special Promise"* as Teachers: Scholars of Religion and the Politics of Tolerance

Nothing can be less politically innocent than a denigration of politics in the name of the human.

Those who regard plurality as a value in itself are pure formalists, and have obvisouly not noticed the astonishingly imaginative variety of forms which, say, racism can assume.

—Terry Eagleton (2000: 7, 15)

In 1995 *The New Yorker* magazine carried a detailed survey and assessment of the various efforts to explain the twentieth-century phenomenon of Adolph Hitler (Rosenbaum 1995; see also 1998). According to the article's by-line, "[i]n the fifty years since his death, generations of experts have produced wildly competing theories that attempt to account for every aspect of his identity." The highly charged nature of any scholarly assessment of Hitler, let alone possible explanations for his behavior, views, and potent charisma, should be obvious to everyone. Noting this at the outset of his article, the author, Ron Rosenbaum, cites a powerful line from Primo Levi's account of his time at Auschwitz; Levi simply writes: "There is no why here." Contextualizing this remark, Rosenbaum reports that this "is a line—a decree—that was delivered to Levi by an S.S. death-camp guard."

For Rosenbaum, Levi's quotation represents a position we can term the "slippery slope of empathy": "any attempt to understand [and subsequently to explain] Hitler inevitably degenerates into an exercise in empathy with him. [In other words, according to this position] to understand all is to forgive all . . . [and the] first steps down this slippery slope to understanding are impermissible" (1995: 50). Or, as a more recent biographer of Hitler, Ian Kershaw, warns his readers, the "inbuilt danger in any biographical approach is that it demands a level of empathy with the subject which can easily slide over into sympathy, perhaps even

155

hidden or partial admiration" (1999: xxi; see also Craig 1999). However, this same decree against explanatory analysis—that is, "There is no why here"—is understood rather differently by yet another Auschwitz survivor who is also cited in Rosenbaum's article: the psychoanalyst Dr. Louis Micheels. "It is wrong, Dr. Micheels told me," writes Rosenbaum, "to adopt an S.S. decree in a death-camp as the final verdict on our quest to understand Hitler. 'There *should* be a why,' [Micheels] insists."

Opening an essay on the role of the scholar of religion as teacher with these references to the politics of explaining Hitler may strike some as, at best, odd or, at least, in very poor taste. However, in keeping with J. Z. Smith's insight that gains in knowledge come about by means of unexpected, interesting, even provocative, juxtapositions, I juxtapose these two sites to make a point regarding attempts to explain religion *per se*, as opposed to theological and humanistic scholarship that, taking religious impulses as merely given, simply aims to describe the diversity of religions, to identify the factors that contribute to religious change and conversion, and to interpret the deep and enduring meaning of religious symbols. By employing such a clearly politicized and emotionally ladened starting point for my chapter, I simply aim to suggest that the longstanding debate in the academic study of religion over the role to be played by explanatory analysis is itself just as politicized; sadly, the origins and implications of this politicization often pass undetected.

This generally obscured politics can be detected in a lecture Jacob Neusner delivered at the University of Wyoming, which was subsequently published in one of the field's main professional newsletters, *Religious Studies News* (Neusner 1997). In his lecture Neusner advised that, given the way in which some questions and certain types of scholarship can hamper efforts to strengthen and unite the nation-state, the scholar of religion *qua* teacher should exclude certain kinds of questions and types of analyses from their classrooms. In the article's opening paragraph we read that "the special promise of the academic study of religion is to nurture this country's resources for tolerance for difference, our capacity to learn from each other, and to respect each other." With this so-called special promise in mind, we then turn to the second of Neusner's three theses, which states: "The classroom study of religion in our generation has to limit its agenda, explicitly excluding provocative political topics for the time being." Given the manner in which this thesis limits the study of religion to the task of "comparison and contrast" in the service of helping people just to get along, it appears that one such provocative topic to be avoided is the effort to explain religion as an all too human doing. Instead, after *identifying* differences by means of description and comparison, it appears that, as teachers, we are called upon simply to *manage* and *minimalize* this difference for the benefit of the abstract notion of a nation-state; our role as teachers, Neusner argues, is to nurture mutual understanding and religious dialogue across what might otherwise be our students' exclusivistic boundaries. It appears that the scholar asking "transgressive questions" (Eagleton 1992: 83) has little place in such a classroom.

Although the role of Neusner's ideal teacher may strike many readers as entirely admirable—much like baby-kissing politicians who are in favor of such abstract values as 'freedom', who could imagine disagreeing with promoting 'tolerance' in our classes?—I think that his recommendation deserves a closer look. However, because I am sometimes accused of doing battle with windmills and strawmen (Rennie 1998; McCutcheon 1999), I should say from the outset that Neusner is hardly alone in holding this view on our field's "special promise." I am therefore somewhat apologetic for singling him out in the way that I have at the opening of this chapter. More than likely we can all think of a department—possibly our own?—whose public justification for existence (at least in terms of its dealings with its own university administrators and local communities) revolves around the scholar of religion's supposed ability to enhance the students' own religious life, teach them tolerance and respect for difference, and thereby enhance religious and cultural diversity. Simply put, the study of religion—whether understood as a theological or humanistic endeavor—is often portrayed as a socially redemptive, existentially salvific exercise (a portrait of the field with a long history). With this in mind, my colleague Jack Llewellyn and I have informally kept our eyes peeled for what we take to be the politically loaded rhetorics of tolerance and pluralism that are commonly found throughout the field, from Gerald Larson's book, *India's Agony over Religion*, where Larson recommends the development of an "All India Institute for Research on Religion" as one possible means for mediating public political clashes in India (1995: 292–93), to the various writings of our field's most vocal liberal commentator, Martin Marty (in particular his recent book, *The One and the Many* [1997]) and, most recently, to Harvard's mammoth Pluralism Project, headed by Diana Eck, which has produced the much heralded CD-ROM resource for classes on world religions in the United States, *On Common Ground*. Much like religion itself—when conceived in a somewhat naive fashion as an obvious and timeless cultural or moral good instead of as a rhetoric that authorizes diverse and competing conceptions of "the good"—scholarship on religion is presumed to provide the means for transcending social, historical, political difference insomuch as it enhances morality, teaches tolerance, and increases compassion and diversity. This is none other than a repackaging of the old social gospel movement, something akin to Eliade's reactionary "new humanism."

But is generating tolerance the goal of teaching the study of religion? And if it is, then, ought it to be the goal? Precisely how do we measure our students' supposed increased tolerance for diversity? Who gets to decide just what constitutes intolerant views? Does our *a priori* opinion on religion having everything to do with 'being good' and 'morally upright' lead us simply to assert, without evidence, that the study of religion increases a student's tolerance? Does this, in turn, prompt us to distinguish good from bad, or functional from disfunctional, religion? What do I make of the students who take my courses to better arm themselves to missionize throughout the world? Are their commitments somehow wrong?[1] Such unanswered questions should prompt us to ask if the values that motivate the goals of tolerance, pluralism, and inclusivity are as unproblematic and as neutral as some colleagues seem to think? Just what role does the scholar of religion play in all this—as opposed to the theologian or the liberal humanist, both of whom are equally committed to normative discourses on such immaterial things as the gods, endtimes, salvation, Justice, Freedom, and the celebration of some essential Human Nature?

To address these generally overlooked questions—and I hope to persuade the reader that they are overlooked for very good reasons—I wish to open with two thesis statements of my own:

i. calls for the exclusion of theorizing and intellectual provocation from the classroom are among the most potently political of all claims;

ii. the tolerance nurtured by limiting teaching to nuanced description followed only by comparison, phenomenological understanding, and mutual, deep appreciation is a monolith that obscures far more than it reveals: it obscures both the theory that drives the selection and juxtaposition of data as much as it obscures the larger social values— in a word, the politics—that equally drive the selection process.

My point? To put it bluntly, by means of pluralist rhetorics, what are otherwise geographically, temporally, and materially diverse human agents are essentialized and subsumed under one philosophically idealist, empty rubric 'religious', making diverse peoples all simply differing species of the universal genus 'believers', thereby ensuring that the observable 'many' is finally resolved into an invisible unity. The political implication of the essentialist strategy I detect in religiously pluralist rhetorics should be clear; as I phrased it in *Manufacturing Religion*, "such strategies . . . produce the image of subjects in the fullest political sense of the word: human beings more easily categorized, defined, [isolated,] and, possibly, ruled. People then become possessions to be understood as disembodied and monolithic minds of little or no social and historical consequence" (1997c: 164).

To understand seemingly apolitical rhetorics of religious plurality in their proper political context, we must connect up a number of dots and take into account the otherwise obscured politics of liberal individualism and the manner in which it nicely dovetails with dominant conceptions of religion as a matter of personal creed or faith. As William Arnal puts it in an article on the modernist and nationalist context in which scholarly discourses on religion inevitably take place, "religion, as such, is the space in which and by which any substantive collective goals . . . are individualized and made into a question of personal commitment or morality. This phenomenon is a feature of modernity, and as such it will be found in the political theories of centuries past" (2000: 32). It makes sense, then, to suspect the individualization and compartmentalization that come with discourses on ethereal sameness that we find when we engage in studies of such things as culture, faith, and the sorts of deep personal experiences, discourses that are often called upon to justify seemingly benign social boundaries.

Now, should we not recognize the complex relations between the politics of liberal individualism, on the one hand, and conceptions of religion as an essentially private, privileged faith, on the other, we may very well be teaching an easy brand of tolerance in our classes, one that obscures material, historic difference by celebrating insubstantial, timeless unity. This is why I am generally suspicious of pluralist discourses on beliefs in invisible beings that take place from within—and simultaneously obscure that they take place from within—very specific class or nationalist settings. Despite some disagreements with Karen McCarthy Brown's reflexive approach to ethnography, I fully agree with her when, in an article on how she teaches the introductory course in the study of religion, she noted that, despite the possibly well-intentioned arguments of those who believe that

> the cross-cultural study of religion has a genuine, if limited, contribution to make toward the saying of this larger 'we' . . . , it seems important to suggest that such an admirable goal, when adopted as the reason for beginning the study of another religion, may end up undermining more than supporting that goal.

She concludes by stating a general principle, well known to those who have, for some time now, seen liberal pluralist ideologies as powerful hegemonic social forces: "Premature resolution of differences between world views somehow always ends up being a resolution on our terms" (1991: 226).[2]

Perhaps we require a case in point to help give this critique some teeth. Take, for example, the above-mentioned CD-ROM classroom resource, *On Common Ground*.[3] In one of the web articles that states the goals of the project, Diana Eck writes: "Pluralism requires the cultivation of public space where we all encounter one another."[4] On one level this all sounds well and good for, as one might ask Who could ever be against a public space where we all encounter one another? Despite the fact that I can easily imagine a few groups who might not wish to be included, for the time being I'll grant to the proponents of this kind of pluralism that they have well-intentioned visions of some idealized, even cosmogonic, public forum where citizen-equals once mounted the proverbial soap box and freely spoke their piece. But it's not—nor ever was—as simple as this, is it? Precisely what does it mean to "encounter" each other? What undisclosed ground rules stipulate the nature and extent of this encounter? More than likely, the soap box isn't open to just anyone. After all, to participate in any so-called public space, one must already be operating by a set of sociopolitical values and rhetorical standards that make it possible, attractive, meaningful, and compelling to 'encounter', 'understand', and 'appreciate' *the other* in just this manner, in just this context, for just this end. Does one get to be part of Eck's 'we' and her 'public' if these values and rhetorics are not a priority? While I may personally find it commendable to work toward some sort of social inclusion—much like being in favor of 'freedom' or 'family values', ill-defined inclusion is easy to be in favor of—I would be terribly remiss if I understood or portrayed the ground rules of such a supposedly inclusive, public forum as somehow being ahistorical, self-evidently meaningful, commonly shared, and utterly persuasive. It would be somewhat akin to celebrating the Internet as a universalist, democratic public forum, a celebration that has much at stake in failing to recognize the Internet's military-industrialist origins and the degree to which one must be a government agency, corporate entity, or member of the middle class with money and time to burn to gain access to it. In presuming a disengaged 'public' to which everyone automatically and equally belongs, and to which everyone wishes to belong, strikes me as already resolving in 'our' favor the issue of 'the many' long before ever seriously entertaining it.

To see the slippery nature of this logic, consider the book that preceded and, in many ways, is the basis for *On Common Ground*. In *Encountering God*, Eck distinguished pluralism from exclusivism and inclusivisim (1993: 168) and argues that it is more than the recognition of a plurality and is far more demanding than mere tolerance of difference: one must *participate* within (i.e., encounter, engage, etc.) a plurality to count as a pluralist. As rightly observed by Eck, tolerance is, after all, an expression of privilege, and it therefore stands in the way of what she considered to be true pluralism. As she argues,

> If as a Christian I tolerate my Muslim neighbor, I am not therefore required to understand her, to seek out what she has to say, to hear about her hopes and dreams, to hear what is meant to her when the words, "In the name of Allah, the Merciful, the Compassionate" were whispered into the ear of her newborn child. (1993: 192)

But there is a difficulty in seeing such a wide divide between, on the one hand, exclusivism and pluralism, and on the other, tolerance and pluralism, a difficulty that writers such as Eck and Martin Marty fail to recognize, perhaps because their own hegemonic position blinds them to the contingent basis of their commonsense notions of engagement and understanding. What they fail to recognize is that one can't have it both ways: one can't call for an engaged pluralism among those committed to deep values while at the same time arguing that this pluralism is more than mere tolerance, for the difference between pluralism and tolerance is merely rhetorical. The only way to have such co-existing differences is if the other is already well on the way to playing one's own game, making the leftover, minor differences something you can easily put up with. Case in point: Eck's dialogue partner in the above example is busy whispering sweet nothings into a baby's ear, not trying to contest late capitalism's worldwide hegemony.

Simply put, there are many 'real commitments' with which encounter is, for Eck's and Marty's well-meaning liberal sentiments, downright impossible. As characterized by Marty, so called tribal life is exclusive and dangerous:

> [T]he invention of modern weapons and the efficiency of communications now renders tribalism potentially lethal. Groups need only a few dollars for supplies and a few recipes for how to mix them to produce devastating explosives to advance their threats.
>
> Tribalism on the world scene in its extremist forms takes a monstrous human toll. (1997: 14)

For whatever reason (more than likely because they wish to reallocate resources and power), some people have little interest in encountering and understanding anyone; such people want to change the rules of the game by—at times—violent or outright coercive means. They choose not to play nice, and this upsets liberal sentiments a great deal. That makes these so-called tribalists and extremsits rather dangerous—not, as Marty implies, in some abstract sense but dangerous in a very practical way, dangerous to a very particular way of conceiving of the world and its socioeconomic relations. In the above passage it seems as if Marty's conception of the world conveniently forgets just who usually sells the weapons and who designs the communication technologies that are being put to such dangerous uses. In other words, the critique of the extremist, dangerous other all too easily avoids the kind of self-implication that comes with understanding that the performance of 'our' mutual funds in part depend on a rather profitable worldwide trade in technologies.

If, as Eck asserts, "in a world of religious pluralism, commitments are not checked at the door" (1993: 193), then what do we do with those commitments that, for example, lead people to kill doctors who perform abortions or to work toward the violent overthrow of this or that regime? Are these commitments allowable in a pluralistic world, a world where we supposedly take seriously differences among competing core values? Or do such commitments so deeply offend some obvious standard of decency to which all humans—insomuch as they share some nonempirical Human Nature—give assent? Which commitments are to be left at the door, then? If *real* pluralism requires openness and commitment, as Eck argues, then, given the colorful ideological spectrum on today's political map, it is more than obvious that only a rather narrow party line of commitments will gain admission to this public square of open engagement. Specifically, they will be those commitments that occupy people's attitudes, their hearts and minds, but that are not manifested in organized political action. In other words, by framing the question as follows, "How are we all to live with one another in a climate of mutuality and understanding?" Eck has loaded the dice in her favor. As she goes on to say, "Those who live according to an exclusivist paradigm frankly do not wish to live closely with people of other faiths and would prefer to shut them out . . . or convert others to their own view of the world" (1993: 191). *Unless I am terribly mistaken, these so-called exclusivists, extremists, and tribalists are precisely the people who have the very real and yet different commitments; they are exactly the people with whom Eck claims to be interested in living on an engaged basis!* Apparently, though, these are just the wrong strongly held commitments. As in the case of Marty's *One and the Many* (1997), only those accepting the dominant ground rules of conversation and storytelling—as opposed to organized political action and contestation—are invited to mount the public square's soap box and tell their tale.

Those not in favor of these rules and the social world they make possible are understandably yet in suitably illiberal fashion, branded as exclusivists by Eck or as radicals, militants, extremists, tribalists, agitators, people with strident voices who are inspired by belligerent leaders, by Marty (1997: passim). Such name calling strikes me as eliminating from serious consideration the very groups whom liberals claim to include in their pluralist umbrella. At this juncture, readers must be clear on one point, however: I am not offering a criticism of this tactic, only a description of a particularly effective rhetoric that portrays self-beneficial, tactical maneuvers as timeless, abstract principles. As Stanley Fish has recently observed, "[s]witching back and forth between talking like a liberal and engaging in distinctly illiberal actions is something we all do anyway; it is the essence of adhocery, which is a practice that need not be urged because it is the only one available to us" (1999: 72).⁵ In arguing for an ill-defined engagement and an encounter that recognizes the necessity for 'real commitments' that just happen to fall within a rather narrow party line, liberal social critics fabricate a toothless other whose seeming differences—"They call God 'Allah,' and we call God 'God'"—are easily resolved on our terms.

Resolution on our terms is indeed a powerful indictment of the pluralist ideology that currently reigns in the study of religion; Eck's hairsplitting discourse on pluralism versus tolerance notwithstanding, her pluralism sounds to me a lot like 'tolerance'. Given the above identified politics I find operating within these discourses, it strikes me that our classes can do considerably more than that which is recommended by Neusner. Consider, for a moment, just what we generally mean by 'toleration'; as phrased by Peter Brown when writing on the Christianization of the Roman empire, toleration generally means "disapproval or disagreement coupled with an unwillingness to take action against those who are viewed with disfavor in the interest of some moral or political principle" (1995: 30). Or, as phrased in a recent theologically liberal cover article in *Christianity Today*: "True tolerance means I voluntarily withhold what power I have to coerce someone else's behavior" (Taylor 1999: 44). Toleration, therefore, implies three things: (i) significant disapproval, (ii) the very real sociopolitical authority, even coercive power, to do something about this disapproval, and (iii) suspension of action for some practical reason. To tolerate is to put up with something, something you know to be wrong, and something you could indeed do something about. Tolerance is therefore part of a normative discourse of dominance and is the trace of an ongoing sociopolitical contestation. If the above analysis holds, then Eck's pluralism is simply the friendly face of tolerance, and both are virtues of the powerful, not of the weak, for, by definition, politically oppositional, as well as socially marginalized, groups cannot be expected to tolerate anything since they do not set the standards for what gets to count as a real commitment nor can they change their situation, even if they wanted to. Tolerance does not take place on their terms. Instead, they are themselves tolerated. Seemingly benign discourses on tolerance therefore have a subtle irony at their very core: they are discourses of the powerful.

Because tolerance is a virtue of the powerful, there is always something very real at stake in deciding just what to tolerate, in deciding the practical limits of the public square's seemingly endless boundaries. As Neusner phrased it, in terms similar to Eck and Marty, the future of the nation-state seems to be at stake in all this. Our question is this: As university professors, are we to police these nationalist limits (i.e., must our motto be, To Protect and Serve the Nation-State?) or are we to teach our students some of the skills necessary for identifying these usually invisible limits, naming and dating their manufacturers, and scrutinizing their implications? I am presuming in all this that, like the seemingly benign pleas for pluralism and tolerance that fail to identify the interests served by this or that limit on toleration, calls for preserving the nation-state are not as simple as they first appear. After all, as historians of nationalism have convincingly demonstrated, the imagined community of the nation, like all social formations, is an abstraction whose existence depends on the suppression of competing narratives of unity and difference (Anderson 1991);[6] it is an abstraction reproduced through devices as diverse as flag-waving parades, anthems, common school curricula, shared economic systems, and centralized access to the tools of coercive violence. As I say to my own students, if you were showing the United States to a visiting anthropologist from Mars, *which* United States would you show? Would you interview bankers on Wall Street or children in an inner-city housing project? Would you visit a food bank or a lunch meeting in Silicon Valley? Or would you point to a symbol of the nation—say, the flag or the Constitution, rather than a ghetto or a mansion—and engage in a discourse on America as a state of mind? My point is not to lament inequity but to press students to consider just what these otherwise distinct sites—some empirical, some nonempirical—have in common and to provoke them into considering how the act of social formation actually takes place—how it is that we can so easily homogenize such obviously different sites into one seamless, shared idea? How and why is it that attention gets focused on abstract unity ('the American Dream', 'the American Experience', or 'the American Century') at the expense of those empirical and often dramatic differences that cut across the ethereal unity of any social formation? When Marty ponders "how the nation as a whole relates to the groups within it" (1997: 9), I am left wondering whether he understands that the idea of a nation-state is hardly some preexistent, level playing field upon which disparate groups interact and move, but rather, as virtually any historian of nationalism will tell you, the result of this and just this group's interests being portrayed and accepted as universal and inevitable.

Because there are so many empirical 'Americas', and because the values of 'tolerance' and 'pluralism' are a far more complicated than writers such as Neusner, Eck, and Marty seem to allow, could we not as teachers instead study whether discourses on religious and cultural tolerance and pluralism are but mechanisms used to help focus collective attention, whether for good or ill, thereby actually concocting and authorizing specific ideas of the nation-state and, by extension, authorizing those social worlds made possible by just these ideas? After all, discourses on religious and cultural plurality could be considered a means for distracting attention from material difference (such as economic plurality?) by disengaging it from the historical and resolving it on a cultural or spiritual level. Despite what modern day Tillichians might say, what is ultimately important about discourses on religion may very well turn out to be their ability to focus attention on nonempirical differences by means of discourses on such ahistorical, nonobvious objects as the gods, end times, salvation, and so on. Empirical differences, however, are not so easy to overcome for they require massive and sustained redistributions of physical resources; but, by means of its focus on a supposedly other-worldy realm of pure ideas and beliefs, mythic discourses resolve these differences and contradictions on a new plane by individualizing that which is all too social and collective. By means of internal and private religious pluralist rhetorics, commonality appears only on the level of attitude, idea, and belief, thereby allowing the label of *exclusivist* and *other* to fall upon those who seek to reorganize modes of practice, behavior, and structure. To appeal to Kershaw writing on the ways in which the rise of Hitler is explained, we see in discourses on personalistic, essential unity (whether they come in the guise of religious or cultural pluralist rhetorics) an "over-personalizing of complex historical developments [that] over-emphasiz[e] the role of the individual in shaping and determining events, ignoring or playing down the social and political context in which those actions take place" (1999: xxi). Religious pluralist/tolerance discourses focus attention in a very specific manner on extraordinary and so-called ultimate concerns at the expense of all too practical and mundane concerns.

Because they lend the guise of resolution on the spiritual level to what cannot be resolved so easily in the material, historical world, such discourses are indeed of ultimate importance to any social formation because of the efficient means by which they turn attention away from historical to ahistorical matters, thereby leaving untouched the very springs that allow patterns of dominance in all social formations to be smoothly reproduced. It is none other than mythmaking, the very mechanism that enables such abstractions as nation-states to exist over time and place. Emphasizing and promoting a specific type of tolerance, one based on ethereal sameness, is therefore at the heart of reproducing any social formation for it focuses attention on a specific site, leaving unaddressed differences in ownership and access.

If promoting this sort of tolerance is accepted as one of the goals for the modern field, then this establishes a field of study preoccupied with policing the limits on what is now taken for acceptable, and classes in the study of religion become a civics class that conveniently avoids the kind of work that novel juxtaposition and intellectual provocation often carry. Taking what is merely given not only as the starting point but also as the end point of our work breeds a culture of couch potato or sound bite scholarship, a context in which—as Pierre Bourdieu names them in his little book *On Television* (1998)—"fast thinkers" rule the airwaves in a society where, as Noam Chomsky told us long ago, concision and enforced consensus constitute the limits of the thinkable. In the previous two chapters I referred to this sort of scholarship—one that aims for mutual understanding and rules out of bounds transgressive, so-called militant questions—as more akin to mere color commentary and the work of caretaking for the institutions under study.[7] It is a brand of scholarship in line with what theologians and humanists accomplish in their work. In place of this, I suggested that the role of the scholar of religion is that of culture critic and that our data are the all too ordinary mechanisms whereby social groups authorize, reproduce, and contest the limits of the meaningful, the thinkable, and the doable. To borrow a phrase from the opening of Michel de Certeau's little book *Culture in the Plural* (1997), I simply recommended that we see ourselves as anthropologists of credibility.

Clearly, the viewpoint I am critiquing would understand my position as undesirable precisely because it is downright dangerous to those who have investments in reproducing just this or that "obviously proper" limit on credibility and common sense—whether those investments are intellectual, social, economic, or, more than likely, all three. As suggested by Rosenbaum, the type of explanatory scholarship I am defending risks historicizing and humanizing that which some people cannot (or refuse to) understand as all too human and *ad hoc*; in the case of scholarship on the psychological causes of Hitler-the-person, as well as the social or economic causes of Nazi rise to power, what is in jeopardy is the ability of some people to dehistoricize and thereby distance the admittedly terrible events we associate with World War II, a distancing that acts as a crucial mechanism in reproducing some people's sense of normality and therefore their current social identity (the idea of Hitler becomes for them the great Other, which thereby makes possible their sense of Self). With this in mind, I recall the playwright and essayist David Mamet, and his commentary on Steven Spielberg's film *Schindler's List*. In voyeuristically peering from the darkness at the deeds of both the overtly evil Amon Goeth—the film's murderous Nazi villain—and Oskar Schindler—the flawed hero—"the audience . . . leaves the theater feeling they have looked down on actions that they have been assured—this is the film's central lesson—they would never commit." Or as recently phrased by Tim Cole in a book that tracks the various contemporary political uses to which discourses on "the Holocaust" are put,

> By situating this murder [i.e., the mass murder of Jews during the Second World War] within the classic categories of hero and villain, Spielberg effectively takes the Holocaust out of history. . . . Spielberg's 'Holocaust' ends with the hanging of Amon Goeth and the arrival of Schindler's Jews in a filmic Jerusalem. The hanging of Goeth effectively brings the murders to an end because it spells the end of the protagonist of evil. The equation is simple: No people like Goethe, no murders. . . . [The lesson is that Goethe] is not like us. He is not simply inhuman. He is unhuman. (1999: 83)

However, as Mamet goes on to write: "This 'lesson' is a lie. The audience is not superior to 'Those Bad Nazis.' Any of us has the capacity for atrocity—just as each of us has the capacity for heroism" (1996: 142).[8] Cole agrees: "We leave the movie theatre . . . comforted that we are nothing like the perpetrators. We are left 'outside the film, admiring one man, condemning the other' and therefore we are 'never implicated in the moral economy of the film' nor forced to examine our 'own social and political ethics'" (1999: 84).[9]

Both Mamet's essay and Cole's book are powerful precisely because they pull moviegoers from their dark hiding spots and places their liberal guilt squarely in the historical light of day. Mamet and Cole see the dangers of Speilberg's stance on the politics of genocide precisely in its distancing, dehistoricizing effect, which enables the comfortable viewer to sit alone in the dark, aloof from history—a distance that simplifies, reifies, and individualizes otherwise complex historical, material events as if they were simply the outcome of either good or bad people, either victims or perpetrators.[10] In the process we are freed from ever confronting not only that we are all too ordinary, complex, contradictory, historical agents, but also that history often reflects not the deeds of great men but the results of structurewide systems of organization with which we ourselves are complicit.

Just as there is a politics to the re-presentation and narrativization of the Second World War, so too in the case of the study of religion; people both in and outside of the academy maintain that naturalistic explanations diminish some inherent or transcendent meaning and sameness to certain sorts of human beliefs and behaviors, insomuch as such analyses account, in purely historical terms, for an aspect of human experience and behavior that participants claim transcends the historical, human situation. In both cases, then, offering historically based explanations contextualizes what might otherwise be understood as ahistorical, powerful, mysterious, and therefore unexplainable dispositions, states of mind, or feelings. In offering answers to questions deemed *a priori* unanswerable, such analysis is clearly troublesome to many; perhaps Neusner had something like this in mind when he advised that our role as teachers is to enhance both the nation-state and interreligious dialogue, *not* to provoke students into examining the discursive preconditions of mythmaking and the institutions it supports. Because theological schools, places of worship, and countless television and radio commentators from across North American are deeply involved in the kind of mythmaking Neusner recommends for scholars of religion, I think that there is hardly any need for us to enter this business too.

Luckily—or maybe I should say, oddly enough—I do not find myself alone in questioning the mythmaking that many others take to be self-evidently meaningful. With regards to Marty's *One and the Many*, consider Tim Murphy's reading:

> Marty's metaphors for unity utterly fail. Marty himself is merely the bearer, the spokesperson, and ultimately the advocate, of one, distinct, specific cultural content of the United States, namely, Anglo-Protestantism (or, more broadly, Euro-Christianity). However hegemonic this specific, cultural content is or has been, it nevertheless remains only one cultural content among many in the United States. The very problem which Marty is attempting to answer here—but instead dismisses [i.e., the problem of the many]—is created by precisely the historical condition of the hegemony of that one cultural position. This kind of position Marty's book takes contributes to this hegemony, and frankly, in a rather brutal, if not fully intended, way. Rather than pushing for a genuine plurality, Marty, in the very name of tolerance, simply reasserts the old hegemony once.more. The very plurality imagined by Marty is already a form of religious exclusion. (1998: 39–40).

Murphy concludes that "[t]he very fact that a claim to unity must be asserted presupposes disunity. Marty voice poses as the voice of the One. But in truth, his voice is but one among many."[11] Concerning Eck's *On Common Ground*, consider two reviews that appeared in a recent issue of the *Journal of the American Academy of Religion*. After discussing the technological features of the CD-ROM resource, and questioning its creators' choice of content and emphasis, Rodger Payne and Braine Turley conclude their review by posing a number of rhetorical questions of considerable import.

Is the pluralism advocated by *OCG* to be found in an Anglican minister giving a Christmas gift to a rabbi, or in a person speaking to a Buddhist neighbor about recycling? Or is it exhibited in the contention expressed by one narrator that Christianity cannot offer a comprehensive way of life for Americans. Or the intimation by another that Christian evangelism is a misguided effort? . . . Is the pluralism advocated in *OCG* an argument about the nature of civil society or theological truth? Is the "common ground" of *OCG* a metaphor for American national life or a wishful plea for recognizing some meta-religion common to all?

Payne and Turley then go on to answer their own questions by concluding that

[t]here is a sense throughout *OCG* that its executors were sympathetic to the words of Victor Kazanjian, Director of Religious Life at Wellesley College, who states in one of *OCG*'s audio clips that "truth rests in between us always." Regardless of how much sympathy one may hold toward the need for "religious" pluralism in the public square, the recurring implications that the religions themselves need to be less theologically divisive suggests a secular [or, as I would rather say, a liberal humanist] evangelism that some users will find problematic. (1999: 646–47)

Although not agreeing with necessarily all of their comments (both for and against the CD-ROM's usefulness), Fred Denny echoes a number of Payne and Turley's comments, concluding that *On Common Ground* is primarily a civics lesson and only secondarily a work of scholarship (1999: 659).

Despite my disagreement with representing contentless inclusivity and tolerance as proper goals for our academic field, there is a lesson for the scholar of religion in all this: acts of theorizing and attempts to offer causal explanation in the realm of human practices do not take place simply in neutral, scholarly contexts. Surely, the days when we would have presumed that our work occupied such purely intellectual domains have been behind us for some time. Our work clearly takes place in the historical, public context of both the university classroom and the social world of the subject under study, for, after all, our students (and many of our colleagues as well) are themselves part of the social communities about which we theorize. Like colleagues throughout the human sciences, we often straddle two worlds; we invite our students to find curiosity in what they take to be self-evident and, thereby, to make themselves and the wider communities to which they belong data in need of analysis. (Don't many of us still rely on Horace Miner's wonderful little essay, "Body Ritual among the Nacirema" to accomplish just these goals?)

But I do not use Miner's essay to teach my students to become good or compassionate citizens who tolerate the quirky differences in others' behaviors. Instead, I use this old but still wonderfully useful chestnut to begin to persuade my students that the world they take for granted is just as complex and multilayered as any other. This insight does not teach tolerance for difference but, hopefully, instills a curiosity in students for mechanisms that successfully mediate and gloss over this complexity—mechanisms that allow their worlds to appear as continuous, simple, and utterly meaningful. By means of this and other devices, I aim to accomplish something J. Z. Smith has already described so well that I can do no better than simply quote him at length:

> What we seek to train in college are individuals who know not only that the world is more complex than it first appears, but also that, therefore, interpretive decisions must be made, decisions of judgment which entail real consequences for which one must take responsibility, from which one may not flee by the dodge of disclaiming expertise [or, I might add, by the dodge of asserting that something is a mystery, inevitable, necessary, or good for the nation]. (1991: 188)[12]

Despite many agreements with Louis Althusser's thoughts on the role of the university in glossing over the contradictions built into the very heart of the modern nation-state, I think that some of us are also in the business of provoking unreflective participants in social systems into becoming reflective scholars of social systems. If this distinction holds up, then it naturally follows that producing good scholars is not necessarily the same as producing good citizens nor necessarily the same as producing good people. First and foremost, my own interest is in producing good scholars.

When it comes to decrees against certain forms of scholarly analysis in the public university, the question that must be asked is *who* gets to decide, and based on *what* criteria, which questions and avenues of inquiry can and cannot be asked and investigated—whether in the classroom or in our research. In other words, how are the limits of our collective, public reality set, and what are the relations between scholarly claims concerning the shape of this public reality and the claims of the very people we study. In his deceptively short essay on pedagogy from which I just quoted, Smith suggests that the goal we aim to achieve in our classrooms is "training in argumentation about interpretation," a type of training that requires one to be vigilant about such matters as who decides on the practical limits of the credible. Determining the answers to these sorts of hows and whys—moreover, teaching students the tools necessary for them to set about answering these sorts of questions long after they leave our classroom—are, in my mind, rightfully understood as scholarly activities.

Although Neusner's claims concerning our 'special promise' may play well with some audiences—especially those with tremendous investments in reproducing just this lived world—it should now be clear that this promise has little in common with what can be accomplished by the academic study of religion as I conceive of it. Instead, as noble as this brand of social toleration may sound, I see it as part of a generally liberal and religiously pluralistic agenda that often passes for the academic study of religion. As already suggested, then, it is a toleration that just happens to operate within rather strict and narrow bounds, one that is intolerant to a set of questions I happen to find of great interest. If, as I believe to be the case, blindfolded religious pluralists in search of their proverbial elephant and liberal humanists discoursing on such ethereal matters as the human spirit are actually but one additional instance of data for the scholar of religion, then we must seriously reconsider our field's special promise.

With this in mind, I return to my question concerning who gets to set the bounds of meaning and significance and the limits of tolerance. More specifically, should scholars of religion be allowed to draw their students' attention to the fact that the bounds of any public, lived world (and all lived worlds are by definition public, no?) are socially set and not natural or beyond question? For some members of our classes, posing this very question concerning how these boundaries are set is itself an act of transgression and provocation. Should we curtail this analysis because of this? Must participants and their meaning systems be understood on their own terms? This is *the* methodological issue that remains at the very heart of our field: it is the old insider/outsider problem. It is therefore the very issue that we ought to be teaching and critically discussing in our classes. Despite the wishes of participants in social systems indebted to narratives of mythic origins and uniqueness, as public scholars and teachers, it is our responsibility to introduce students to a pervasive human phenomenon: the manner in which dehistoricization is routinely employed as a social authorizing practice, generating legitimacy for whichever group is doing the dehistoricization (dominant *or* oppositional).

Given the world in which I teach (the United States), I can think of no better example of such practices than the familiar words used in the U.S. Declaration of Independence, "We hold these truths to be self-evident." In the classic sense, there is a rhetoric embedded here that generally passes unnoticed; these words *do* something, but what? Following Smith once again, in my efforts to redescribe "Scripture" for my students, I have placed this usually *sui generis* or privileged body of so-called religious literature within a much wider, more familiar genre, a genre identified by the particular manner in which various texts and discourses authorize not only themselves but also the social, economic, and political institutions from which they arise and to which they contribute continued legitimacy. Much as we see this happening in the case of so-called scriptures, the opening to the Declaration of Independence effectively removes readers from the tug-and-pull of the contingent, historical world, placing them instead in an abstract, ahistorical realm where such things as "truths" are self-evident. Through this rhetoric of self-evidency, then, the long European history of philosophical, political, and social debate and development, which greatly influenced this document's composition—and the nation-state eventually founded upon it—is completely obscured, as if the Declaration and later the Constitution as well spontaneously arose from the ground fully formed. After all, self-evidencies do not have a history, and they are not manufactured; instead, they simply appear and proclaim their existence to the senses.

Whether or not we have the "eyes to see, and ears to hear" these self-evidencies is, of course, a separate question—the so-called framers of the Constitution apparently recognized those self-evidences that were lost on many of their predecessors. Along with rhetorics of self-evidency, then, there comes a rhetoric of discernment. Just as the preexistent Veda was simply heard by the *rishis* of old, just as the preexistent Qu'ran was recognized and recited by Muhammad, just as the preexistent voice of Yahweh prompted a response in only some listeners, and—at least according to the Gospel of John—the "Word of God" preexisted all of creation, so too the content of the Declaration of Independence not only benefits from (is authorized by) a rhetoric of self-evidency but presupposes the privileged status of those wise or lucky enough to have paid attention to it. To put a finer point on this, it is actually misleading to talk of the document being authorized; rather, the social world of its framers is what ultimately received legitimacy. More than this, it is a very contemporary re-presentation of this long since past social world that is legitimized. Just as cosmogonies are devices for recreating a very particular present by steeping it in the supposed time of the ancestors, when the gods walked the earth, we see the same devices employed in the construction of nationalist identity. To stick with the U.S. example, every time the Supreme Court judges put on their black robes, a cosmogony is acted out and a judgment on a very particular present is richly steeped in appeals to that mythic time when the reified framers and founding fathers walked the earth. To bring in Smith once again, an economy is being exercised in this elaborate performance—an economy not of money, of course, but one of significance. The limits of seemingly uniform social space are being established in their acts of interpretation, and those limits are authorized and contested by means of appeals to the mythic past. Culture, to return to de Certeau, is a structural *place* distinguishable from mere empty *space*; they are distinguished precisely by means of this enforced economy of credibility, an economy that allows a place to exist in which human agency takes its cues from otherwise invisible boundaries that allow the exercise of constrained agency as if it were some form of free play. As de Certeau phrases it, culture is nothing other than "a proliferation of inventions in a limited space." How geographic and chronological spaces are transformed into social places with limits and meanings, how inventions are signified, authorized and eventually contested by means of mythic discourses on origins, nonobvious beings, and endtimes is, for me, the domain of the scholar of religion.

Considering the manner in which many of the United State's founding fathers continued their practice of owning slaves, the supposedly self-evident, timeless rights of equality, liberty, and the pursuit of happiness are, to our eyes, circumscribed in terms of the blatantly obvious interests of a rather narrow ruling elite of landowning white males. Hence, the rhetoric constitutive of the Declaration initially authorized a very particular social world. But who among us is able to see how the complex relation between interpreters and text continues to authorize yet more specific social worlds in the present? Those who happen to have watched Clinton's impeachment hearings may recall Chief Justice Renquist's reported weakness for Gilbert and Sullivan operettas, the source of his black gown's three gold bars (they were added in 1995 according to a *New Yorker* article from last year); although the bars appeared from nowhere on the sleeves of his gown, we read them as altogether proper, natural, in place, self-evidently meaningful, virtually eternal. Can we not teach our students that what makes the rhetorics of self-evidency and discernment so powerful and enduring is that they— like gold ribbing on gowns—are utterly empty signifiers, making them infinitely malleable and endlessly useful for material purposes that might diverge completely from one another. The more basic point I work toward in some of my classes is that, insomuch as it posits a discernable yet obscured meaning that can be discerned by the careful reader, the very "art" of hermeneutics (whether carried out by Eliade reading "archaic symbols"or a chief justice reading "the Constitution") is by definition a cosmogonic and hence political activity.

Teaching the study of such human artifacts as meaning systems in a phenomenological manner leaves this sort of analysis untouched. However, theoretically based redescription allows us to juxtapose what was previously thought to be incomparable; it shifts the ground and allows scholars to arrive at novel conclusions. I think once again of juxtaposing scholarship on Hitler with scholarship on religion. In both cases we see the rhetoric of mystery and insolubility used to manufacture an other, rhetorics crucial to the maintenance of social identities. In both cases a line is drawn in the otherwise shifting, ambiguous sands of history and social life; thus far and no further. De Certeau's empty space thereby becomes a place of significance and limit where agency is enacted—a so-called public square, if you will. Here is where we etch and authorize the maps that not only guide our movements through history but also make movement possible to begin with, movements in which we distinguish between and thereby concoct us/them, safe/unsafe, good/evil.

To come all the way back to Neusner's thesis, I maintain that without evidence to the contrary—and what is needed here is a conversation on just what would count as this evidence, apart from *a priori* assertions—there should be a why to accompany our current abundance of phenomenological research into the how, where, when, and who of religion; otherwise, we will be forced to abandon our efforts to generalize about the sources of complex human behavior, curtail our efforts to sort through and organize such events by means of analytic categories, and cease enquiring into the observable factors that may have led to just this as opposed to that characteristic or outcome. If we challenge the legitimacy of those who disavow the politics of setting limits to the questions we ask and, instead, continue to pursue our investigations into the causes and implications of human actions of all sorts, then we will examine the social, nationalist, economic, political, and so on, claims that lie camouflaged and thereby sanctioned within the undefended decrees of those who insist upon ending our efforts to explain. Instead of supporting nationalist and religious rhetorics concerning the social autonomy and privilege of human communities, we will thereby live up to a long and important tradition of scholars as social provocateurs.

In my opinion, the dangers of unilaterally exempting just this or that human claim, action, or organization from explanatory analysis strike me as far greater than the benefits to be had from privileging and thereby protecting the supposed integrity of certain human events, the certain sense of what it is to be a "good citizen," and just this or that conception of the modern nation-state. For me, efforts at naturalistic explanation therefore have an intellectual *and* political warrant. To explain is to situate an event, a belief, an assertion, and so on, within a complex nexus of antecedent historical factors and examine it in terms of one of a number of predetermined rational frameworks brought to the table by the scholar. Accordingly, to situate historically is to risk deprivileging—to see the apparently universal as local, the necessary as contingent, the self-evident as manufactured. Although it is a risk understandably not taken by participants in the social formations we study, it is a risk that is mandated by public, rational discourses where claims about the observable state of affairs around us must be open to continued debate and testing. Whether it is in the classroom, our scholarly publications, or various contributions we make to wider public forums, our role as scholars is not to encourage the rhetoric of privilege, protection, and credibility that we inevitably find throughout all cultural settings but to engage in the kind of analysis that seeks the historical beginnings and material implications of such privilege.

Contrary to Neusner, then, I suggest that our classrooms ought to contribute to the systematic search for the why of public human behavior; as scholars, we should leave it to the members of the communities we study to build up (or tear down) their own social boundaries, and we should instead be busy studying the manner in which they accomplish such boundary maintenance and contestation. We are anthropologists of the credible, presuming that social authority and identity are generated and regenerated by means of social rhetorics that extract claims, practices, and institutions from historical pressures and causes. Who, then, but scholars of religion are equipped with tools to comment on these intriguing practices? For a scholar of religion to limit this type of inquiry based on religious or nationalist presuppositions is to fall well short of the critical contribution to be made to the human sciences by scholarship on religion.

NOTES

1. For example, when introducing themselves in my religious studies majors' capstone course, one student recently spoke quite plainly of his goal "to convert Russia."

2. Having stated my agreement with McCarthy Brown, I should add that I am suspicious, however, about just how one judges the difference between resolving and *prematurely* resolving difference. In other words, to take differences between worldviews seriously means being prepared to entertain the possibility of the radical incompatibility of two or more worldviews. *Premature resolution* may well turn out to be an ideological phrase.

3. One should, of course, note that McCarthy Brown is on the editorial advisory board for the Pluralism Project. This suggests that, in the preceding quotation, emphasis should be placed on the word *premature*, suggesting that "resolution of difference . . . on our terms" can be avoided if resolution occurs at the proper time.

4. The article, entitled "Challenge of Pluralism," originally appeared in *Nieman Reports*, "God in the Newsroom," 47/2 (1993), and can be found on the web at: http://www.fas.harvard.edu/~pluralsm/html/article-cop.html.

5. I am deeply indebted to Fish's *The Trouble with Principle* (1999) for my analysis of Eck's and Marty's rhetoric, in particular Fish's chapter "Boutique Multiculturalism" (56–73).

6. It is interesting how Eck appropriates Anderson's materialist use of the "imagined communities" metaphor for clearly idealistic, theological uses (1993: 226–27).

7. For the debate that followed this article, see Griffiths 1998a, 1998b; O'Connor 1998; and McCutcheon 1998b. See also Cady 1998.

8. My thanks goes to Joby Taylor who pointed out Mamet's essay to me.

9. Cole is quoting Horowitz 1997: 138.

10. Despite the much-heralded gritty portrait of war that is found in Spielberg's *Saving Private Ryan*, it too individualizes complex historical events. The "Nazi bad guys" receive no character development whatsoever, serving either as faceless snipers impeding the mission of mercy undertaken by the selfless U.S. soldiers whose individual characters are developed in detail or as inhuman targets deserving of their graphic fate.

11. See Marty 1998 for his reply to the review symposium on *The One and the Many*, in which Murphy's article appeared. It should come as no surprise that, in his reply, Marty characterizes Murphy's criticism as *ad hominen*; "Who can refute a sneer?" Marty rhetorically asks, in commenting on Murphy's article. In my experience, the accusation of "bad form" all too often accompanies liberal replies to well argued criticisms of their position.

12. In an editorial to the *CSSR Bulletin* (28/3 [1999]), I attempted to elaborate this very point in commenting on the recent U.S. Congress decision to "allow" publicly funded institutions to post the Ten Commandments. In that editorial I concluded:

> One of the goals of teaching in the liberal arts tradition is to persuade students that the world is far more complex than they might at first think it is. Biology, geography, and political science classes all work toward this general goal quite effectively—after all, no one comes out of those classes thinking the world works in quite the same fashion as they did when they went in to them—so why shouldn't our classes achieve this goal as well? If this is indeed our goal, then we certainly have something to say about the Congressional vote—both in our classes and, possibly, in other public settings as well. But just what can we say? Well, given that this decision on the Ten Commandments came as the Congress debated the issue of youth violence, I think of Carol Delaney's recent book, *Abraham on Trial: The Social Legacy of Biblical Myth* (Princeton University Press, 1998). Her book asks, how and why did an ancient story about a father's willingness to sacrifice a son (rather than, say, his desire to protect his child at all costs) come to stand for the pinnacle of faith in three religious traditions? Delaney argues that Biblical stories are hardly immune from social and physical violence; after all, the willingness to kill one's child is crucial to the Abraham story. Her general question is: What kind of social world do we build when such stories form the foundation? Despite Rep. Ader-

holt's [the Republican sponsor of the Ten Commandments bill] belief that posting Biblical passages in public "is an important step to promote morality and an end of children killing children," Delaney's analysis suggests that the situation is far more complicated than Congress may wish to think, for scholars know that many of the stories considered by adherents to be most central to their religion presuppose at their very core the kind of violence that many today find unacceptable. Social life is ironic and complex, no?

CHAPTER 11

Redescribing "Religion and . . ." Film: Teaching the Insider/Outsider Problem

THE "RELIGION AND . . ." COURSE

Anyone even partially familiar with the course offerings of most departments of religion will recognize the ever-present "religion and . . ." courses: Religion and Human Culture; Religion, Self, and Society; Religion and Women; Religion and Ethics; Religion and the Law; Religion and Literature; Religion and Film; Religion and Music, Religion and Politics; and so on. The list is virtually never ending. If one were to delve into the histories of these courses and the institutional contexts from which they were originally conceived, my guess is that many came into being in an effort not simply to cover a new content area but as an explicit attempt to gain a little more institutional turf for struggling programs; the basic elasticity of the religion and . . . rubric makes it an ideal site for extending a department's offerings. We have seen this all too well in the ever-growing industry of teaching courses on religion and world cultures or religion and globalization (thinly revised versions of world religions courses, our old standby) aimed at the business colleges on our campuses as well as religion and ethics courses that challenge the philosophy department's traditional proprietorship over studying ethics.

The elasticity and popularity of such religion and . . . courses, however, come with a price that many in the field will likely know firsthand. Such courses confirm that departments of religion have a tenuous place in the university curriculum, for they often exist only insomuch as they fulfill the breadth requirements of other departments. As Jonathan Z. Smith has noted,

> courses in religious studies largely function as "service courses" (a despicable term, which remains, in this instance, useful for designating the fact that the majority of enrolments in religion courses are one-time

electives, either fulfilling some distribution requirement or meeting a student's interest). Few programs in religious studies have numbers of majors commensurate with their enrolments; few majors go on to graduate studies in religion. (1995a: 409)

From the viewpoint of someone convinced that academic study of religion is one of an increasingly small number of sites in the modern university where detailed, comparatively based scholarship on the complexities of human behavior and institutions can be taken seriously, this is hardly a good sign. For the frightening degree to which some departments depend almost completely on enrollments in such courses suggests that the field is able to reproduce itself as a viable institution only by continuing its own institutional marginalization—it is a catch-22 of the very worst kind. Although I recognize that the luxury of more specialized upper-level courses in large part depends upon the existence of a sufficient number of religious studies majors, which in turn often depends on the student numbers generated in our more user-friendly introductory courses—it is simply a question of cost/benefit—I fear that in many cases the upper-level classes we purchase by means of the currency of lower-division student numbers suffer from the same lack of theoretical rigor that so often characterizes the religion and . . . genre of courses.

As I recall him phrasing it in an address at the 1996 meeting of the American Academy of Religion, Smith sees the religion and . . . rubric as sufficient evidence that the ghost of Paul Tillich yet haunts the field. Or, as he put it elsewhere, "Tillich remains the unacknowledged theoretician of our enterprise" (1990a: 6). The point seems to be that insomuch as the religion and . . . rubric juxtaposes coherent, autonomous religious systems over against such other equally coherent, identifiable phenomena as culture, ethics, literature, or politics, it perpetuates a rather naive, and simply outdated, view that religions are socially autonomous, acontextual systems that make manifest an essential impulse or drive of deeply numinous value. In other words, from the outset this rubric presupposes that religion can hardly be *explained* as a result of social, political, or psychological processes and instead can only be *understood* to *manifest* in culture, in politics, in literature, and so on, essentially religious or transcendent values and feelings. Despite the fact that the troublesome circularity of this reasoning has been known for some time, it nevertheless continues to dominate the field.

Elaborating on this point, we can simply say that the continued emphasis on the religion and . . . rubric demonstrates that we have failed to develop analytically useful definitions and theories of religion (the object, or 'it', of our studies). Instead, presuming we all intuitively know what we are talking about, we have opted simply to look for 'its' effects in other aspects of culture and history; much like Plato's philosopher coming out of the cave, we search among the shadows for hints of the sun. Undoubtedly, if pressed to identify the 'it' we were actually talking about, we would resort to sheer assertion in maintaining that 'it' was essentially undefinable and only discernable through 'its' various manifestations in culture, politics, literature, etc. (what Eliade termed hierophanies). In other words, while 'it' cannot be defined, it can somehow be recognized by the trained eye.

Should one think that my critique of this position is misplaced, being applicable only to the modern field's prehistory, consider a recent collection of essays on the category of "the sacred" (Idinopulos and Yonan 1996).[1] After citing Nathan Söderblom's early-twentieth-century views on the centrality of the notion of 'holiness', the editors go on to say:

> It is difficult to see how one could study religions without some working notion of the holy or the sacred; it is equally difficult to fix on one, universally agreed upon definition of the sacred. The aim of this book of essays is to focus attention on the importance of the sacred in the study and teaching of religion, and to seek for newer and more compelling ways to conceive of the sacred. (1)[2]

Despite maintaining that certain concepts are essential to the study of religion, the editors acknowledge that no one actually agrees on what such terms mean or on what they signify. Given this, the two-fold aim of their volume—"to focus attention on the importance of the sacred" and "to seek for newer and more compelling ways to conceive of the sacred" are rather difficult to accomplish—how can one focus attention on an undefined, free-floating signifier? Moreover, how is one to judge how compelling a conception is when we have no idea what we are trying to conceive? If we have no widely accepted definition of our object of study, let alone a term to signify 'it', then we have no way of deciding if we are all talking about the same thing. Either we are all groping toward some enduring yet undefined mystery—like the proverbial blind men and the elephant—or we are studying an agreed upon aspect of human behavior. We cannot have it both ways. Some years ago, members of many English departments generally abandoned the quest for finding the enduring values of "Literature" in particular works of literature—it is about time we abandoned this pursuit ourselves.[3]

THE COMMODIFICATION OF SCHOLARSHIP

Although I do not completely reject the traditional religion and . . . approach to the study of religion, I would like to suggest that, because such courses are often based on a suspect theory of religion, there is something to be gained by redescribing what we mean by religion, thereby rethinking what we hope to accomplish in our classrooms.[4] Such a redescription is all the more necessary when one recognizes the degree to which the dominant presumption that religion is essentially good, or in the least, an independent variable, fits the current model of the university as a place where student *customers* purchase a nonthreatening commodity that has immediate, practical value. As phrased by Gustavo Benavides:

> Like most buyers, the majority of prospective students are interested in purchasing the most desirable goods and services at the lowest possible price; conversely, like most sellers, colleges advertise themselves as providing the best possible education at the lowest cost. Should one be surprised, then, to discover that the advertising frenzy that surrounds us—a frenzy that not only fuels the process of production and consumption that keeps our world going, but that seems to constitute our very subjectivity—is very much at work in the educational process? . . . [A] commodified "College Experience" is advertised [in our catalogs] using the same elements—plentiful smiles against a green background—[that are] employed in advertising cruises and retirement communities. (1997: 89)

Despite the fact that it rightly reminds us that students and their families are indeed paying their hard-earned money for the opportunity of attending our classes and working through our syllabi, the student/customer model unfortunately also reminds us that the kind of intellectual and social provocation once associated with the university classroom may no longer be acceptable or even possible. Let's face it, no one goes to MacDonalds to ponder such issues as the relations between world hunger and the global rise of capitalist hegemony.

This commodification of education suggests that courses that prompt critical thinking and question dominant assumptions (such as religion being a pure, politically independent variable) will prompt many students to, as the old saying goes, vote with their feet and leave our classes. But to sacrifice intellectual/social provocation for the security gained by increased enrollments may be just as dangerous to the long-term health of the field as it would be to try to eliminate the service component of the field in favor of courses that engaged simply in rigorous theorizing and critical thinking. While acknowledging that this is an issue of costs and benefits to be calculated by each individual department, I happen to think that we can walk this tightrope better than we have in some cases. Therefore, in an effort to help us redescribe the role of the religion and . . . rubric, I would like to focus attention on one particular and often popular site: the religion and film course. Or, better put, I would like to examine the use of feature films in our classes in an effort (i) to demonstrate how unresolved theoretical issues have led to conflicting models for the use of films and (ii) to revise how we employ films so that our classes teach our students the skills needed by critical commentators on the mechanisms of culture. I offer these suggestions because I believe that redescribing what we can accomplish by routinely using films in our classes will bring benefits to our entire curriculum.

RELIGION AND FILM AS SITES OF SOCIAL FORMATION

I have selected the relationship between religion and film for a specific reason: the way in which films are often used in our classes reflects the kind of antitheoretical stance that sometimes characterizes our field. More often than not, films are used to communicate to students, in suitably circular fashion, that religions are about essentially religious matters such as sin, redemption, grace, salvation, transcendence, ultimacy, sacredness, and so on. What makes a particular film a candidate for our courses, then, is usually limited to whether it addresses such grand issues as suffering and evil or such supposedly enduring human values as forgiveness and love. The religion and film course, then, is premised on phenomenological categories largely derived from Christian theology. While such categories may be of great use to the Christian theologian, they are of little or, at worst, no analytic value for the scholar of religion, for they limit scholarship to mere description of the insider's claims. By developing a special vocabulary removed from the other human sciences, such descriptive scholarship effectively reproduces and thereby entrenches the participant's claims of social and political autonomy, as if religions are somehow a special case, that one site where humanity confronts the really big issues. The question we must pursue is whether the scholar of religion should be constrained by the insider's claims, interpretations, and vocabulary.

For instance, take the case of Richard Attenborough's film *Shadowlands* (Savoy Pictures, 1993), starring Anthony Hopkins as C. S. Lewis; this film is sometimes used in our classes to illustrate the problem of evil, for, as the film's video advertising phrases it, "a heart awakened to great love is also opened to great pain." To those who come on the scene with a rather liberal and uncritical understanding of just what religions are and do, it is no doubt entirely self-evident that such a theme is a religious theme. However, if our classes are about cultivating historical, cultural analysis of complex human behaviors and institutions, then it will not do for us to assert that religions are essentially about transcendent or immanent matters. We will surely want to redescribe the claims and behaviors of the people we study in terms of critical vocabularies shared throughout the human sciences. What's more, it will not do to employ films as a way to get students thinking about how they could be relating to the universe or how to figure out life's big puzzles. Instead, we could be prompting them to inquire as to just why it is that human communities generally find life to be such a puzzle in the first place and why it is that human beings are generally so concerned to believe that the natural world of objects they bump into, let alone the universe as a whole, somehow cares for them. Focusing on just these issues will likely provoke some students, as well as provoke those among our colleagues and administrators who take religion in general (let alone any one in particular) to be an obviously nurturing, salvific power in human history; as suggested above, such provocation is precisely our role as scholars.

Because I often use feature-length films as a means for prompting students first to think and then to rethink theoretical and methodological issues, instead of using them as illustrations of phenomenological categories, I tend to think that the religion and film course is one site where a redescription of our field can profitably take place. For example, as noted in the following chapter, I have used some of Bill Moyers's videotaped interviews with Joseph Campbell (PBS's *The Power of Myth* series) in my courses on theories of myth and ritual; the point of using them, however, is not to study myths but to critique the ease with which such issues as gender and politics are subsumed and thereby ignored within totalized discourses on monomyths and personal bliss. Accordingly, Campbell the myth theorist and 1980s cultural icon is effectively redescribed as a mythmaker and a myth, thereby becoming but another piece of data in need of study. Therefore, rethinking our use of film resources requires first a conceptual shift on the part of the instructor, a shift from seeing religion as a self-evident, autonomous system symbolizing timeless values to seeing religion as an active process and part of the sociocultural mix. This entails a redescription of religion itself. Second, it requires instructors to see the medium of film as not simply manifesting enduring religious values but, rather, to see film—much like myth itself—as a contemporary medium whereby human communities construct and contest their ever-changing and emotionally charged social identities. Think no further than the very different Americas portrayed in *Forrest Gump* and *Pulp Fiction*, both of which went head-to-head for best picture of the year. Not only did *Gump* win, so too did a particular (re)vision of twentieth-century America.

When using films in our religion courses, then, we should not be concerned with teaching students to recognize the sacred in its celluloid manifestations but to see in religious systems as well as in our own society's films the all too common mechanisms of social formation. Such a shift opens the way for questioning how, as scholars of religion, we can contribute to studying the complex processes whereby sociocultural formations begin (emergent social formations), successfully reproduce themselves (dominant social formations), and eventually come to an end in the midst of prompting yet new emergent social forms (residual social formations). Such a shift (i) fully inscribes religion *and* film within a wider field of cultural practices, (ii) prompts us to develop an explicit social theory of religion, and (iii) draws on and develops our ability to accomplish creative, cross-disciplinary work. Making such a shift, then, prompts the scholar of religion to become a commentator on a wide array of cultural practices—both historic and contemporary.

For example, take the case of Monty Python's now classic film *The Life of Brian*, a film that many in our field have surely seen but probably only the brave have used in their classes. The film pokes a great deal of fun at the dominant Christian myth of origins, no doubt confirming for many that it is hardly the kind of film to use in a class designed to uncover religions' enduring values. But if such a class was redesigned in the manner suggested above, then *The Life of Brian* would be a powerful example of how social formations more than likely actually arise— in a haphazard manner that only later comes to be authorized and mythified.[5] For some time, scholars of religion have known that, with the benefit of hindsight and in light of continually changing social pressures, participants in social movements generally construct elaborate narratives of origins that presuppose (i) some sort of *Geist* manifested within, and working itself out of, human history and therefore (ii) the direct relevance of originary events for the current historical era. For the scholar, however, the historic *beginnings* are to be distinguished from later myths of *origins*, for these later narratives are themselves social constructs that legitimize current social formations by casting their values into the distant, authoritative past.[6]

The tension between historic beginnings and mythic origins is also captured in *The Life of Brian*; it nicely demonstrates the *ad hoc* manner in which social formations splinter and begin, a manner dramatically different from the myth of origins that later comes to dominate within developed traditions. When we see the crowd as well as the soldiers hounding Brian, when we watch people debating whether to follow the one who has Brian's cast-off sandal or the one who has his cast-off gourd, and, at the film's end, when we witness his friends and family leaving Brian alone on the cross to pursue their own convoluted agendas (agendas that, all along, have had virtually nothing in common with Brian's own self-conception), we are seeing the generally blind dynamics of social formation prior to their investment with mythic, teleological significance.[7] I think here also of the scene in *Forrest Gump* where, after having jogged all over the country and attracted a group of devoted followers (Gump's disciples? his *sangha*?), the usually silent, bearded Gump stops running, turns around, and, to the utter puzzlement of his followers, simply says that he is tired and wants to go home. The crowd parts, and Gump starts walking back in the direction from which he came. It is clear from this scene that the "meaning" his followers had invented for themselves had nothing to do with his own (possibly unknown) reasons for running.

A wonderful example of how stories of origins legitimize current social formations can be found in Barry Levinson's film *Avalon*, where an extended family's Thanksgiving dinners provide recurring opportunities to tell the old, old story of nationalist and familial origins. In the opening words of the family patriarch, Sam Krichinksy: "I came to America in 1914, by way of Philadelphia. That's where I got off the boat. And then I came to Baltimore. It was the most beautiful place you've ever seen in your life. There were lights everywhere. What lights they had. It was a celebration of lights. I thought it was for me. 'Sam was in America. Sam was in America'." The power of the film as a class resource is greatly enhanced by Bruce Lincoln's insightful article on the film (1996b); reading it along with viewing the film, students become aware of the sometimes subtle, and usually overlooked, ways in which narratives, practices, and enduring social identities fit together and reproduce each other.[8] In Lincoln's words:

> This particular group of people [the Krichinsky family of the film] comes to this particular Thanksgiving dinner and listens to this particular story because they are members of one family, a family that is not only defined but actively constructed through the stories they tell and the ceremonies they share. Moreover, these occasions are important . . . precisely because they provide the opportunity to share the stories that actively remind their hearers of what holds them together and makes them who and what they are. (1996b: 166).[9]

Lincoln's essay is a fine example of the scholar of religion breaking free of the self-imposed limits that constrained our predecessors, a freedom that enables him to make significant contributions to the wider analysis of how individual and social identities are constructed and maintained over time and place (see also Lincoln 1989, 1994). Because human values arise, operate, and have meaning within the context of such communities, then, for the scholar of religion, *Avalon*, *The Life of Brian*, and parts of *Gump* afford us a glimpse of communities busy creating and then recreating themselves by means of value systems communicated through authorized stories and behaviors. Such films, then, are not examples of enduring values manifested in celluloid, values the viewer must correctly recognize, but are examples of how values are created and socially authorized in the first place. These films should find a place in our classrooms, for what else are religious systems but highly efficient means for authorizing socially reproduced values.

COMPETING MODELS FOR RELIGION AND FILM

As should by now be apparent, the difference between these two understandings of film as a resource in the religious studies classroom boils down to a difference over an old theoretical topic in the field: the insider/outsider problem. Whereas one group reproduces the insider's claim when maintaining that films can embody essentially religious themes, the other attempts to develop an outsider's viewpoint by questioning what sense it makes to posit anything as being essentially religious in the first place. This theoretical dispute was surprisingly apparent in the book review section of a recent issue of *JAAR* (65/2 [1997]: 496–98; 498–501). In back-to-back reviews, two books on religion and film were discussed: *Screening the Sacred* (Martin and Ostwald 1995) and *Seeing and Believing* (Miles 1996). The first volume, a collection of essays, is concerned with the influence of religion on movies (i.e., religion as independent and causal) and therefore devotes considerable space to examining what it terms the "theological, mythological, moral, and archetypal" themes manifested in such films as *Apocalypse Now*, *Platoon*, and *The Seventh Sign*. Its title alone, *Screening the Sacred*, is sufficient to suggest its editors' approach to the study of religion. Contrary to this approach, the second volume is explicitly concerned with the analysis not of isolated or purely religious themes but with how religions function to authorize social values: drawing on a social theory of religion, Miles maintains that religion is "centrally and essentially about the values according to which people conduct their relationships" (1996: 15). We see here the notion of *sui generis* religion being bypassed somewhat for more of a social understanding of religion, one close to Tim Fitzgerald's own understanding of religious systems as one among many cultural sites where institutionalized value systems are created, authorized, and reproduced (1997, 1999). Whereas the first volume takes it for granted that religious themes are concerned with making sense of the world, the second draws the lens back even further and problematizes the social and ideological mechanisms whereby this or that counts as sensible in the first place. To put it another way, where the first volume examines, in its reviewer's words, "the dramatic presentation of fundamental values" in film (Johnston 1997: 497), the second uses the analysis of films to examine how it is that human societies go about making and contesting so-called fundamental values to begin with.

It should be evident, then, that these books represent two rather different approaches to the study of religion: the first takes the reports and behaviors of religious insiders at face value, limiting the field to mere description; the second understands such reports and behaviors as part of the data in need of analysis, and therefore its approach is analytic and redescriptive. This difference of approach is all the more evident in the review of Miles's *Seeing and Believing*, where the reviewer happens to be one of the editors of *Screening the Sacred*. There is little surprise, then, that in only the second paragraph of this review we read:

> [B]ecause her value-centered approach tends to ignore mythic patters and theological meanings, it suggests that her approach to religion and film needs to be supplemented with those of other scholars who attend to other dimensions of religion. . . . Indeed, because religion itself is multidimensional, we need hybridized forms of criticism to explore *how it manifests itself* in and through film. A focus on values is necessary but insufficient. (Martin 1997: 499; emphasis added)

Predictably, Martin recommends that the reader interested in such a hybridized approach consult the works of, among others, a Christian theologian (for its theological meanings) and a post-Jungian (for its mythic meanings). However, what is particularly troubling about his review of Miles's book is how Martin apparently misses her point. It is only on the basis of his undefended, and merely asserted *a priori* knowledge that religion is indeed a unified, objective, yet nonempirical whole that is made real (is manifested) in the material world, that he could even mount such a criticism. For Martin, the so-called multidimensional nature of religion far exceeds what social scientifically grounded, interdisciplinary work can study, for this nature presupposes the need for studying such nonempirical phenomena as universal human feelings and universal problems of human existence (to borrow the words of Johnston, reviewing the co-edited *Screening the Sacred*).

Undoubtedly, Miles "ignores" the so-called mythic and theological meanings of the films she examines precisely because both mythic and theological discourses are two of the primary sites where social values are authorized to begin with! To make this point, we can appeal to the structure of Martin and Ostwald's volume: it is organized into three sections: theological, mythic, and ideological (by ideological, they mean the social and political aspects of film). Once again, the ghost of Tillich (perhaps joined by Joseph Campbell this time) has passed through the classroom (or, in this case, the movie theater), for, instead of understanding discourses on transcendent values (i.e., theology) and discourses on origins, grounding prototypes, and timeless archetypes (i.e., myths) as just a few of the many cultural sites of sociopolitical behavior, *Screening the Sacred*'s structure suggests that these discourses are somehow privileged because they operate autonomously, free from, and juxtaposed to, the tug and pull of historical existence (what they term "ideology"—a use that hardly does justice to this category). I suggest that positing such a zone of free-floating privilege is itself—to rehabilitate the critical edge of the term—ideological.

Before proceeding, I must point out that such a stark juxtaposition of Miles's work to that of Martin and Ostwald is not entirely accurate, for Miles's commitment to a thoroughly social theory of religion is ambiguous. For instance, she understands religion in film to contest and present alternatives to so-called secular values (1996: 15, 25) and also characterizes religious commitment as "interior and invisible" (43). Positing a fundamental distinction between so-called sacred and secular values, not to mention understanding religion as essentially concerned with interior and private feelings, flies in the face of a social theory of religion. It is not that there are religious vs. secular values but that this very division of values is itself one sociorhetorical technique essential to social formation. As I read Durkheim, he argues that the sacred/profane distinction is one of the primary classificatory schemes whereby social communities are maintained; he does not argue that the world is actually divided up in this manner: "The division of the world into two domains, one containing all that is sacred and the other all that is profane—such is the distinctive trait of religious thought" (Durkheim 1995: 34). To classify and divide the world in such a way is to construct social identities in a particular manner, a manner that, for the sake of description, Durkheim terms "religious."[10] This criticism notwithstanding, *Seeing and Believing* nicely suggests just how promising a culture studies approach, when consistently applied, can be for our field.

THE INSIDER/OUTSIDER PROBLEM

If the use of film in religious studies courses is meant merely to chronicle and describe the sacred's varied, allegorical manifestations,[11] then Miles's approach needs to be supplemented, for it overlooks what a number of devotees themselves might say; however, if our courses are designed to problematize and analyze devotees' reports, then Miles's approach needs no supplementation whatsoever. If religious systems possess timeless truths either of the theological or mythic sort (though I am not convinced there really is any difference between these two), then her book will be of little use, for it rightly problematizes the seemingly transparent authority upon which both sorts of discourses depend! No wonder Martin's review opens by appreciatively quoting Eliade's *Sacred and the Profane* and ends with a detailed apology for his own approach to this special subject matter. Sadly, he fails to see—or, because he sees all too clearly, he contests the view—that scholars of religion working with an explicit social theory of religion will take the so-called dimensions of religion as data in need of analysis.

Instead of closing this chapter by outlining an entire syllabus for a religion and film class (the interested reader is referred to Miles's chapters, which do precisely this, each tackling two or more films on related topics), I would like to focus attention on the key issue that, I have suggested, haunts our rationale for using films: to borrow Miles's apt phrasing, it is the question of whether scholars should maintain a "spectatorial distance" from their object of study (1996: 31). In my own support of a social theory of religion, the insider/outsider problem is of direct relevance, for I presume, from the outset, that the participants' understanding of what they might term a "religious system" does not constrain my analysis of it as a social system. In fact, as should be obvious at this late point in this book, I would go so far as to say that the participants' self-understanding and discursive rules are themselves but two more pieces of information in need of scholarly analysis and study.

However, regardless of how each of us views and solves the problem in our own scholarship, in the classroom our role is to introduce students to the problem and its many possible solutions. In a nutshell, then, we must assist students in confronting whether, and to what extent, someone can study, understand, or explain the beliefs, words, or actions of another. In other words, to what degree, if any, are the motives and meanings of human behaviors and beliefs accessible to the researcher who may not necessarily share these beliefs and who does not necessarily participate in these practices? Do students of culture have virtually unimpeded access to the intentions and meanings of the people, societies, or institutions they study, or, to take the contrary view, are all human observers cut off from ever being able to see past their own biases, contexts, and presuppositions? Or is there a solution somewhere in the middle? The future of the human sciences depends on how our students answer these questions.

Simply put, *must we*, or better put, *can we*, climb out of our skin and, as the old saying goes, walk a mile in someone else's shoes? This is a problem that must be faced by all scholars of the human condition: psychologists, sociologists, anthropologists, historians, and political scientists, among others, must confront not only the question of *how* to study the intentions and actions of human beings and groups but *whether* such a study can take place at all. The first involves a question of *method* (what tools must we use to access the meanings and motives of our subjects); the second requires us to defend the *theory* of human cognition, behavior, and organization upon which our methods are based. Is the person we study, often termed simply as "the other," an open book, an enigma, or simply a neutral screen onto which the observer projects his or her own desires and fears? Depending on which of these three theoretical options we choose, our study will proceed in dramatically different ways, relying on different tools and methods, reaching significantly different ends.

When, in suitably humanist fashion, religion is conceived as a universal human impulse and positive value, the insider/outsider problem is rarely confronted, for, or so it is assumed, we all have religions and can therefore identify (*understand*), with varying degrees of success, with each other's claims. After all, religions are said to be essentially about such universal human issues as redemption and grace; being human beings ourselves, how could we as scholars not understand other people's thoughts on these deep issues? Accordingly, there really is no problem of understanding the insider. (Joachim Wach provides a classic example of this argument [1967].) However, I would argue that such an approach is not characteristic of the academic study of religion but, rather, the practice of interreligious dialogue.

Where the insider/outsider problem is confronted in a sophisticated manner is in scholarship that has been influenced by feminist, postmodern, or postcolonial theorizing, where the situatedness of human discourse is taken seriously. This suggests that only when and where dominant modes of re-presentation are no longer presumed to be transparent and authoritative is the insider/outsider problem apparent. Therefore, in all three of these theoretical contexts, the traditionally distanced, detached relationship between subject and object, spectacle and spectator, ruled and ruler, female and male, has been quite effectively called into question. This became all the more apparent to me over the course of the past year while I was developing a class anthology on this very topic (1998b): the modernist approach to the problem (be it of the antireductionist or reductionist kind) differs dramatically from what we can simply term the "reflexive tradition" associated with work carried out by feminists, postmodernists, and postcolonialists. Accordingly, a degree of theoretical sophistication is presupposed for one even to confront, let alone solve (if indeed one can), the insider/outsider problem. It is precisely this sophistication that our students will take with them from our courses and apply in countless sites.

Although reading texts and articles can help a great deal in detailing for students the ins and outs of this issue,[12] I have also found three feature-length films that offer a different entry into the issue. In attempting to have students redescribe their own position as scholars of—rather than just participants in—human behavior, the following three films hold much promise, for, instead of solving the insider/outsider problem, they present it, in all of its complexity, for the viewer to mull over and consider. By incorporating these films into many of my courses, I would like to think that I have succeeded not only in overcoming the traditionally ghettoized nature of the "religion and film" course but also in prompting students to confront, in a creative manner, a pervasive theoretical topic that is sadly bypassed by many of our colleagues.

Rashomon

For those conversant with the history of Japanese cinema, Akira Kurosawa's Academy Award winning film *Rashomon* (black and white, 83 minutes, 1952) will be a familiar title. Kurosawa presents a film in which audience members find themselves continually drawn deeper into a number of converging and diverging narratives, none of which, as it turns out, is completely trustworthy (what tale is?). *Rashomon* is the tale of a woodchopper and a priest in medieval Japan, who, while seeking shelter from a heavy rain storm under a large ruined gate into the old imperial city of Kyoto, recount their stories to a commoner who has also sought refuge from the rain. The stories involve the woodchopper's and the priest's recollections of their appearances before the local authorities earlier that day, where each recounted tales of (in the former's case) finding a dead man in the woods a few days earlier and (in the case of the latter) of previously passing on the road a man who matched the dead man's description and who was at that time accompanied by his wife on horseback. After bearing witness to these matters, they told the commoner how they had remained to listen to the stories of other people involved in the case: the infamous bandit who was captured in the possession of the dead man's horse, bow, and arrows; the dead man's distraught wife; and the dead man himself testifying through a possessed medium. Although the viewer knows that the husband has died and that the woman was attacked by the bandit (for all accounts agree on these basic matters), by the end of the film he has witnessed each participant recounting (and the participants acting out) a significantly different story as to who killed the man, how, and for what reason. Much like Plato's dialogues, *Rashomon* comes with a multilayered narrative; however, contrary to Plato, Kurosawa does not do us the favor of placing an unfolding, unified message or *Geist* in his text.

For instance, the bandit portrays himself as daring and courageous in defeating the husband in a dramatic sword fight. However, in her version, the wife, portraying herself as an appropriately subservient and therefore passive victim, is compelled to stab her husband with a dagger, when, after her rape, he casts a cruel, unfeeling gaze at her. Finally, the husband's story told through the medium focuses on his wife's betrayal of him (he recounts how she willingly took up with the bandit and abandoned him), which drives him to commit suicide. Clearly, someone is not telling the truth. Even the woodchopper turns out to be a liar, for, late in the film, he drastically revises his original story of finding the husband's body some days later only when the commoner presses him on certain conflicting details. In his revised tale, he turns out to have witnessed the entire affair from the bushes, where he saw what now turns out to be the inept and cowardly men fight, a fight that takes place only due to the prompting of the wife, who has belittled them both by questioning their manhood. However, is the woodchopper to be trusted now? The commoner presses him on why it was that the man's pearl-inlay dagger was never found at the scene. Could the woodchopper also be a thief? By the end of the film, viewers know little of what really might have happened in the woods that day: none of the insider's versions are trustworthy, and if the woodchopper lied once, why would he not lie again?[13]

Blow Up

Blow Up (color, 111 minutes, 1967), directed by Michelangelo Antonioni, is the story of a young fashion photographer (Thomas) in London in the 1960s. Early on in the film we understand that his life and work both inhabit a hectic world with little commitment or sense of responsibility. Like *Rashomon*, *Blow Up* suggests an existentialist reading of life, devoid of stable meanings and grand narratives, where actors have little choice but to create their own stories. While randomly photographing in a public park one day, Thomas happens on a couple in the distance who seem to be in love and who may very well be having an illicit midday rendezvous. Unbeknownst to them, he begins taking pictures of them. After being seen and then confronted by the woman, who is rather insistent that he give her the film, Thomas returns to his studio, and, curious as to her interest in the film, he eventually develops the pictures. Becoming increasingly preoccupied with the story seemingly told in the photographs, he blows up the black and white prints, arranges them around the walls of his apartment, and begins reconstructing (or constructing?—now *that's* the question our classes must address!) a coherent and logical narrative sequence. Placing the blow ups in "order" around the room, he stands in their midst, looking back and forth between them, making ever larger, grainier copies, replacing one with another, changing his position in their midst, thereby changing his viewpoint.

Soon he has identified what he considers to be not only a troubled or apprehensive expression on the woman's face, but, among the bushes (in a photo tacked to the wall across his room) and in the direction in which she seems to be looking, he sees in the grainy blow up what appears to be a hand with a gun pointing toward the man and the woman (in the photo back across his room). In yet another picture, "later" in his constructed sequence, we see the lone woman by now in the distance, standing over what appears to be the man's dead body partially obscured by the distant trees. But in Thomas's attempts to tell his friends and his manager that he has "witnessed" a murder, his news consistently falls on deaf ears (the London underground culture of 1960s rock and roll and drugs is effectively used to symbolize his friends' lack of interest in compelling narratives). After returning to the park later that night by himself, where he does in fact find the man's body, he returns once again in the morning, this time armed with his camera, but only to find the body has now disappeared. Bewildered, the movie ends with Thomas wandering through the park in the early morning, camera in hand. We leave him watching, and later becoming more deeply involved with, two mimes who are playing an imaginary game of tennis. As the lens pulls back, we hear the imaginary tennis ball bouncing between their imaginary rackets.

Blow Out

Last is Brian DePalma's remake of *Blow Up* entitled, *Blow Out* (color, 107 minutes, 1983), a movie that also mirrors the earlier U.S. film *The Conversation* (directed by Francis Ford Coppola and starring Gene Hackman, 1974), in which a surveillance expert makes and analyzes tape recordings. However, instead of a photographer (re-)constructing a narrative sequence from still photographs, *Blow Out* is about a movie sound engineer (played by John Travolta), who, while out one night gathering sound bites of assorted noises (such as owls hooting, people chatting and strolling, etc.), happens to record the sound of an oncoming car whose tire blows out, sending it crashing through a barrier and into a river.

Although he is able to rescue the female occupant of the car, he is unable to rescue the man, who soon drowns in the submerged vehicle. The pace of the movie quickly picks up, for we soon learn that the man who has drowned is a governor favored to become the next president of the United States, that the woman was not his wife (making this all a politically embarrassing situation), and that, upon his analysis of the sound recording, a gunshot can be heard on the tape recording immediately prior to the tire's blow out. Thrown into an apparent assassination (with John Lithgow convincingly playing the assassin), and fearing for his own safety, the protagonist has little choice but to try to save himself and the woman by reconstructing the narrative sequence on his audiotape and determining who it is that has committed the murder.

TO WHOM DO WE GIVE THE BABY?

What all three of these films effectively call into question, making them particularly useful for initiating class discussions on the insider/outsider problem, is the ability of either insiders or outsiders to provide ultimately authoritative accounts of a particular event. Implicitly, such films prompt class discussions on the relations between historic beginnings and mythic origins, for they suggest that, as scholars, "ultimately authoritative accounts" are themselves the subject we study rather than the outcome of our studies. For the scholar of religion is aware that, despite the playful and *ad hoc* nature of all social interaction, social actors are busy normalizing, rationalizing, routinizing, mythifying, and authorizing their interactions.

Although our students are often immersed in data that takes for granted the routinized and absolute nature of both social relations and even the workings of the universe, these three films allow teachers to reintroduce this playfulness to the study of human affairs. In all three films it is obvious that *something* has taken place. But what? In *Rashomon* it is all too apparent that no insider has a complete or a trustworthy account of what transpired (since every account disagrees with all others and each of the participants tells a story in which he or she is flattered). In *Blow Up* and *Blow Out* the sometimes invisible gap between the observer/listener and the actual event itself is painfully apparent—just as apparent as in the case of the viewer of *Rashomon* not knowing what has actually happened. Despite the fact that by its end *Blow Out*, like most Hollywood films, provides complete closure, making it somewhat less attractive for use in our classrooms (for reality never provides us with closure), students not acquainted with either subtitled or older films find it the most accessible of the three, possibly because of its more contemporary look and, for some students, the generally recognizable American actors. However, for those willing to tackle the more difficult films, the uneasy, off balance feeling of indecision, disorientation, and even frustration that the viewer feels at the end of both *Blow Up* and *Rashomon* provides most useful teaching aides.[14] Despite all three films being available in video format at many rental stores (especially video stores with well-stocked foreign film sections), I have found that having students view the film together, in or outside of normal class time, is best, for this disorientation is usually heightened when the lights go up at the film's end and everyone looks around, wondering who could have made sense of it all.

Seeing Thomas watch the mimed tennis match from behind the fence that separates court from not-court, watching his eyes follow the "ball" as it flies outside, over the fence, following him as he retrieves "it," with his realist 35 mm camera in one hand and the "ball" in the other, and tracing its path as he throws the ball back into the court prompts students to question just what does and what does not constitute reality not only for the film's protagonist but also for the people whose behavior they describe and study in their other courses. Who is to say what counts as real? Can this problem be solved? If so, how should we set about doing this? If not, how are the human sciences even possible? These are the questions that become possible after viewing these films. Despite being the explicit focus of one or two class periods, they are questions that fuel virtually all of my classes.

After confronting the problem of insiders and outsiders, it is little wonder that students, much like the priest in *Rashomon* may begin repeating to themselves, "I just don't understand. I just don't understand." Although our goal-oriented student/customers often want sure and quick answers (e.g., "But what do we have to know for the test?"; "How can I use this information?"), I tend to think that a little puzzlement and timidity in the face of complex human behaviors and institutions is a good thing. For if the realm of the insider is one where meanings are certain and order is self-evident, then it makes sense that the student of human behavior, when confronted with the utter uncertainty of motives and stories, is deeply troubled and, dare I say, provoked. For some students it is therefore the priest who presents a figure with whom they can identify, for, throughout the film, his efforts are directed toward making sense of it all.

Near the end of *Rashomon*, after the various tales have been told but prior to the rain letting up, a previously unseen, abandoned baby suddenly cries out from around the corner. The commoner, after finding it, steals some of its clothes—reasoning that if he does not do it someone else will—and then runs off in the rain, leaving the woodchopper and the priest alone once again. I have found this to be the most useful part of the film for the commoner, who, much like the students themselves, is the only true outsider to all these sordid and assorted tales, turns out to be unethical and therefore entirely untrustworthy. Cradling the baby, after the commoner has run off into the rain, the priest makes a leap of faith in trusting the baby's safety to an admitted liar (the woodchopper), who says that one more mouth to feed in his large family is not a problem.

The image of the baby is a powerful metaphor for the position in which we as scholars may very well be when it comes to observing and then analyzing human behavior, for we too must make a leap: not the priest's leap of faith that Meaning awaits us around the next corner, but the scholar's theoretical leap of trying to understand human behavior based on theories and models of the scholar's own making: devotees, much like the mysterious couple in Thomas's photographs, do not wear their intentions and meanings on their sleeves. In fact, if we accept anything that Freud told us, we know that the people we study—much like Gump jogging back and forth across the United States—are probably aware only of certain manifest reasons for, and the implications of, their behavior. It falls to us as teachers to help our students grasp the *ad hoc* nature of human communities and to learn to describe, compare, and finally analyze and redescribe the complexities and uncertainties of people's intriguing actions based on the theories of human behavior that we as scholars in the human sciences bring to the scene—that is our theoretical leap. Regardless of which option one selects in resolving the insider/outsider problem—i.e., to whom do we finally give the baby?—these three films prove to be extremely useful class resources for bringing a complex theoretical issue into focus in a manner that engages our students while simultaneously provoking them into being better scholars of human cultural practices.

NOTES

1. Idinopulos and Yonan were also the editors of the previous collection of essays on the topic of reductionism (1994; see also Idinopulos and Wilson 1998).

2. I certainly imply no overall criticism of the individual essays included in this volume. In fact, I am in general agreement with Stewart Guthrie, who concludes his essay, "The Sacred: A Sceptical View," by noting that the "current popularity of 'the sacred' as a universal index of religion, then, appears unjustified. . . . At the very least, we should employ it with caution, and only in those cultural contexts where it is at home" (135–36).

3. As I have noted elsewhere, it continually amazes me how the rhetoric of autonomy found in traditional English departments is precisely the same rhetoric that we find in departments of religious studies. This first dawned on me when reading Terry Eagleton's ideological critique (1989) of "Literature" as a sociopolitically free-floating value.

4. I have been influenced here by Ann Baranowski's novel critique (1998) of "ritual and" theories of ritual (e.g., ritual and dance, ritual and myth, etc.).

5. My favorite sociological moment in *The Life of Brian* is when, after Brian has lectured the crowd concerning the need for them to stop following him, to think for themselves, and to be individuals, they bellow out in unison that they are all individuals. Then, one meek-voiced member adds, "I'm not."

6. In his presentation to the 1997 annual meeting of the North American Association for the Study of Religion (NAASR), Jonathan Z. Smith nicely drew on Edward Said's useful distinction between historic *beginnings* and ahistoric *origins*.

7. By using the metaphor *blindness*, I simply mean to imply that, despite being the cumulative results of intentional beings, social systems are themselves without intentions. In the words of the British sociologist Anthony Giddens, "human beings act purposefully and knowledgeably but without being able either to foresee or to control the consequences of what they do" (1986: 217–18). The study of the ongoing process of social formation, then, "is involved in relating action to structure, in tracing, explicitly or otherwise, the conjunction or disjunctions of intended and unintended consequences of activity and how these affect the fate of individuals. . . . For the permutations of influences are endless, and there is no sense in which structure 'determines' action or vice versa" (1986: 219). As noted in chapter 2, Giddens names the reciprocal relations between individual action and social structure "recursive reproduction"; in studying the dynamics of social formation, then, we must attend to the interface of individual actors and the systemwide constraints in which they think and act.

8. Or, in the words of Mack, "social formation and mythmaking fit together like hand and glove" (Mack 1995, 11).

9. Think of the ways in which funerals and weddings are used in other films as devices for chronicling the ups and downs of social formation (e.g., the film *Cousins*, starring Ted Danson and Isabella Rosallini [which contains three weddings and a funeral], or, come to think of it, the comedy *Four Weddings and a Funeral*).

10. I think here of Guthrie's article once again, where he nicely summarizes and advances scholarship that fails to find the sacred/profane distinction as a universal aspect of human cultures. In Guthrie's words, the distinction is overburdened. This is not to say, however, that the distinction is not a key sociorhetorical technique used in many societies.

11. I think here of how many commentators seem satisfied with identifying, for example, that one of the characters in the film *The Matrix* is named Trinity, making it a religious film. Such an allegorical reading is rather conservative given the manner in which it is constrained by a dominant yet underlying insider text. My thanks to Willi Braun for helping me to articulate this point.

12. Although few articles are more effective than Horace Miner's now classic, and often anthologized, essay "Body Ritual among the Nacirema" (1956), David Macaulay's wonderful children's book *Motel of the Mysteries* (1979) comes in a close second. Set in the year 4022 C.E., it is about a future amateur archeologist, Howard Carson (who looks and acts remarkably like a nineteenth-century gentleman scholar), who stumbles upon a completely intact, ancient "burial chamber" dating from the late twentieth century. Even the most unsophisticated readers immediately recognize his find simply to be a motel, complete with a "Do Not Disturb" sign on the door knob and "Sanitized for Your Protection" strip across the toilet seat; the former Carson identifies as the outer chamber's "sacred seal," and the latter, as a "sacred headband" worn by the

ranking official at the burial. In my experience, both the illustrations and the text of the book have led to some wonderful class conversations not only on the assumptions that guide all interpretive scholarship but also on why it is that members of our culture do some pretty interesting things (such as why hotel housekeepers fold the ends of new rolls of toilet paper into little points). Despite being a children's book (a large-format, soft-cover volume of ninety-six pages), it is a fun and effective resource in the university classroom. My thanks to Tom Ryba for first bringing it to my attention.

13. Ann Baranowski first introduced me to *Rashomon* via Marvin Harris's comments on the film. See Harris 1979: 321.

14. To some extent, *Blow Out*'s morbid ending does cause the viewer to consider the issue of what kind of closure life presents. The film opens with a movie in the movie—a screening of a teen horror movie for which the protagonist has been hired to add screams and various other sound effects. However, he is not satisfied with the particular screams in his collection of sounds. *Blow Out* then closes by returning to the screening room where the same horror movie is being edited once again, but this time the perfect scream has been used in the film—as the scream rings out, we see the somber protagonist, silently watching in the darkened screening room. The attentive viewer quickly recognizes this to be the scream of his friend as she was murdered. To help solve the mystery of the assassination, he had followed her, wired her with a hidden microphone, and recorded her conversations with the man that indeed turned out to be the assassin; although he was not able to prevent her death, he captured her scream on tape.

CHAPTER 12

Methods and Theories in the Classroom: Teaching the Study of Myths and Rituals[1]

In Kees Bolle's *Encyclopedia of Religion* article, "Myth: An Overview," we read that a myth "is an expression of the sacred in words: it reports realities and events from the origin of the world that remain valid for the basis and purpose of all there is. Consequently, a myth functions as a model for human activity, society, wisdom, and knowledge" (1987: 271; see also Bolle 1983). This is precisely what many of us have learned from those who have studied myths:

> [myth] explains and justifies at the same time the existence of the world, of man, and of society. . . . In sum, the governing function of myth is to reveal exemplary models for all rites and all meaningful human activities. (Eliade 1991: 4)

> myth is a narrative of origins, taking place in primordial time, a time other than that of everyday reality. (Ricoeur 1987: 273)

> myth is a distinctive expression of a narrative that states a paradigmatic truth (Long 1986: 94)

Such a uniform conception of myth has been extremely influential in our field; it is a conception that emphasizes these tales' normative, explanatory aspect, an aspect that is somehow distinctive, for it "cannot be expressed in simple propositions" (Sharpe 1971: 43). Too often this approach to myths as steps along a personal, existential quest has ignored addressing the sometimes subtle mechanisms and often occluded social implications of such normative claims. In other words, how is it that one account/practice as opposed to another counts as a valid model in Bolle's definition, as exemplary and meaningful in Eliade's, as original and primordial in Ricoeur's, and as distinctive and paradigmatic in Long's?

A very different tradition has tried to answer just these questions. This scholarly tradition has tended to de-emphasize the supposed

essence or substance of these tales and, instead, examines the active processes that do the authorizing in the first place. It deconstructs the privilege usually afforded the category of myth over against other sorts of
tales. In fact, it breaks down the usually unquestioned boundary
between myth-as-narrative and myth-as-human-practice. It moves from
simply describing what is or is not authoritative and exemplary in these
narratives/practices to attempting to explain what it is that makes something real or valid in the first place. In other words, it has taken the
problem of myth for its focus as opposed to the problem of the *meaning* of myth. There may be no better example than Roland Barthes's collection of essays *Mythologies*, and Bruce Lincoln's creative application
of Barthes' work (1989, 2000b), where we learn that myth "is not
defined by the object of its message, but by the way in which it utters its
message: there are formal limits to myth, there are no 'substantial ones'.
Everything, then, can be a myth? Yes, I believe this" (Barthes 1973:
117).

The distance between these two readings of the term *myth* are great
indeed. Where the former represents a relatively standard history of religions approach in which myths are understood as narratives about origins that set standards for contemporary meaning, most notably as
found in cosmogonies, the latter avoids all questions of content or substance and instead finds myth to be a rhetorical process, an ideological
act. For Barthes, *mythification*, or even *mystification*, might be the more
appropriate term because when he identifies myths he does not speak of
nouns but of verbs, of networks of actions, assumptions, and representations. In other words, his interest in myth concerns the "'naturalness'
with which newspapers, art, and common sense constantly dress up a
reality which, even though it is the one we live in, is undoubtedly determined by history" (Barthes 1973: 11). A little closer to home, we find a
surprisingly similar use of 'myth' in the recent work of the scholar of
Christian origins, Burton Mack, whose latest book is subtitled *The
Making of the Christian Myth*. For Mack, myths "turn the collective
agreements of a people into truths held to be self-evident" (1995: 301).
No wonder, then, that the rhetorical mechanisms that have constructed
the seemingly self-evident meaning, authority, and reality of both the
Bible and the U.S. Constitution equally interest Mack. Both documents
are particularly powerful instances where active processes have
"turned" and "dressed up" what might otherwise be mundane and for-
gettable historical moments.

The implication of this for scholars is that if we take for granted the
already established meaning and unquestioned authority of 'myth' we
too may have come under its spell. In so doing, we miss out on asking,
What is going on when we, as historically bound agents, constantly

dress up our own creations in "decorative displays" to make them pass for what Barthes labels "what-goes-without-saying"? How can the descriptive 'is' so smoothly become the prescriptive 'ought'? If anything, I presume that Bolle's use of the phrase *expressions of the sacred in words* would attract Barthes's interest in demystification just as much as does professional wrestling, the striptease, and even margarine, only to name a few sites that occupy his attention in *Mythologies*. Where Bolle represents those who are content to employ a phenomenological method simply to determine what this or that people hold to be "sacred" (whatever that may actually mean), Barthes' and Mack's critical methods question the strategies that construct the set-apartness of these very things, acts, conventions, beliefs, and so on, in the first place.

It was in the middle of these two very different approaches to 'myth' that I found myself in the summer of 1993 when, newly hired as a one-year lecturer at the University of Tennessee, Knoxville, I was asked by Charlie Reynolds to teach Stan Lusby's already popular upper-level course entitled "Myth, Symbol, and Ritual." Because my own area of interest is the history of methods and theories in the field, and because I was under the impression that my new job would simply entail teaching introductory courses in comparative religion, I was not that prepared to teach such a course. However, in the current academic labor market, jobs do not come along every day; so, when my new department head asked me on the phone if I could teach their myth/ritual course, my answer was, "Of course I can!" It was only then that the problem of these two competing approaches to the study of myths became most apparent to me. Needless to say, I had some library work to do.[2]

What I quickly discovered was that many of our courses in the study of myths and rituals presume both of these two categories to be unique and interrelated practices that the historian of religions alone can study—after all, the definitions cited earlier make it exceedingly clear that myths are distinctive, exemplary, and paradigmatic. Despite the fact that courses on myth might be found in classics departments and that anthropologists study rituals, we in the study of religion seem to claim some special ownership of both of these categories. The course on myths and rituals, often described in university catalogs simply as "the study of distinctive modes of religious expression," is not only a mainstay of our curricula, but it is one of the few places our classes depart from tradition-based models (courses on "the religions") and venture into wider statements about religion in general. However, such courses often entail a semester's worth of reading and storytelling, employing a definition of myth similar to Bolle's, in which the student learns to appreciate exoticness in the "familiar" and meaning in the "strange" (what Wendy Doniger once advocated as scholarship for "receiving and accepting the myths from other people's religions" [O'Flaherty 1985: 236]). Sadly, though, such courses can usually be characterized more as celebrations than as scholarly investigations into theoretical questions about the study of religion in general. For example, questions such as the adequacy of the very terms *myth* and *ritual* are never raised; instead, we assume, "often without testing, that there is some sort of universal construct—i.e., 'ritual'—and the task is to figure out how it works and why" (Aune and DeMarinis 1996: 8). In the widespread absence of undergraduate and sometimes even graduate courses on critical thinking, as well as the history of methods and theories in the field, the myth/ritual course stands out as one of the few sites where theoretical and methodological issues could be, but generally are not, made explicit and examined.

Given my own interest in methods and theories, coupled with the fact that I was not particularly committed to one understanding of either myth or ritual over any other, I soon settled on a syllabus that acted as a menu of different approaches and theories. For a general road map to the course, I was able to draw on such works as Brian Morris's *Anthropological Studies of Religion* (1987), Marcel Detienne's survey of nineteenth- and twentieth-century theories of myth (1991), William Doty's helpful survey of the literature on myth and ritual (1986), and Catherine Bell's detailed overview of scholarship on ritual (1992).[3] We started with Plato's criticism of the poets, as well as his tale in the *Republic* concerning our common origins in the earth (where, it seems, some of us are just a little more equal than others), and we moved through the work of the nineteenth-century intellectualists, the social and psychological functionalists, anthropologists, existentialists, historians of religions, structuralists, and feminists. Of course, Müller, Frazer, Tylor, Durkheim, Mauss and Hubert, Malinowski, Eliade, Turner, Douglas, Geertz, and Campbell made their customary appearances—the last by means of his Bill Moyers popular interviews—but we also had an example of Barthes's approach applied to the politics of mythmaking in popular culture (Jack Zipes's "Breaking the Disney Spell" [1994]). Albert Camus's use of Sisyphus demonstrated just how malleable these stories can be, and Bruce Lincoln's work (e.g., 1986, 1989, 1991) provided us with a number of opportunities to discuss the social, political, and economic work they can carry out without our ever knowing it. As a contemporary example of Plato's thoughts on myths as lies, we read portions from Naomi Wolf's bestselling critique of the ideology of "female beauty," *The Beauty Myth* (1992). Marshall McLuhan's (1995) and Noam Chomsky's thoughts (1991; Rai 1995) on the role of the modern mass media in shaping social identities and public opinion occupied our attention;[4] we flirted with the possibility "that ritual is pure activity,

without meaning or goal" (Staal 1993: 131) or that ritual behavior simply represents the very cognitive structures that underlie all human perception (Lawson and McCauley 1990); Jay (1992; see also Delaney
1998) helped us to reframe the study of sacrifice by not simply questioning the relations between sacrifice, violence, and anxiety, but by
linking sacrificial practices to issues of gender and social organization,
and the work of Catherine Bell (1992) and Talal Asad (1993: 57–79)
provided us with the opportunity to pull back the lens even further by
seeing the very category of "ritual" itself as part of the problem to be
studied.

The rationale for the course anticipated the theoretical position I
came to hold several years later, a position laid out in the preceding section of this collection: If one of the goals of a university education is
acquiring skills necessary for independent, critical reading and thinking,
or what Chomsky simply calls "intellectual self-defense," then a course
on myths and rituals should aim not simply at appreciating the seemingly distinctive or essential aspects of "myths" and "rituals." Instead, it
should suggest to students that research in the human sciences is just as
theory-driven as in the natural sciences, that there are ways to distinguish better from worse theories, explicit from implicit ones as well, that
the so-called facts and hard data are both a function of the theory you
happen to be using at the time, and that critical intelligence is one thing
that scholars have to offer their societies. Simply put, I took full advantage of the fact that the classroom is the one public site where engaged
scholars of religion have a tremendous impact. After beginning with the
distinction between Bolle's and Barthes's approaches, then, the course
turned out to be an introduction to the incredibly rich, interdisciplinary
literature that uses as its starting point the categories of myth and ritual.
In a word, the course deconstructed the usual unquestioned privilege
these categories carry for many scholars of religion.

Despite the fact that our students constitute a captive public, I
quickly discovered that applying this is sort of critical scholarship in the
classroom is easier said than done. The emphasis on theory and critique
made the course rather different, for drawing the students' attention to
theories and critical argumentation is generally not what our undergraduate curricula do very well. Whereas they enrolled expecting to sit
back and enjoy "the old old stories," they soon found themsevles debating the merits of theories of myth and defending their own choices and
interests in classifying this or that as a myth. But most were ill prepared
to discuss theory; for example, it was to my own amazement that my
students were simultaneously intrigued *and* troubled to learn that the
chalk will not necessarily drop into my hand the *next* time simply
because it dropped every time *in the past* (the problem of induction).

They were just as perplexed to learn that without preexistent theoretical perspectives, methods of research are utterly useless.[5] They seemed to crave self-evidencies and certainties and had an aversion to finding the possible motives and implications of their own assumptions and actions come under scrutiny. (As should be clear from the preceding sections of this book, many of our colleagues have the same aversion.) In a word, they seemed to desire what I can only call a "mythic" or "ritualized" approach to the problem of myths and rituals, suggesting to me one likely reason for the popularity of our many courses taught in line with either Eliade's or even Joseph Campbell's noncritical scholarship in this area. Deviating from such approaches sometimes made this class an uphill battle, for, in a word, theory is dangerous—especially when brought into an institution whose primary goal is to reproduce itself rather than ask troubling questions about social structures. Theory makes you question and defend that which is often taken to be beyond question and therefore in little need of scrutiny.

If the students were ill prepared to entertain that studying myths and rituals is to study scholars with differing and even competing theories of human cognition and behavior, this same approach rendered the vast majority of current resources on the market of little benefit. Possibly the most useful book was Alan Dundes's collection of essays entitled *Sacred Narrative: Readings in Theory of Myth* (1984).[6] Unfortunately, the twenty-two essays in this volume stress the rather one-sided reading of "myth" as an ahistorical category concerned with origins. This is a point that has been convincingly argued by Graeme MacQueen (1988); he understands the Dundes collection to emphasize such things as social consensus at the price of identifying the roles played by domination and coercion in the construction of social identity. In other words, when we read people telling us that myths "reveal exemplary models for all rites and all meaningful human activities," we must problematize the universal nature of their claims and ask the simple question For whom are they exemplary, by what standard, by what criteria? When it came to the study of ritual I encountered the same problem: if one happens to think that rituals simply dramatize so-called sacred moments, some of which usher people through social passages, then the market has a number of resources. Or if you happen to think that myths and rituals will help you to save yourself and enhance your life, every bookstore is filled with self-help books capitalizing on this now popular approach. But if one holds 'ritual' to be a tool some scholars use to distinguish one set of human practices from another, for some specific theoretical reason, then a readable survey of the varying theoretical reasons for using 'ritual' in the first place just did not exist.

Given the virtually hegemonic role that the seemingly self-evident construct "*sui generis* religion" has played in the North American field since the 1960s, the number of scholars interested in teaching theory may not be large, but I am convinced that it is growing. Evidence of this might be found in the increasing number of books devoted to theories of religion (e.g., Boyer 1994, Burkert 1996, Fitzgerald 1999, Guthrie 1993, and Pals 1996). No longer can we simply rely upon circular arguments and sheer assertions, such as Eliade's infamous definition of the sacred as that which is not profane or Tillich's widely repeated yet still empty claim that "the ultimate concern is a concern about that which is truly ultimate." Such claims have often passed unquestioned simply because of a consensus among scholars intent on protecting one aspect of human behavior from theoretical, social scientific analysis. But, given the inter-disciplinary nature of the modern study of religion, affected as it is by skeptical postmodern dispositions, and coupled with the rather tenuous position some departments of religion now hold, I would think that an emphasis on theoretical precision, definition, and method will charac-terize the field's research, as well as teaching in the twenty-first century.

Given this increased awareness of the role played by theory, we now find new teaching resources that should be of great use to instructors who are interested in surveying the many different ways in which implicit and explicit theories direct research in the academy. Specifically, I know of two resources that should be welcomed by those who teach courses in myths and rituals: Robert Segal's six-volume series entitled *Theories of Myth: From Ancient Israel and Greece to Freud, Jung, Campbell, and Lévi-Strauss* (1996) and Ronald Grimes's one-volume collection, *Readings in Ritual Studies* (1996). What I find most interest-ing about these volumes is that they immediately draw the reader's attention not only to the fact that 'myth' and 'ritual' are complicated scholarly tools but that the manner in which they are used may tell a stu-dent far more about researchers and their pre-operative theories than they do about the data.

If teaching such critical thinking skills is our goal as university instructors, then, along with his other works on the reductionism debate, Segal's series on myth belongs in all of our libraries.[7] Each of the six volumes in *Theories of Myth* covers one classic area in which myth research has gone on: psychology; anthropology and folklore; philoso-phy and religious studies; literary criticism; myth-ritual school; and structuralism. In this collection there is no one metatheory of myth offered; this series, much like *The Feminist Companion to Mythology*, "is not striving for the grand Victorian overview, the 'Key to all Mythologies'" (Larrington 1992: x).[8] Instead, the Garland series pre-sents what are often competing approaches, which can then be com-pared and applied in class. As Segal writes in his series introduction:

"Theories of myth are never theories of myth alone. Myth falls under a larger rubric such as mind, culture, knowledge, religion, ritual, symbolism, and narrative. The rubric reflects the discipline from which the theory was derived." Given that four of the volumes are explicitly organized around a disciplinary approach (as opposed to the final two volumes, which focus on theories, e.g., the myth-ritual school and structuralism), the series' interdisciplinary nature nicely draws attention to the highly tactical nature of yet another scholarly category, namely "discipline," allowing the instructor even to venture into the role played by institutional turf wars in the production of knowledge.

Each volume contains a brief introduction by Segal (to the series as well as to the individual volume, accompanied by a brief bibliography of general essays that survey theories of myth) followed by roughly twenty essays, each of which is presented in its original typeset format (making the volumes slightly uneven in visual appearance). The essays represent both classic works in each of the six areas, as well as pieces that interpret, elaborate, and critique the various approaches. Take, for example, the volume entitled *Philosophy, Religious Studies, and Myth*, a volume that emphasizes classical and ancient Near Eastern data. Here one finds articles by Bultmann and Cassirer, Eliade and Pettazonni, Kirk, Doniger, Ricoeur, and Widengren. Perhaps even more interesting is the selection in *Structuralism in Myth* where we find, among others, Barthes's concluding theoretical essay from *Mythologies*, "Myth Today," along with two essays each from Georges Dumézil and Claude Lévi-Strauss ("The Structural Study of Myth" and "The Story of Asdiwal"), as well as essays by J-P Vernant, Vladimir Propp, Mary Douglas, and Edmund Leach.

The price of the *Theories of Myth* series is, sadly, rather high (between $60 and $68 per volume or the complete set for $388 U.S.). This and the fact that the volumes are all in hardcover makes this series ideal for library purchase but an unlikely candidate for purchase as a class text—although a graduate class might employ one or two. In large part, the series acts as a repository of hard to find and out of print articles that are essential to the study of how scholars have defined and studied myth. It would be an ideal resource for reserve readings or as a basis for constructing in-class readers that cover such topics as the history of anthropology or psychology and the study of myth.

Where the Garland series is designed mainly for library purchase and use as a reference or supplementary resource, Prentice Hall's *Readings in Ritual Studies* will likely be used in a number of classes, and I wouldn't doubt very soon. When it comes to ritual, there are not all that many options for undergraduate survey classes, and this one does such an effective job of placing a wealth of resources in the student's hands that it deserves to be widely used. In a softcover volume of 575 pages, Grimes has collected some forty-three essays, varying from Freud's classic "Obsessive Actions and Religious Practices" to an excerpt from Bell's *Ritual Theory, Ritual Practice*. All the notables are present, such as Burkert and Girard on sacrifice, Diane Bell on Australian aboriginal women, Eliade on myth and ritual, Douglas on purification, Durkheim on magic and ritual, Turner and van Gennep on rites of passage, an excerpt from Lévi-Strauss's *Structural Anthropology*, Geertz on Balinese cockfighting, and Staal's "Meaninglessness of Ritual" (see below). Apart from such "classic" works, Grimes has come across a number of essays that effectively put into practice these various theoretical perspectives: contemporary sociological, political, feminist, anthropological, and so on, analyses of specific practices. As well, students will find a number of creative essays on such topics as the ritual aspect of the Olympic games, ritual clowning, neurobiology, Israeli kindergartens, death and dying, abortion, and even the ritualized aspects of both the American legal system and Thanksgiving Day.

One practical example of how rather sophisticated theories of ritual can be incorporated into a class based on Barthes's and Lincoln's emphasis on myth as rhetorical technique deserves brief attention here: I think specifically both of Marshall McLuhan's well-known dictum, "The medium is the message," and Frits Staal's conclusion that Vedic ritual—indeed, all ritual—is meaningless, patterned activity to which meaning is only later ascribed (1993).[9] In Staal's words, when asked why they perform their rituals, brahmin participants answer as follows:

> [W]e do it because our ancestors did it; because we are eligible to do it; because it is good for society; because it is good; because it is our duty; because it is said to lead to immortality; because it leads to immortality. [Most frequently, however, the answer is that] we act according to the rules because this is our tradition. . . . The effective part of the answer seems to be: look and listen, these are our activities! To performing ritualists, rituals are like dance, of which Isadora Duncan said: "If I could tell you what it meant there would be no point in dancing it." (1993: 115–16)

This approach to seeing meaningful content as a function of rhetorical structure and form can be applied all throughout the study of popular culture, something with which our students are thoroughly acquainted. Moreover, if religion is conceptualized not as a *sui generis* phenomenon but as simply one instance of how systems of symbols and their attendant social worlds are made possible and reproduced, then one would anticipate that the very tools used to study religion would have application all throughout the study of culture. Take, for instance, Staal's approach to ritual as applied to the music of the contemporary alternative band Blues Traveler, a group whose work strikes me as a far more sophisticated form of cultural analysis than what many scholars of religion produce. For example, consider just the first two verses of their 1994 hit song "Hook":

> It doesn't matter what I say
> So long as I sing with inflection
> That makes you feel that I'll convey
> Some inner truth or vast reflection
> But I've said nothing so far
> And I can keep it up for as long as it takes
> And it don't matter who you are
> If I'm doing my job it's your resolve that breaks
>
> Because the hook brings you back
> I ain't tellin' you no lie
> The hook brings you back
> On that you can rely
>
> There is something amiss
> I am being insincere
> In fact I don't mean any of this
> Still my confession draws you near
> To confuse the issue I refer
> To familiar heroes from long ago
> No matter how much Peter loved her
> What made the Pan refuse to grow
>
> Was that the hook brings you back.[10]

What attracts me to this song is that it offers moral judgments coupled with explicit contradictions and outright lies, making its criticisms self-implicating and thoroughly ironic. Given the manner in which the chorus's admittedly catchy tune is overlapped with the glib lyrics concerning the shallowness of pop music hooks, it is both a critique of and the triumph of form over content. When studying this song in class it is apparent that students like it very much, but they do not know the words and they have no idea what it is about—as Staal tells us, *rituals are not about anything* (i.e., they have no meaning or content); if they are about anything at all, it is simply following the rules (form) properly. And this the song does admirably, for in following the rules of pop music (it was a hit after all), it draws attention to the usually invisible rules, critiques them thoroughly, and finally reinforces them. The utility of this example is that it creatively demonstrates to students that, by means of their theories, scholars of religion study active cultural process and not dead symbolic systems. Simply put, scholars of religion are relevant, not museum pieces.

To return to Grimes's reader, its essays are arranged alphabetically by author, and each opens with an extremely helpful abstract of the article accompanied by a brief biography of the author, a list of some of his or her other published works, as well as, in some cases, a brief quotation that personalizes the piece by outlining some of the author's more recent studies and general interests. (The quotation found at the outset of Richard Schechner's essay is well worth finding and reading.) Unlike Segal's volumes, Grimes's comes with a very useful appendix where each article's topics and themes are classified under such rubrics as *ritual action, ritual time, ritual space, ritual in dance, purification, passage, sacrifice, civil ceremonies, healing,* the various religious traditions from which an article's examples might be drawn and the various disciplines involved in that particular study of ritual. Using this appendix, instructors could profitably tailor their use of Grimes's volume either as a primary text or, more likely, as a secondary text that develops and applies approaches learned in other class work. This volume would work very nicely in any number of settings: alongside a world religions textbook in a comparative religion course, as a primary resource for an upper-level course on the study of rituals, or, as I have used it, along with Pals's *Seven Theories of Religion* (1996) to provide practical examples of the various types of theorizing in the history of the field. For, apart from Pals's opening chapter on the intellectualists (Tylor and Frazer), each of his subsequent chapters provides an introduction to a specific type of theorizing nicely represented (sometimes even critiqued) by several essays in Grimes's volume. In fact, the sheer variety of the essays in Grimes's reader, coupled with his very helpful introductory abstracts for each essay, made the book quite a hit in my course. Not only did students read a large portion of the volume as preparation for our class discussions, but they also used the essays we were not covering as the basis for their own writing and abstracting assignments. Although the volume's price ($38.75) may seem to some an impediment, the sheer variety of the essays, coupled with a creative, well-planned syllabus, allowed us to use most of the book. The students all felt that they got more than their money's worth.

Readings in Ritual Studies will likely be competing with such other well-known collections as *Reader in Comparative Religion* (Lessa and Vogt 1979) and even *Magic, Witchcraft, and Religion* (Lehmann and Myers 1993)—the latter being one place where Horace Miner's classic essay, "Body Rituals among the Nacirema" has been reprinted; the former is a reader not in comparative religion but in classical anthropology of religion. The obvious advantage of Grimes's volume over these is that it avoids a homogenous anthropological approach and does not get mired in dated pieces of scholarship. Instead, it presents the work of classical *and* contemporary anthropologists, along with the work of psychologists, feminists, political scientists, historians of religions, and classicists, to name only a few. Accordingly, the category of "ritual" comes across as a diverse, interdisciplinary tool used in as many ways as scholars have used the tool "myth."

Although not as explicitly built around theoretical articles as is Segal's *Theories of Myth*, *Readings in Ritual Studies* presents a large number of essays concerned with issues of theory, method, and definition; even those articles addressing more specific descriptive, ethnographic, or historical data are fine examples of certain approaches to the material. Much like Segal's series, then, Grimes's volume presents, in his own words from the introduction, "a theoretical . . . basis for interdisciplinary teaching and research" (xv). In a way, the self-conscious theoretical perspective of both these volumes can be contrasted with Cassell's new ten-volume series, *Themes in Religious Studies*. Each volume is approximately two hundred pages in length and presents essays, by different authors, on eight religious traditions (Buddhism, Christianity, Hinduism, Islam, Judaism, Sikhism, Chinese religions, and Japanese religions). Although the series includes edited volumes organized around such topics as worship, women in religion, attitudes to nature, sacred writings, and sacred places, the two volumes of interest for the present purposes are *Myth and History* and *Rites of Passage* (Holm and Bowker 1994a and 1994b). In the former volume, Douglas Davies's introduction provides a standard history of religions definition of myth: "stories which enshrine religious and social ideals expressed through the activities of divine, human or animal figures within an environment where astonishing things may take place" (1994a: 2). Just what makes an ideal religious as opposed to social is left largely unexplored—it is just this issue that a theoretically engaged resource should explore. In the volume on rites of passage, we find the equally traditional strategy of equating rituals simply with changes in social status and responsibility. Or, to put it another way, it is significant that the series features a volume on myth but no volume on ritual and, instead, limits the notion of religious practice either to worship or to rites of passage.

I have suggested that these two volumes seem to diverge from the theoretical advances seen in the Segal and Grimes volumes, for, as should be apparent, the Cassell series reflects the traditional "world religions" approach so familiar to our students. However, it is an approach that is a rather suspect (both theoretically *and* politically) way of dividing up the world and the curriculum (as argued by Fitzgerald 1990). However, in support of this series, the essays are explicitly aimed to develop descriptive and comparative skills, skills that are no less theoretically demanding than those of interpretation and explanation. In this way these volumes can actually replace the traditional, phenomenologically based world religions textbook and, through the diversity of the ten volumes, can provide professors with much greater flexibility in designing a thematic, comparative course in the study of religion. John Lyden's edited volume, *Enduring Issues in Religion* (1995),[11] also comes to mind as another such resource—Lyden collects primary source excerpts from writers representing eight different religions (including, among others, North American Sioux, Confucianism, and Taoism), all of which address such questions as "What Lies beyond Death?" Perhaps if used alongside such a book as William Paden's highly useful introduction to comparative religion, *Religious Worlds* (1994), these resources would challenge professors and students alike to explore the theoretical and methodological issues entailed in practicing nonevaluative description and comparison (on Lyden's and Paden's books, see also chapter 13). After all, the academic study of religion originated with the efforts of such scholars as F. Max Müller and C. P. Tiele to describe, compare, *and* explain the diversity of narratives, institutions, and practices (a topic to which the final chapter returns).

It is to the beginnings of our own field that we must now return, for even though we find ourselves at the centenary of Müller's death in 1900, scholars of religion are still acting as apologists for the study of religion in the public university—this very collection of essays is evidence of this. Many readers can easily recall a North American department with which they are familiar that has recently had to engage in such apologetics. Most recently, the case of the University of Pennsylvania comes to mind as one example where members of the field have successfully rallied to spare a religion department from the budget axe.[12] But in some of these cases such victories may very well be short lived, making it something akin to winning the battle when the war may soon be lost.

I say this because the manner in which some scholars continue to conceive of, and therefore defend, the field, as well as its central analytical tools (e.g., religion, myth, ritual, etc.), is highly suspect and desperately in need of critical attention. Although arguments concerning the field's institutional autonomy seem to have worked for the past three decades, these very claims may have, ironically, brought us to this current impasse. For in some modern defenses of the field we hear echoes of undefendable assertions relying on such troublesome notions as the sacred, *sui generis* religion, and the privacy of religious experiences. The fact that this field, like all other human sciences, is based on particular theories of human minds and communities and that these theories must continually be articulated clearly in order to be applied, critiqued, and defended, is all too often lost on scholars of *sui generis* religion fighting to retain not simply their data but, more important perhaps, their institutional, cultural, and even political turf.

If, as I happen to think is the case, the future health of the field will be linked to the ability of its practitioners to develop and defend theories as opposed to intuitions, then the work of cross-disciplinary cooperation will be essential to our survival within the academy. Because theories of religion are so often built upon theories of myth and ritual (a point identified nicely by Pals in his commentary on E. B. Tylor [1996: 24]), there may be no better place to start rethinking the theoretical foundations and future of the field than with books such as those of Segal and Grimes. With such resources as these in their hands, the next generation of students and scholars may find past assertions concerning the unique and autonomous nature of the study of religion, myths, rituals, and symbols not only to be antiquated but also to be terribly misguided. Who knows, they may even study the possible reasons why a previous generation of scholars troubled to dress up "religion," "myth," and "ritual" as self-evident, ahistorical categories. Only then will they begin to demystify the myth of religious uniqueness.

NOTES

1. My thanks to the members of the Department of Religious Studies at the University of Tennessee at Knoxville (notably Stan Lusby); between 1993 and 1996 they encouraged me to experiment with how to rethink the study of myths and rituals. This chapter receives considerable elaboration in my survey of the history of scholarship on myth (McCutcheon 2000).

2. This anecdote provides a good example of the unplanned, ad hoc nature of social interaction and change—a presumption central to much of my work. Prior to the summer of 1993, I had not thought all that much about theorizing rituals and, in particular, myths. As a result of Tennessee's needs, I taught the course every semester and in the summers for three years. I have made it a central course in my schedule since then, and, apart from this chapter, I have written other pieces on the topic as well.

3. *The HarperCollins Dictionary of Religion* (Smith 1995b) provides a useful introductory survey both to theories of myth (749–51; the historical, rationalist, functionalist, symbolic, and structuralist) and to theories of ritual (930–32; Rational and Expressive). On the *Dictionary*, see chapter 13.

4. I have had great success using the two-part film/video *Manufacturing Consent: Noam Chomsky and the Media* (Wintonick and Achbar 1993) in classes on myths and rituals, for there may be no better place than the media to

begin looking for the sociopolitical role played by shared narratives/practices in modern, technological society.

5. I have often used, to great effect, a teaching strategy suggested by Karl Popper in his *Conjectures and Refutations* (1962). He would request that the class perform a simple experiment: "Take pencil and paper; carefully observe, and write down what you have observed!" (46). Soon it becomes painfully obvious that without some clearly articulated set of criteria that assign relative importance to our many experiential events, no one knows precisely *what* to observe. Popper concludes: "Observation [or, for that matter, comparison, interpretation, and explanation] is always selective. It needs a chosen object, a definite task, an interest, a point of view, a problem." For scholars, such a frame of reference is provided by their theories.

6. Bierlein (1994) tries to combine the standard approach to myths (conceived of as "a pattern of beliefs that give meaning to life") with introductory surveys of modern theories of myth. Typically, however, the theory chapter comes at the book's close, as if myths are self-evidently there and only later do we develop theories of their meaning. That theories generate the very category "myth" in the first place is lost to the student who uses this book.

7. Apart from this new series, Garland also produces the *Theorists of Myth* series, now numbering near ten volumes and also edited by Robert Segal. Examples from the series include Robert Ackerman, *The Myth and Ritual School*; S. Daniel Breslauer, *Martin Buber on Myth*; Richard Golsan, *René Girard and Myth*; Segal's own volume on Joseph Campbell; and Christopher Flood, *Political Myth*.

8. Larrington's volume is intriguing precisely because its many contributors do not romanticize mythology. Instead, they confront the political and imperial purposes mythology serves in a number of geographic, historical settings, going so far as to identify the mechanisms whereby contemporary feminist scholarship often produces its own mythologies. For example, "work on the 'Goddess' . . . frequently blurs important differences, generalizing, often inaccurately, about the goddess of different cultures, in order to assimilate them to a single supreme figure, often Eurocentrically conceived" (Larrington: x).

9. The following example derives from "Theorizing at the Margin: Religion as Something Ordinary" (McCutcheon forthcoming).

10. Words and music by John Hopper, from Blues Traveler's CD, *Four* (1994).

11. As part of their *Opposing Viewpoints* series, Greenhaven Press also produces a collection of primary source materials entitled *Science and Religion*, which, among other topics, reproduces portions of the debate between Galileo and the Roman Curia, as well as the debate over whether evolution should be taught in U.S. public schools (involving Clarence Darrow and William Jennings Bryan).

12. For those interested in the recent institutional health of the study of religion, consult the 1995 special issue of *Method and Theory in the Study of Religion* (guest edited by Gary Lease) for six case studies (three from Canada, three from the United States).

CHAPTER 13

Theorizing in the Introductory Course: A Survey of Resources

Knowledge of any set of phenomena, whether natural or cultural, comes about not primarily from the application and development of taxonomies, but from explanatory theorizing.
—Jonathan Z. Smith (1995b: 1102)

THE INTRODUCTORY COURSE AS PRIMER IN CRITICAL THINKING

As is evident from the preceding chapters, I attempt to engage students in theory at every step of the way; this has always been challenging, often rewarding, sometimes very frustrating—for both the students and myself! In earlier chapters, I reflected on the ways in which religious pluralist discourses, the traditional myth and ritual course, as well as religion and film classes can become effective sites for engaging in self-conscious theoretical and methodological scholarship. In this final chapter I would like to take time to draw attention to some of the resources that I have found to be of use in teaching the introductory course in the study of religion. Specifically, I have in mind the kinds of undergraduate courses that often complement our courses in world religions—those courses that introduce the study of religion in a more thematic manner. This alternative course holds great promise not only as a general introduction to the study of religion but also as a primer in theoretical critique. Such a course would be one site where we can achieve much, if indeed we understand our role not simply as helping students to understand and appreciate so-called extraordinary and ordinary religions but instead as providing our students with critical thinking, debating, and writing skills upon which they will draw long after they have left our classes. The study of religion, then, becomes a convenient opportunity (but by no means the only opportunity) to challenge students to articulate and defend publicly their implicit theories about human minds, behaviors, and institutions.

217

I use a four-part model for such an introductory course that includes units on *defining, describing, comparing,* and, finally, *redescribing* religion. I settled on just these four because each of these methods of analysis presupposes not only a number of theoretical issues deserving discussion in all of our classes but also specific methodological tools with which students should be competent. Such a typology also lends itself particularly nicely to the classroom, for together they comprise a grouping that develops in order of increasing theoretical scope and sophistication. Moreover, the interrelated, almost circular, nature of these four seemingly distinct operations provides an opportunity for instructors to discuss the intellectual contexts of scholarship. For by the time students have developed skills to discuss some of the merits of theories of religion, they are also able to discern the way in which definitions themselves presuppose theories, making definitions virtually theories in miniature.

Despite the fact that this typology bears some resemblance to the way in which the late Walter Capps divided and understood the field in his book, *Religious Studies: The Making of a Discipline,* there are some significant differences. Capps portrays the field as comprised of an overall intellectual and methodological paradigm containing six "large, controlling questions," each of which can be traced to the Enlightenment distinction between revealed and natural religion. These controlling questions revolve around discerning the essence, origin, description, function, language, and comparison of religion. Accordingly, his main chapters are organized around the contributions of assorted scholars to each of these six topics, the development of each being portrayed primarily as an unfolding, almost Hegelian, narrative or intellectual adventure. Differing from Capps,[1] the framework proposed here does not attempt to identify different intellectual currents or developments in the history of the field; instead, it aims to discern the fundamental theoretical and methodological operations that are implicitly and simultaneously at work in all research on human beliefs, behavior, and institutions. Rather than seeing these as large, controlling questions or paradigms, definition, description, comparison, and redescriptive analysis are four interrelated tasks that together comprise the ongoing work of the scholar of religion.

Although we must of course recognize the practical limitations to such a framework for the introductory course, whether taught over a single semester or during a full year, we can still go a long way toward providing our students with a useful introduction to the theoretical issues involved in the study of human practices, as opposed to providing them simply with the kind of "show-and-tell" phenomenological survey that presently dominates our introductory curricula.

DEFINING RELIGION:
IS IT PIOUS BECAUSE THE GODS APPROVE IT?

In his efforts to define piety for the ever-inquisitive Socrates, Euthyphro offers the following definition: piety is that which all the gods love. Predictably, Socrates poses a question in reply: is something pious because the gods love it, or do they love it because it is pious? Far from being a "chicken or egg" question, Socrates' query nicely sums up what might be considered *the* issue at the heart of the academic study of religion: is our object of analysis a preexistent essence we simply recognize, or is it instead the product of social practices and institutions? If we see in the ancient Greek *eusebia* something at least in part akin to what we mean by 'religion' when defined as a social mechanism—even though it may in fact be more similar to the Sanskrit notion of *dharma*—we have here the issue most in need of discussion in any introductory class in our field: when studying religion—or anything, for that matter—in the public university, are we engaged in intuiting transhistorical nonempirical essences, feelings, experiences, and so on, or are we studying certain intellectual, historical, social, political, and economic—in a word, human—practices and their public, observable effects?

We can rephrase Socrates' question as follows: is it the task of the observer to *reconstruct* the actual event, complete with its actual meaning for the actors, or to *construct* an event based on the observer's own theoretical interest and point of view? Do we argue for an objective, realist position, or must we adopt the kind of reflexive stance so characteristic of some recent trends in postmodern and feminist anthropology? Although it is perhaps more than apparent which of these options Plato himself preferred, it is not entirely obvious for students what the correct option is for the contemporary scholar of religion. That this debate will hardly be solved in the introductory class is more than obvious, for it is far from being solved in the field at large; however, demonstrating to students that there is something at stake in the way in which we go about defining and classifying objects in the world is an important start. It provokes them to reflection and provides them with intellectual tools they will take to a number of other classes and activities.

Starting with Socrates' question to Euthyphro, then, the effort to define religion can be divided into the two major categories: essentialist and constructionist. The first section of John Lyden's anthology, *Enduring Issues in Religion* (1995), provides seven excerpts that attempt to define religion in one of these two ways. With this two-fold typology as their guide to reading these selections, students can work through the arguments of Schleiermacher (from *The Christian Faith*), Otto (the opening chapters from *The Idea of the Holy*), Tillich (from his *System-*

atic Theology), Barth (from *Church Dogmatics*), Marx and Engels (from *On Religion*), Freud (from *New Introductory Lectures in Psycho-Analysis*), and Sartre (from *Existentialism and Human Emotions*). Although the excerpt from Barth provides a unique case study, the others easily fall into one of Socrates' two categories: Schleiermacher, Otto, and Tillich all make self-evident assertions regarding religion's private, experiential nature, while Marx and Engels, Freud, and Sartre find religion to be the effect of specific human (mis-)practices. Although many students will no doubt find some of the arguments rather difficult to work through, in large part because of the inevitably brief and abstracted nature of the excerpts, the fact that they have such a concise selection of definitions juxtaposed to one another (from Schleiermacher's "feeling of absolute dependence" to Marx and Engels's "sigh of the oppressed creature") makes Lyden's book highly useful in the classroom.

Similar to Lyden's selection of definitions is Andrew Greeley's (1995) edited collection of readings in the sociology of religion. Where Lyden's book is specifically geared to a comparative religions class (a feature to be addressed below), Greeley's collection is focused on sociological analysis, in large part concerned with the American scene (as in its essays on civil religion, African American religions, Judaism, Catholicism, Protestantism, and Fundamentalism in America), and contains a number of quantitative studies (some of which are Greeley's own work). Like Lyden, the opening section of Greeley's book is devoted to canvasing a series of formative attempts to define religion. However, unlike Lyden, the attempts of religious devotees do not figure prominently at all; instead, the sociological approach dominates with three selections from Marx (including his *Theses on Feuerbach*), and one each from Freud (from *Moses and Monotheism*), Durkheim (from *The Elementary Forms of Religious Life*), Malinowski (from *Magic, Science, and Religion*), Weber (from *The Protestant Ethic and the Spirit of Capitalism*), Parsons (from *Essays in Sociological Theory*), Geertz ("Religion as a Cultural System"), and Otto (from *The Idea of the Holy*).

Unlike Lyden, Greeley is explicit about his own perspective: religion, he notes in his preface, starts with "hope-renewal experiences" that are "coded in narrative systems that purport to explain the meaning of life and provide templates for living" (1995: ix). These experiences, he maintains, are shared among and shaped within a community, which thereby provides its members with readymade symbols and interpretations of the world at large, symbols and meanings that are dramatized in ritual performances. Indeed, the very effort to trace this explicitly articulated theory of religion throughout the volume, determining how it is related to the book's various selections (e.g., does it account for an entire section devoted to Eliade and entitled "The Lure of the Sacred"?), would be a worthwhile end of term class assignment.

To the best of my knowledge, there does not exist a class resource that collects and reproduces those essays that one would consider central to the effort to the task of defining religion. Although most every class text has an introductory section on the difficulties of defining religion, there seems to be an absence of resources that collect the many scholarly analyses on just what is involved with the effort to define religion. Although it is important to study attempts to define religion (and both Lyden's and Greeley's selections provide interesting examples), students also need to be made aware of the assorted meta-issues involved in the definitional exercise itself, such as the various types of definitions (e.g., substantive, functional, etc.) and what is at stake in category formation. Until such a time, however, professors will continue to construct their own in-class readers.

DESCRIBING RELIGION:
EAST IS EAST AND WEST IS WEST?

After coming to some decision as to just what religion is, is not, or at least what is involved in even making this decision, instructors will need to apply these various theoretical issues to the study of "the real world." Presuming that the definitional issue is settled and that 'religion' continues to be a useful heuristic for studying a certain aspect of human practices and institutions, there are any number of resources that phenomenologically describe the major and minor aspects of religious traditions. Although such resources are extremely problematic when used on their own, when used as part of a wider approach they can be useful tools.

Representative of a large number of textbooks is the recent two volume work from Oxford University Press, *World Religions* (edited by Willard Oxtoby 1996a and 1996b). Divided in terms of the rather suspect categories "East" and "West," the volumes cover what Oxtoby terms "traditional religions": Hinduism and Jainism (Vasudha Narayanan), Buddhism (Roy Amore and Julia Ching), East Asian religion (Julia Ching), Sikhism and Primal Religions (Oxtoby), and Judaism (Alan Segal), Christianity and Zoroastrianism (Oxtoby), and Islam (Mahmoud Ayoub). In addition, Oxtoby provides several essays on such topics as religious contact and dialogue, religious revivals (such as new age religions) and an essay entitled "The Nature of Religion." Clearly the two volumes are meant to be purchased together, for these additional thematic essays are not reprinted in each of the volumes (e.g., the essay on the nature of religion is discussed in the Eastern volume). However, given the wealth of material covered (each volume is over 550 pages), it is questionable whether many semester courses could justify using both volumes.

Like the contributors to *Our Religions* (Sharma 1993), *World Religions'* "authors speak in some sense for their identities" and attempt to "walk the tightrope of disciplined empathy without falling into the abyss—of advocacy on the one side, and of debunking on the other" (1996a: 4–5). What is most intriguing about this is that any attempt to redescribe religion in terms of nonreligious categories is understood as debunking or an abyss into which one might slip—not a good thing at all. Oxtoby notes that "among scholars of religion [there] are quite a few who have become profoundly alienated from the faith communities in which they were raised" (1996a: 4). The student is told, then, that to study religion nonreligiously entails alienation and an interest in debunking, both of which constitute a dark and deep abyss into which students of religion might slip if they are not careful. The norm that is presented to them is, therefore, the sympathetic religious insider, while the abnormal position is occupied by the alienated, nonreligious outsider. Such characterizations are reminiscent of Mary Pat Fisher's criticism of Marx and Freud as being cynical toward religion, an attitude that today, in her opinion, is giving way to a search for spirituality (1994: 11).

Although no critique should place too much on an author's choice of words, I cannot help but find Oxtoby's thoughts on the so-called abyss into which nonreligious studies of religion fall to be in need of comment. In his chapter on the nature of religion, Oxtoby tells us more: "Lurking in many efforts to define religion is an implicit attempt to explain it" (1996a: 493). That all definitions are by their very nature entrenched in a particular theory (whether an implicit or explicit theory) is well worth pointing out to students, for a definition is simply one's theory in brief. But this is not what Oxtoby suggests. Instead, he suggests that explanations of religion's origins and function lurk in many, but of course not all, definitions. This presumes that good definitions avoid explanation. What is a good definition, one free of lurking theories? Apparently, Oxtoby's own:

> Religion is a sense of power beyond the human, apprehended rationally as well as emotionally, appreciated corporately as well as individually, celebrated ritually and symbolically as well as discursively, transmitted as a tradition in conventionalized forms and formulations that offers people an interpretation of experience, a guide to conduct, and an organization to meaning and purpose in the world. (1996a: 493)

We see here the troubling heritage of van der Leeuw, Otto, Cantwell Smith, and Eliade: a primary emphasis on senses, feelings, and emotions manifested in actions and institutions. Oxtoby's clear debt to the phenomenological tradition is evident, right down to this effort to construct a definition that is actually a description that empathetically communicates what the religious devotees consider religion to be, not what scholars consider it to be. In fact, his emic descriptions are perhaps more problematic than the term he is attempting to describe; after all, just what is a "sense of power," and how is it an advance on Otto's analytically vacuous "sense of a tremendous mystery"? Moreover, to ask what might be a silly question, is his use of the term *power* in line with van der Leeuw's or Foucault's understanding of it? And, let alone studying it, just how does one "apprehend rationally and emotionally" something that is supposedly "beyond the human"? If anything, allowing such vagaries to pass as scholarship is, in my opinion, to risk slipping into the abyss of ambiguity.

Given the resounding critiques of the universalist tendencies of such grand categories as "world religions," as well as the manner in which an exclusive reliance upon matters of personal "belief" determine the boundaries of "West" and "East," it is somewhat surprising that such volumes as this continue to be used. Regarding the West/East dichotomy, Oxtoby finds this particular way of dividing up the world to be useful: whereas "we can speak in a fairly coherent fashion about the West and its role in the world," the East "is a hugely diverse region" (1996a: 6)—here we find the old colonialist associations between identity/order/unity (all of which are implicitly aligned with the rationally ordered West) and difference/disorder/diversity (all of which are aligned with the mysterious East). After noting that we "could even go so far as to suggest that 'the East' is a Western construct, existing as a coherent entity only in the mind of the West," Oxtoby makes it clear that admitting as much is to go *too* far, for he immediately goes on to maintain that because what we today call "Hinduism" influenced what we call "Buddhism," which in turn influenced Confucianism and Taoism, let alone Shinto in Japan, we can organize these three into the category "East." That each of these so-called coherent and distinguishable religions is the product of European scholarly cataloguing, that the region and history of the world organized by the category "West" is just as complex and incoherent, and that this type of homogenizing clearly overlooks (ignores?) material criteria such as economics (who owes what to whom?) and politics would all suggest that the traditional West/East division has little use for contemporary scholars. If one were to take economic, industrial, and political factors into account, rather than simply issues of belief and doctrine, then many have suggested that a North/South division would make much more sense.

It is most intriguing that in arguing that West/East differences are finally resolved, melted, and subsumed into the one "human common denominator," which is, after all, "human experience" (yet another category that effectively eliminates all class, gender, and race differences), Oxtoby quotes Rudyard Kipling's 1892 "The Ballad of East and West":

> Oh, East is East, and West is West
> and never the twain shall meet
> Till Earth and Sky stand presently
> at God's great Judgment Seat.
> But there is neither East nor West,
> border, nor breed, nor birth
> When two strong men stand face to face,
> tho' they come from the ends of the earth!
> (1996a: 8)

The utter irony of a contemporary world religion textbook appreciatively citing a writer whose works are so intimately connected to the history and justification of the British attempt to control, dominate, and own huge expanses of the globe is, for the critic, too good to be true. For Kipling was, in the estimation of Edward Said, one of the most imperialistic and reactionary writers of his era (1993: xxi). Finding Kipling here of all places is yet more evidence that liberal scholarship continually fails to recognize the manner in which its grand, teleological narratives of social unity and political homogeneity are far from free-floating, apolitical statements and neutral observations.

To presume that what Kipling was talking about—as well as what we as scholars of religion are studying—is the "universal appeal to human experience" that somehow unites slave and owner, imperial powers and subordinated populations, and women and men (after all, Kipling is talking about "two strong men") all at "God's great Judgment Seat" (a rather effective universal signifier, no?) is to entertain and entrench what can only be termed an ideological fantasy. Such casual talk of universal human experience, wiping out differences in "border, breed, and birth," is sufficient evidence that feminist, critical, and cultural theorists have had little or no influence among some of our colleagues. I cannot state this forcefully enough: *one of the great perils of our field is that we continue to ignore the fact that we exist in large part due to the needs of the nineteenth century's imperial nations for powerful controlling and cataloguing mechanisms and categories for addressing and dominating the inhabitants of distant lands.*[2] Therefore, that a quotation from Kipling turns up in a world religions textbook is hardly surprising—as psychotherapists can tell us, latent tendencies sometimes drift to the surface in the most surprising places; it provides evidence of "an astonishingly durable imperial worldview" (Said 1993: xx) or what Said terms the "imperial dynamic."

A very different resource for describing the data of religion can be found in Gary Comstock's *Religious Autobiographies* (1995), which contains chapters that each present two autobiographical studies of people in seven different religious traditions, including Lakota Sioux, Honduran Catholics, and African American Protestants. Where the "world religions" textbook emphasizes (and constructs) universal sameness in both history and geography (as if it makes sense to talk about one transcendent thing named Christianity, let alone human experience), Comstock's book emphasizes context, particularity, and individuality. As he notes in his preface: "No religion is monolithic, and no single Catholic story can possibly represent all Catholics's stories" (xi). When used as an end in itself, such anecdotal and autobiographical reporting is just as problematic as the traditional world religion textbook, for it simply amounts to show and tell; however, when used as the basis for higher-level redescription, contextualization, comparison, and finally explanation, Comstock's volume is highly useful. The message is that the utility of such a volume is to be found in the way in which an instructor uses it; in and of itself such a volume is useful only in a certain clearly articulated theoretical framework.

By making the kinds of critiques that I have made on these descriptive works, I do not mean to imply that we need not describe the data of religion. All I wish to suggest is that when, as J. Z. Smith has already noted, show and tell is understood as the primary goal of our study, such scholarship is severely lacking, for it presumes that our data preexists our methods and theories, making it self-evidently meaningful and accessible only through careful inductive research. However, when we acknowledge that the descriptive exercise is but one component of our overall study and that description is intimately tied to our prior definitions of religion, let alone our eventual efforts to compare and redescribe it, then our scholarship and teaching will become more sophisticated and defensible.

COMPARING RELIGION:
TO COMPARE OR NOT TO COMPARE . . .

Like description, students must realize that comparison is based on classificatory categories of the scholar's own making. To arrange and understand our data in terms of such widely used phenomenological categories as myth, ritual, festival, symbol, Scripture, totem, and so on, often entails failing to recognize that the data does not conveniently arrange itself in this manner, that it does not arrive on the scene already neatly packaged as myth or ritual.[3] I am far from the only one to have gained this basic insight from J. Z. Smith. In the hands of those who have yet to recognize this, however, comparison quickly eliminates all issues of context, replacing it instead with the search for intuited essences.

The popular use of the comparative method to accomplish the essentialist goal of overcoming religious diversity is the primary aim of Dale Cannon's *Six Ways of Being Religious* (1996). Unlike William Paden's two highly successful ventures in drawing the student's attention to the theoretical, nonreligious nature of comparative work (1992, 1994), Cannon's book is explicitly aimed at studying religions "from within." In other words, for Cannon the problem is not the fact of religious beliefs and practices but the fact of religious *diversity*. Cannon is unapologetic about this purely religious pluralist goal: as he states in his preface, the book "is written to improve the climate of inter-religious relationships, of how in practice we understand and relate to one another in the religiously plural world we now live within." As if this were not clear enough, he immediately adds: "That is why the academic study of religion, as understood and practiced here, shades imperceptibly into inter-religious dialogue" (Cannon 1996: 12).

Unfortunately, Cannon's comparative work, which is based on examining, in detail, Christianity and Buddhism in terms of six phenomenological categories (sacred rite, right action, devotion, shamanic meditation, mystical quest, and reasoned inquiry) adds little to the already long list of phenomenologically based resources intent on reducing religious plurality to religious unity. As part of this tradition, his book does not address what sense it even makes to talk of religion in the first place, for his categories already presume it sensible to talk about such things as sacred rites, devotion, mystical quests, and ultimate reality. That these very categories presuppose the existence and sense of religion makes it hardly surprising that in Cannon's comparative scheme both Buddhism and Christianity turn out to have remarkable similarities.

Take, for example, his use of the common parable of the blindmen and the elephant. Although I have identified elsewhere the problem of using this story as an illustration of the task of the scholar of religion, it is worthwhile repeating it here, this time using Cannon's text as the example.[4] After asking "What is the elephant of human religiousness anyway? Is there a way of comprehending unity in all of the diversity," Cannon proceeds to tell the story of the six blindmen in surprising detail (thereby anticipating his own six ways of being religious). Unwilling to entertain the validity of the knowledge possessed by the others, the moral of his tale is that each of the blindmen lacks "an awareness of the limits of his own quite genuine acquaintance." Put another way,

> what each man lacked was a sense of the transcendence of the elephant beyond his own limited acquaintance, hence his need (in order to know the elephant in the round) to explore empathetically the other men's knowledge of the elephant. What initially seemed to contradict each man's knowledge and understanding would thereby turn out to complement his own limited perspective. (1996: 7)

The many problems associated with Cannon's work all come to light in this one passage. Failing to acknowledge the role played by theories, as well as pretheoretical commitments, in generating our data, a role that permanently marks scholars of religion as the blindmen groping by means of hypothesis and empirical testing, Cannon's viewpoint slides all too easily from the perspective-bound blindmen to the omniscient narrator—a move not available to the scholar of religion but one that is more than open to the religious pluralist who, by faith, posits an nonempirical unity that transcends the empirical diversity.

What I mean is that the narrator's, or Cannon's, point of view, one that "know[s] the elephant in the round," is precisely the viewpoint that we as scholars of religion *do not have* but one that our subjects *claim to have*—specifically, religious pluralists make this claim, making them no less data for the scholar of religion than other people making grand universalist claims. Fully recognizing the contextual nature of all claims to knowledge, while also acknowledging the unsupported nature of claims concerning the big picture, the scholar of religion engages in studying those who fail to set these limits on their knowledge claims. We are, then, the blindmen studying people such as Cannon, who claim their perspective to be all-encompassing and fully adequate. By arguing that religion is the same case as the elephant, Cannon betrays his own unarticulated faith claims concerning the big picture, claims that he needs to argue for rather than simply presume. But since these claims involve knowledge of religion, or reality, "in the round," a knowledge that more than likely surpasses Cannon's perspective, it seems unlikely that he will be very successful in persuading readers who do not already hold this same unarticulated assumption. The story of the blindmen and the elephant, then, is a story for religious pluralists and *not* comparative religionists.

That we as scholars routinely use theoretically based frameworks as the basis of comparison is not a problem, for this is what comparative work entails. That scholars such as Cannon fail to make explicit and defend such frameworks, however, *is* a problem, for then they are making the same error as the people we as scholars of religion study: they are presuming that their maps of reality have a one-to-one correspondence with reality itself. Scholarship requires us to recognize and then analyze the theoretical and therefore tentative and playful nature of all maps and grids, as opposed to simply reporting them as intrinsically meaningful and preexistent.

Accordingly, for comparative approaches to continue, we must develop a way of engaging in the work of classification and comparison that differs from previous efforts so as to avoid the pitfalls of what can variously be labeled as "Eliadean," "modernist," or simply "religious pluralist" studies of religion. In the spring of 1994, the North American Association for the Study of Religion (NAASR) sponsored a panel at the Midwest regional meeting of the American Academy of Religion (AAR) on this very topic (it was later published under the title "The Post-Eliadean Study of Religion: The New Comparativism").[5] Using the work of William Paden as the starting point, the panelists (Marsha Hewitt, E. Thomas Lawson, and Donald Wiebe) explored Paden's attempt to answer a question of direct relevance to all members of the field: "How, after Eliade, and after the critique of the contextless character of classical comparativism, is it possible to recast the viability of cross-cultural analysis?"

Of the three responses to Paden's paper, by far the most relevant for our purposes is Lawson's. His point was a simple but profound one. In the words of the panel organizer, Luther Martin, Lawson observed that

> the act of comparing is a fundamental cognitive property of all human beings and, as such, can be neither old nor new. The issue, in Lawson's view, is not *whether* to compare but *how well* we compare. Lawson is concerned, in other words, to address directly the theoretical framework within which comparison proceeds. (Martin 1996: 1)

Contrary to Marsha Hewitt's fear that comparative work jeopardizes the integrity of others by subsuming difference within identity (which is understood as an act of intellectual and even political imperialism), Lawson reminds us that comparison is not just a *fundamental* but an *inevitable* human operation. As I sit writing this sentence I am constantly classifying, distinguishing, sorting, comparing, and valuing innumerable sensory stimuli; only some of those stimuli rise to the level of conscious thought, and of those many are ignored. What makes scholarly comparison different from the cognitive processes that continually inhabit our minds is the former's self-reflectiveness; scholarly comparison is based on clearly articulated theories and sets of value judgments that have more to do with the interests of the researcher than with some inherent property in the data. In other words, on what grounds am I classifying, comparing, and then ignoring or valuing certain stimuli in my feet, hands, itches on my cheek, or noises outside my window while writing this sentence? The scholar's role is to make explicit and then defend the criteria by which she decides to ignore this or that aspect of a datum in an effort to compare some other aspect.

Accordingly, the art of comparison cannot jeopardize the "integrity of the other," for it is the very art whereby we as scholars actually construct the others of our research, a construction based on our own theoretical interests and questions. Coherent others are not simply out there for the taking; one must first define, classify, and distinguish before one can compare a *this* and a *that*—all these operations must occur before one can even speak of an other. It may be because we do this sorting and comparing so naturally that we continually presume that such things as myths, rituals, and scriptures—not to mention genders or religions—are simply out there, requiring us only to find them using induction and then simply describe and interpret them using the tools of phenomenology and hermeneutics.

It turns out, then, that Hewitt's fears that comparative work subsumes difference into identity may be misplaced. Comparative-based scholarship is the active art of concocting identities and others in the process of addressing some clearly delineated interest, question, or concern. For example, if my particular interest is in the geographic and demographic growth/movement of a particular social formation, then my comparison will in part revolve around a category such as "recruitment"—a category of my making and not an inherent dimension of the data. Many other ways in which my data can be classified and compared will, therefore, gladly fall by the wayside. Unable to describe, compare, or redescribe "the whole," we are left not with *discerning* the meaningful parts but with *constructing* the parts we have an interest in addressing, knowing full well that our sheer interests must be systematically arranged in terms of a coherent theory in need of testing. Where such defensible theoretical concerns are not made explicit, where the researcher simply confronts, describes, and catalogues seemingly preexistent and self-evidently meaningful data, there is no scholarship.

Acknowledging this "new ethos which eschews classification, comparison, and explanation," Smith has recently quoted Kimberley Patton of the Harvard Divinity School as warning, "Thou shalt compare neither religious traditions, nor elements of religious traditions, lest thou totalize, essentialize, or commit hegemonic discourse." His reply is succinct and worth noting: "to which I might add, "Nor shalt thou consider thyself a member of the academy" (Smith 1996a: 26).

The moral of this story? As teachers we do not introduce our students to the study of self-evidences or inherently coherent others.

Instead, we assist them to develop defensible theories of human minds, practices, and societies and, by means of these theories, to define, describe, classify, compare, and redescribe human beliefs, behavior, and institutions. The dangers of totalizing, essentialist, and hegemonic discourses attend efforts to intuit reality rather than to theorize about it.

DESCRIBING AND COMPARING IN THE CLASSROOM

But how does one get an undergraduate student to think about these complex issues? Must we continue to describe and compare religions as if they are self-evidently real phenomena, as virtually every comparative religion textbook does? Some would say that only in a graduate course does one have the luxury of returning to these theoretical concerns, prompting students to think back to the inadequacies of the resources they used at the start of their university education. Although this may be a useful approach, I tend to think that we can begin this kind of meta-theoretical work in the introductory class.

After addressing issues concerning definition and description, my students then use a resource that provides descriptive data from a number of religions as the basis for small group work in comparison. I have found that the last three chapters in *Enduring Issues in Religion* (Lyden 1995) provide students with ample descriptive information that can be used as the basis for very fruitful comparative exercises. Reading the excerpts that Lyden arranges from writers representing eight different religions, all of which address a question Lyden himself imposes (such as, What happens after death?), group members are each challenged first to be able to describe accurately what the informant writes. Each group member then becomes the expert in one particular viewpoint. As each group member reports on and redescribes his particular excerpt, implicit comparison is already taking place in the minds of all members of the group; as experts in another viewpoint, they already have a basis for comparing the viewpoint represented to the group by its other members. My challenge to them is to come up with a set number of creative and informative categories or questions that can help them to classify and then compare the information presented to the group.

For instance, when comparing a number of religions, groups come up with such comparative categories as "founder," "geographic location," "deities," and "year of origin." They soon realize that not all their categories/questions fit all their data, that many of their categories are deeply embedded within one particular religion and therefore are of little use in comparison across religions (e.g., "prophets," "prayer," or "savior"), and that their categories/questions reflect their own interests,

interests that they bring with them to the data, as opposed to teasing them out of their data. The results of their conversations must then take the form of a chart (viewpoints/religions on the vertical axis, comparative categories/questions on the horizontal axis,) that allows them to stand back from their comparison and draw some kind of general conclusion (e.g., All religions . . .).

Although the comparative chart that each group produces, along with their conclusion, is graded, the primary goal of the assignment is for students to interact and experience the responsibility, frustration, and creativity of scholarly analysis. They come to understand their analysis as being driven by their own concerns and interests rather than some preexistent essence in their data. In fact, they sometimes realize that their data *is* data only in light of just this or that question and interest. They come to understand the conflict between those who portray the field as inductively based (the late Ugo Bianchi's support for inductive work is but one useful example) and those who acknowledge the deductive, theory-based aspect to our work as scholars.

Most recently, after constructing and then studying their comparative chart, one group concluded that monotheistic religions also tend to be missionizing religions. How did they arrive at this intriguing conclusion? In part, I believe it was because in their chart the columns for monotheism and missionary happened to be directly beside each other, thereby no doubt drawing their attention to the similar distribution of yes and no answers for each of the five religions they examined in light of these two categories. As their teacher, my interest is not to debate their findings; instead, my aim is to prompt them to make these little discoveries on their own. They, not I, came up with the questions concerning the worship of one or more deities and on their own they came up with the category of missionary activity. Once applied to the religions they studied, they drew their own conclusion, a conclusion that none had previously entertained. Whether they were right or not, the point is that they made this discovery on their own and have experienced firsthand the creativity and sometimes blind luck of scholarship. Or, as J. Z. Smith so appropriately phrases it, "classification, by bringing disparate phenomena together in the space of the scholar's intellect, often produces surprise, the condition which calls forth efforts of explanation" (1996a: 26).

REDESCRIBING RELIGION:
ANSWERING THE "SO WHAT?" QUESTION

All too often it is simply presumed that because religion is a special case, it can only be interpreted and appreciated, thereby disallowing any attempt to determine the "so what?" of the material we study. I recall a class presentation where a student once read out loud to the class, and in great detail, information about Amish life, going so far as to inform his peers about the foods traditionally served at Amish weddings. At no point did it dawn on the student to provide a context so as to persuade his listeners as to *why* it was important for them to know that, for instance, jam and bread often find their way into the wedding feast. Simply put, he hadn't answered the so what question. As I noted above, after students decide on their comparative categories and construct their charts, they are challenged to analyze them, to answer the so what? question. For if the means by which we classify and compare our data are not self-evident, then what our work signifies is not self-evident either. Accordingly, definition, description, and comparison are all directed toward redescriptive analysis. Simply put, so what if there seems to be a correlation between the number of gods a group worships and their likelihood of missionizing? Can you explain this intriguing correlation? What new information has now come to our attention?

For teachers who are willing to venture into the admittedly difficult terrain of explanatory theories of religion, there is one classroom resource that they must all own: Daniel Pals's *Seven Theories of Religion* (1996). Although Paden's *Interpreting the Sacred* (1992) has several chapters of relevance for teaching issues surrounding explaining religion (for example, his chapters on religion and society or religion and the psyche), its overall intention is to situate both interpretation (religious and nonreligious) and causal explanation within larger contexts or perspectives. This goal makes *Interpreting the Sacred* useful in applying issues derived from studying the insider/outsider problem to the realm of interpretation and explanation, but it covers explanatory theorizing only as one among a variety of options—or interpretive lenses—in the field. Although Paden does address the more traditional relations between meaning/interpretation and cause/explanation in his opening chapter, the way in which the book is structured suggests that, ultimately, religious and nonreligious studies of religion are both perspectives open to the student. In other words, the volume is significantly *not* titled *Explaining the Sacred*.

Pals's book is, to my knowledge, the only resource currently available that provides a thoroughly accessible and systematic introduction to the classical efforts to explain religion in terms of causal factors. Starting with the intellectualists of the nineteenth century (e.g., Frazer and Tylor), Pals moves the student through the work of Marx, Durkheim, Freud, and eventually to Evans-Pritchard and Clifford Geertz. Although it is debatable to what extent the last two deserve such a prominent place in a volume explicitly concerned with reductionistic theories of religion's origins, Pals's chapters on the first four are helpful, fairly written, and easily accessible to the undergraduate student. Each chapter moves readers from the biography of the writer in question, to an overview of his work, and then to a specific description of the implications for the study of religion. Each chapter ends with an extremely useful summary of the theory of religion generated by the writer, as well as several fair criticisms of the theory.

Although this text may not be all that useful for those in the field who are familiar with the theorists it covers, for those of us who teach introductory courses in the study of religion, Pals has provided an extremely helpful resource. Armed with the information gained from the definitional, descriptive, and comparative aspects of the course, students come to *Seven Theories of Religion* with a wealth of data in need of analysis. Each chapter allows them to "try on" a theory and see how it fits. In fact, because the format of each chapter is the same, the book makes metacomparative analysis of theories a relatively easy exercise. Students come to see that an economic perspective enables them to ask certain questions that a psychological one precludes and that a psychological perspective is of little use when it comes to larger issues of social formation and change. They come to understand that, once again, their own particular interests and questions will determine which theory they decide to use. Theories, then, are finally understood to be tools that inform methods of analysis, tools that are represented in our very definitions, all of which are driven by questions that curious people bring to their experience and study of human beliefs, behaviors, and institutions.

USING DICTIONARIES OF RELIGION

We have come full circle, from definitions to the methods of description and comparison (which implicitly involves classification), and finally to theories, which are, after all, the intellectual contexts from which definitions and methods arise. The introductory course in the study of religion implicitly touches on all four of these fundamental and interrelated aspects of the field. Because these are operations on which our courses already rely, with a little effort these same courses can become an effective site where methods, theories, and critical thinking skills can be introduced to our students. The preceding has simply been one attempt to survey the resources that can contribute to making such a course.

In an effort to experiment further with this four-part course, on several occasions I have taught the introductory course based exclusively on *The HarperCollins Dictionary of Religion* (Smith 1995b)[6] Using this as a resource might strike the reader as odd, but anyone who has looked at this book in any detail will realize that it might be singularly suited to the introductory classroom. Even the apparently high cost ($45. U.S.) is less than the expense of many textbooks. The advantage of the dictionary is that it provides not only a wealth of interesting reference information but, given the extended entries on "the religions," it easily replaces world religion textbooks. Take the case of Hinduism, for example. Beginning with an entry on Hindu domestic ritual, it moves to entries of varying length on Hindu texts and interpretation, festal cycles, life cycle, mysticism, performing arts, poetry, art and architecture, ethics, worship, and the Hindu renaissance. In the middle of all this is a seventeen-page general entry on Hinduism, complete with maps and a timeline. A similar pattern is repeated for the religions of antiquity, Buddhism, Chinese religion, Christianity, Islam, Japanese religion, new religions, and the religions of traditional peoples.

Moreover, amidst this useful descriptive information, the dictionary implicitly employs a comparative approach when dealing with more traditional, phenomenological categories. For example, under the category of "sacrifice" one briefly learns not only of the term's history and uses, but detailed examples are provided from Aztec religion, Vedic and post-Vedic religion, and Chinese religion. Under "pilgrimage" one finds a detailed general description of the category followed by examples drawn from Hinduism, Christianity, Islam, and Japanese religions. But what is most interesting about the dictionary is that, for example, immediately following the article on pilgrimage, there appears a two-and-a-half-column article on theories of pilgrimage that discuses this practice not only as a rite of passage entailing a liminal stage but also redescribing the indigenous behaviors as fulfilling some psychological or sociological need. Therefore, besides descriptive articles on religions and comparative-based entries on traditional phenomenological categories, under the guidance of area editor Hans Penner, this resource comes with extensive articles on the study of religion itself. While there is a nine-page feature article on the study of religion, there are also helpful articles on theory, religious experience, science of religion, theories of religious language, descriptive versus explanatory reductionism, typology/classification, the definition of religion, anthropology of religion, sociology of religion, phenomenology of religion, philosophy of religion, psychology of religion, comparative religion, hermeneutics, ideology and religion, and so on. Assigned at the proper moment in a course, these articles would provide a specific basis for in-class discussion and exploration.

In my opinion, the dictionary is, in part, misnamed; despite having an alphabetical listing of succinctly defined terminology, its longer articles make it a very useful handbook as well. *The Continuum Dictionary of Religion* (Pye 1994) is an example of a more traditional wordbook, containing entries varying from a few lines to a column in length. Whereas *The HarperCollins Dictionary of Religion* has many such entries on names, places, or concepts, it also contains numerous articles that simultaneously address descriptive, comparative, and theoretical issues (such as the six-column discussion of purity/impurity that tackles such subtopics as the sacred/profane dichotomy in Durkheim's *Elementary Forms of Religious Life*, Mary Douglas's work on dirt/cleanliness, issues of the body, while also providing descriptive data from Hinduism, Judaism, and Islam).

Compared to the role other dictionaries play in our classes (as supplementary reference resources),[7] Smith's dictionary stands on its own as a complete survey of the field. Because of its unique mix of articles, the dictionary strikes me as one of the more interesting resources for the introductory class, where issues of definition, description, comparison, and redescription are already intersecting. Provided that a syllabus includes generous opportunities for creative research assignments that require students to browse through the resource and to use it as the starting point for more detailed investigations, the dictionary might be a wonderful primary resource for our classes. Perhaps one should not be surprised that, under Smith's editorial eye, this 1,150-page resource far surpasses Eliade's massive, sixteen volume *Encyclopedia of Religion*. Where reductionist articles and topics were ruled out from the start in Eliade's encyclopedia (reading his preface makes this clear), the dictionary more accurately reflects the actual research taking place in the modern study of religion by filling in the glaring gaps in the encyclopedia.

CONCLUSION: SO WHAT DO WE WITH "RELIGION"?

I am hardly the first to wonder what we should do with the category of "religion" and how we should address its limits. I would hope that one possible answer is now apparent: although 'religion' may be of some use on the descriptive and comparative levels of analysis, on the analytic and metatheoretical levels we work with students to expose the theoretical origins of the category; we explore the limits of using it as a basis for making claims about human beliefs, practices, and institutions; and we prompt our students to come up with more theoretically sophisticated ways either of defining it or replacing it with a more productive category for research.

These are big tasks that surely will not be accomplished in any one class, let alone the introductory course in the study of religion. However, I think that the rationale and resources surveyed in this chapter provide an opportunity for addressing all these issues at a specific, introductory site, in a way that is accessible to our undergraduate students. What to do with 'religion' as an analytic construct will then be left up to our students once they have gained some of the tools of critical analysis that we have to offer them. As teachers we should recognize that this is as it should be.

NOTES

1. A case in point is Capps's chapter on comparison, which turns out to be a historical survey of largely Christian religious pluralism, almost as if the tradition of comparative religion (or the science of religion) stretching back to Müller had not existed.

2. Most recently, the colonial roots of our field have been examined by the contributors to *Curators of the Buddha* (Lopez 1995); Chidester 1996a, 1996b; and King 1999. The neocolonial roots of the field's North American rebirth in the 1960s is one of the central topics of my own *Manufacturing Religion* (1997c).

3. For an example of the use of such traditional phenomenological categories in doing comparative religion, see Sharpe 1971. Whereas *Critical Terms for Religious Studies* (Taylor 1998) is an odd mix of phenomenological and analytic handbook, the articles in the *Guide to the Study of Religion* (Braun and McCutcheon 2000) consistently address the redescriptive, theoretical nature of scholarship in the study of religion.

4. See chapter 4 of McCutcheon, *Manufacturing Religion* (1997c), specifically, the section entitled, "The Study of Religion and Thick Skinned Mammals," where I address Catherine Albanese's odd use of this story (1981).

5. See *Method and Theory in the Study of Religion* 8/1 (1996).

6. Once, on the University of Santa Barbara's listserve, Andere-L, as an aside I once commented on using Smith's *Dictionary of Religion* as a textbook; I soon heard back from Juan Campo at the University of California at Santa Barbara that he too routinely uses it in his undergraduate classes as a textbook.

7. When teaching introductory world religions courses, I often use *The Penguin Dictionary of Religions* (Hinnells 1984; new edition 1997) as a required yet supplementary class resource.

PART V

Afterword

The trick is to start at the ending when you write. . . . Get a good, strong ending, and then write backwards.

—Woody Allen (1972: 190)

"ad hoc" = (adv.) for the particular end or purpose at hand and ʒ reference to wider application or employment. (lit. "for this")

AFTERWORD

The chapters in this collection have covered a wide number of topics, but—as I suggested in the preface—a simple thesis was applied throughout: Public scholars of religion study the way communities artfully deploy and manipulate discourses on such topics as evil, their mythic past, endtimes, and nonobvious beings in an attempt to authorize their contingent, historical worlds. Because not all events in the natural world can equally attract our attention (remember, it's a hectic place out there, and I've only got so much attention to focus), these rhetorical devices constitute the mechanisms whereby groups concoct and reproduce meaningful, historic worlds by exercising an economy of signification, thereby establishing the limits of credibility. It is an economy efficiently managed by cognitive and social classifications that delineate this from that, important from unimportant, godly from ungodly, pure from impure, exclusivist from pluralist, and, finally, us from them. These are all classifications with explicit political impact.

What should be clear is that the scholar of religion I have named a culture critic is not in the business of nurturing, enhancing, or—despite the caricatures of those who wish to remake the academic study of religion into a liberal theological pursuit—criticizing the communities we study; this is the business of the various groups' members. Neither are we in the business of proposing final, definitive, totalized theories. As a cultural critic, the public scholar of religion's contribution is made as a scholar of classification and social rhetoric. Our work presumes the ambiguous, *ad hoc* nature of all historical activity—our own scholarship included—making the academic study of religion tactical, anthropologically based, problem-oriented, and always conscious of the ironic, self-implicated position of the scholar who seeks to study the mechanisms of their own social formations. For the public scholar of religion, there is therefore nothing irreducibly religious about religion. Religion is simply the label some of us give to various collections of artful but all too ordinary human doings that portray any given historical world as the "world without end. Amen."

Given this conclusion—or, taking Woody Allen's advice seriously, this starting point—I can do no better than end this book by quoting a recent concluding paragraph written by someone who, long ago, helped to get me to start thinking critically about religion as a form of rhetoric:

If history, including its repertoire of symbols . . . is a human production from beginning to end, then there is no place to hide from the imperative to take responsibility for history, both in terms of our lived doings in the present and in terms of how we describe and use "the past" to rationalize our doings, worldviews, social arrangements, and the multitudinous instrumentalities, material and symbolic, by which we contrive powerful tangible worlds in accordance with our imagined worlds. There are no proxies—slippery abstractions such as "nature," "teleology," "God," "Devil," that are reified, i.e., endowed by human imagination with a rock-solid concreteness, and placed in tamper-proof, beyond-argument creeds and canons—which might allow us to avoid exercising our franchise, to cast our vote, as frankly and transparently as we can. Please, do not misunderstand: I am not implicitly pleading for a Promethean view of human performance, which by heroic dint and huff, can unfix and refix the theater of our lives at will. That would be to fall under another spell of fantasy, one which overlooks the complexities of the cultural and material forms and forces that place constraints both on the potential (power) and forms of human doing. No, the point of this little discourse . . . is precisely to begin to expose the complexities of history, then to plead for locating the doings of "theology" and "religious studies" within, rather than beyond, this messy mix of historical human performance, a locating that requires as a start, and at least within the rhetorical situation of the academy, to scrutinize, reconsider, and rectify assumptions that let "theology" and "religious studies" live on as somehow "divine" sciences. (Braun 1999a: 8)

REFERENCES

Albanese, Catherine L. (1981). *America: Religions and Religion*. Belmont, CA: Wadsworth Publishing Company.

——— (1995). "Refusing the Wild Pomegranate Seed: America, Religious History, and the Life of the Academy," *Journal of the American Academy of Religion* 63/2: 205–229.

——— (1996). "Religion and American Popular Culture: An Introductory Essay," *Journal of the American Academy of Religion* 64/4: 733–742.

Allen, Charlotte (1996). "Is Nothing Sacred? Casting Out the Gods from Religious Studies," *Lingua Franca* 6/7:30–40.

——— (1998). "Response to *Bulletin 26/4*," *Bulletin of the Council of Societies for the Study of Religion* 27/2: 45–46.

Allen, Woody (1972). *Without Feathers*. New York: Ballantine Books.

Althusser, Louis (1971). "Ideology and Ideological State Apparatuses (Notes toward an Investigation)." In Ben Brewster (trans.), *Lenin and Philosophy and Other Essays*, 127–186. Monthly Review Press.

Althusser, Louis, and Etienne Balibar (1970). *Reading Capital*. London: New Left.

Alton, Bruce (1989). "Before Method: Cognitive Aims in the Study of Religion," *Studies in Religion* 18:415–425.

Anderson, Benedict (1991). *Imagined Communities: Reflections on the Origin and Spread of Nationalism*. 2nd ed. London: Verso.

Anonymous (1998). Review of *Manufacturing Religion*. *Christian Century* 115/5:187.

Armstrong, Karen (1991). *Muhammad: A Biography of the Prophet*. San Francisco: Harper.

——— (1993). *A History of God: The 4,000–Year Quest of Judaism, Christianity, and Islam*. Alfred Knopf.

Arnal, William E. (1997). "Making and Re-Making the Jesus-Sign: Contemporary Markings on the Body of Christ." In William E. Arnal and Michel Desjardins (eds.), *Whose Historical Jesus?* 308–319. Waterloo: Wilfrid Laurier University Press.

——— (1998a). "Unpopular Items." Posting to Andere-L (February 22); archived at http://ucsbuxa.ucsb.edu/rgstd/local/andere-l/archives.html.

——— (1998b). "What If I Don't Want to Play Tennis? A Rejoinder to Russell McCutcheon on Postmodernism and Theory of Religion," *Studies in Religion* 27/1: 61–68.

——— (2000). "Definition." In Willi Braun and Russell T. McCutcheon (eds.), *Guide to the Study of Religion*, 21–34. London: Cassell Academic Press.

Asad, Talal (1993). *Genealogies of Religion: Discipline and Reasons of Power in Christianity and Islam*. Baltimore: The Johns Hopkins University Press.

Aune, Michael B., and Valerie DeMarinis (eds.) (1996). *Religious and Social Ritual: Interdisciplinary Explorations*. Albany: State University of New York Press.

Baird, Robert D. (1971). *Category Formation and the History of Religions*. The Hague: Mouton.

Baranowski, Ann (1998). "A Psychological Comparison of Ritual and Musical Meaning," *Method & Theory in the Study of Religion* 10/1: 3–27.

Barthes, Roland (1973). *Mythologies*. Annette Lavers (trans.). Hammersmith, London: Paladin.

Becker, Gay (1997). *Disrupted Lives: How People Create Meaning in a Chaotic World*. Berkeley: University of California Press.

Bell, Catherine (1992). *Ritual Theory, Ritual Practice*. New York: Oxford University Press.

—— (1996). "Modernism and Postmodernism in the Study of Religion," *Religious Studies Review* 22: 179–190.

Benavides, Gustavo (1997). "The Study of Religion under Late Capitalism, or Commodity Triumphant," *Bulletin of the Council of Societies for the Study of Religion* 26/4: 88–91.

Berling, Judith (1993). "Is Conversation about Religion Possible? (And What Can Religionists Do to Promote It?)," *Journal of the American Academy of Religion* 61/1: 1–22.

Bianchi, Ugo (ed.) (1994). *The Notion of "Religion" in Comparative Research*. Rome: "L'Erma" di Bretschneider.

Bierlein, John F. (1994). *Parallel Myths*. New York: Ballantine Books.

Bloch, Maurice (1994). *Prey into Hunter: The Politics of Religious Experience*. New York: Cambridge University Press.

Bolle, Kees (1983). "Myths and Other Religious Texts." In Frank Whaling (ed.), *Contemporary Approaches to the Study of Religion*, 297–363. Berlin: Mouton.

—— (1987). "Myth: An Overview." In Mircea Eliade (ed.), *Encyclopedia of Religion*. Vol. 10: 261–273. New York, Macmillian.

Bourdieu, Pierre (1998). *On Television*. Priscilla Parkhurst Ferguson (trans.). New York: The Free Press.

Boyer, Pascal (1994). *The Naturalness of Religious Ideas: A Cognitive Theory of Religion*. Berkeley: University of California Press.

—— (1996). "Religion as an Impure Subject: A Note on Cognitive Order in Religious Representation in Response to Brian Malley," *Method & Theory in the Study of Religion* 8/2: 201–213.

Braun, Willi (1999a). "Amnesia in the Production of (Christian) History," *Bulletin of the Council of Societies for the Study of Religion* 28/1: 3–8.

—— (1999b). "Socio-Mythic Invention, Graeco-Roman Schools, and the Sayings Gospel Q," *Method & Theory in the Study of Religion* 11/3 : 210–235.

—— (2000), "Religion." In Willi Braun and Russell T. McCutcheon (eds.), *Guide to the Study of Religion*, 3–18. London: Cassell Academic Press.

Braun, Willi, and Russell T. McCutcheon (eds.) (2000). *Guide to the Study of Religion*. London: Cassell Academic Press.

Brightman, Robert (1995). "Forget Culture: Replacement, Transcendence, Reflexification," *Cultural Anthropology* 10: 509–546.

Brown, Karen McCarthy (1991). "Religion as Language." In Mark Jurgensmeyer (ed.), *Teaching the Introductory Course in Religious Studies: A Sourcebook*, 221–226. Atlanta: Scholars Press.

Brown, Peter (1995). *Authority and the Sacred: Aspects of the Christianisation of the Roman World*. Cambridge: Cambridge University Press.

Brzezinski, Zbigniew (1993). *Out of Control: Global Turmoil on the Eve of the Twenty-First Century*. New York: Charles Scribner's Sons.

Burkert, Walter (1996). *Creation of the Sacred: Tracks of Biology in Early Religions*. New Cambridge: Harvard University Press.

Cady, Linell E. (1993). *Religion, Theology, and American Public Life*. Albany: State University of New York Press.

——— (1998). "The Public Intellectual and Effective Critique," *Bulletin of the Council of Societies for the Study of Religion* 27/2: 36–38.

Cameron, Ron (1996). "Mythmaking and Intertextuality in Early Christianity." In Elizabeth A. Castelli and Hal Taussig (eds.), *Reimagining Christian Origins: A Colloquium Honoring Burton L. Mack*, 37–50. Valley Forge, PA: Trinity Press International.

Campany, Robert (1996). "Xunzi and Durkheim as Theorists of Ritual Practice." In Ronald Grimes (ed.), *Readings in Ritual Studies*, 86–103. Upper Saddle River, NJ: Prentice Hall.

Cannon, Dale (1996). *Six Ways of Being Religious: A Framework for Comparative Studies of Religion*. Belmont, CA: Wadsworth Publishing Co.

Capps, Walter H. (1995). *Religious Studies: The Making of a Discipline*. Minneapolis: Fortress Press.

Carroll, David (1995). *French Literary Fascism: Nationalism, Anti-Semitism, and the Ideology of Culture*. Princeton: Princeton University Press.

Carter, Jeffrey R. (1998). "Explanation Is Not Description: A Methodology of Comparison," *Method & Theory in the Study of Religion* 10/2: 133–148.

Carter, Stephen L. (1993). *The Culture of Disbelief: How American Law and Politics Trivialize Religious Devotion*. New York: Basic Books.

Certeau, Michel de (1997). *Culture in the Plural*. Luce Giard (ed.). Minneapolis: University of Minnesota Press.

Chidester, David (1996a). "Anchoring Religion in the World: A Southern African History of Comparative Religion," *Religion* 26: 141–160.

——— (1996b). "'Classify and Conquer': Friedrich Max Müller, Indigenous Religious Traditions, and Imperial Comparative Religion." Unpublished paper.

——— (1996c). *Savage Systems: Colonialism and Comparative Religion in Southern Africa*. Charlottesville: University Press of Virginia.

Chomsky, Noam (1987). "The Responsibility of Intellectuals." In James Peck (ed.), *The Chomsky Reader*, 59–82. New York: Pantheon Books.

——— (1991). *Necessary Illusions: Thought Control in Democratic Societies*. Concord, Ontario: Anansi Press.

Codrescu, Andrei (1994). *Zombification: Stories from NPR*. New York: St. Martin's Press.

Cohen, Percy S. (1969). "Theories of Myth," *Man* 4/3, 337–353.

Cole, Tim (1999). *Selling the Holocaust: From Auschwitz to Schindler, How History is Bought, Packaged and Sold.* New York: Routledge.

Coleman, Simon and John Elsner (1995). *Pilgrimage: Past and Present in the World Religions.* Cambridge: Harvard University Press.

Comstock, Gary (1995). *Religious Autobiographies.* Belmont, CA: Wadsworth Publishing Co.

Connerton, Paul (1998) [1989]. *How Societies Remember.* Cambridge: Cambridge University Press.

Craig, Gordon A. (1999). "'Working toward the Führer'," *The New York Review of Books* 46/5 (March 18): 32–35.

Cumpsty, John (1991). *Religion as Belonging: A General Theory of Religion.* Lanham: University Press of America.

Dean, William (1994). *The Religious Critic in American Culture.* Albany: State University of New York Press.

Delaney, Carol (1998). *Abraham on Trial: The Social Legacy of Biblical Myth.* Princeton: Princeton University Press.

Dennett, Daniel (1995). *Darwin's Dangerous Idea: Evolution and the Meanings of Life.* New York: Simon and Schuster.

——— (1996). "Appraising Grace: What Evolutionary Good Is Grace?" *The Sciences* 37/1: 39–45.

Denny, Frederick M. (1999). "*On Common Ground: World Religions in America*: A Review Essay of the Harvard Pluralism Project CD-ROM," *Journal of the American Academy of Religion* 67/3: 649–659.

Detienne, Marcel (1991). "The Interpretation of Myths: Nineteenth- and Twentieth-Century Theories." In Yves Bonnefoy (comp.), *Mythologies,* 5–10. Vol. 1. Chicago: University of Chicago Press.

Doty, William G. (1986). *Mythography: The Study of Myths and Rituals.* Tuscaloosa: University of Alabama Press.

Downing, Christine (1993). "A Somewhat Mitigated Disaster: The Status of the Religious Studies Department at San Diego State University as of February 1993," *CSSR Bulletin* 22/2: 39–43.

Dundes, Alan (1984). *Sacred Narrative: Readings in Theory of Myth.* Berkeley: University of California Press.

Durkheim, Emile (1952) [1897]. *Suicide: A Study in Sociology.* London: Routledge & Kegan Paul.

——— (1995) [1912]. *The Elementary Forms of Religious Life.* Karen Fields (trans.). New York: The Free Press.

Eade, John, and Michael J. Sallow (eds.) (1991). *Contesting the Sacred: The Anthropology of Christian Pilgrimage.* London: Routledge.

Eagleton, Terry (1989). *Literary Theory: An Introduction.* Minneapolis: University of Minnesota Press.

——— (1991). *Ideology: An Introduction.* New York: Verso.

——— (1992). *The Significance of Theory.* Oxford: Blackwell.

——— (1996). *The Illusions of Postmodernism.* Oxford: Blackwell.

——— (2000). *The Idea of Culture.* Oxford: Blackwell.

Eck, Diana (1993). *Encountering God: A Spiritual Journey from Bozeman to Banares.* Boston: Beacon Press.

—— (1997). *On Common Ground: World Religions in America*. Columbia University Press.

Eliade, Mircea (1973). "Myth in the Nineteenth and Twentieth Centuries." In *Dictionary of the History of Ideas*. Vol. 3, 307–318. Philip P. Weiner (ed.). Charles Scribner's Sons.

—— (1984). *The Quest: History and Meaning in Religion*. Chicago: University of Chicago Press.

—— (ed.) (1987). *Encyclopedia of Religion*. 16 vols. New York: Macmillan Publishing Co.

—— (1991). "Toward a Definition of Myth." In Yves Bonnefoy (comp.), *Mythologies*, 3–5. Vol. 1. Chicago: University of Chicago Press.

Evans-Pritchard, E. E. (1992) [1965]. *Theories of Primitive Religion*. Oxford: Clarendon Press.

Fiorenza, Francis Schüssler (2000). "Religion: A Contested Site in Theology and the Study of Religion." *Harvard Theological Review* 93: 7–34.

Fish, Stanley (1999). *The Trouble with Principle*. Cambridge, MA: Harvard University Press.

Fisher, Mary Pat (1994). *Living Religions*. 2nd edition. Englewood Cliffs, NJ: Prentice Hall.

Fitzgerald, Timothy (1990). "Hinduism and the World Religion Fallacy," *Religion* 20: 101–118.

—— (1995). "Religious Studies as Cultural Studies: A Philosophical and Anthropological Critique of the Concept of Religion," *Diskus* 3/1: 35–47.

—— (1997). "A Critique of the Concept of Religion," *Method & Theory in the Study of Religion* 9/2: 91–110.

—— (1999). *The Ideology of Religious Studies*. New York: Oxford University Press.

—— (2000). "Experience." In Willi Braun and Russell T. McCutcheon (eds.), *Guide to the Study of Religion*, 125–139. London: Cassell Academic Press.

Frisina, Warren (1997). "Religious Studies: Strategies for Survival in the 90's," *Council of Societies for the Study of Religion Bulletin* 26/2: 29–34.

Geertz, Clifford (1968). *Islam Observed: Religious Development in Morocco and Indonesia*. New Haven: Yale University Press.

—— (1973). *The Interpretation of Cultures*. New York: Basic Books.

Giddens, Anthony (1986) [1984]. *The Constitution of Society: Outline of the Theory of Structuration*. Berkeley: University of California Press.

Gill, Brendan (1989). "The Faces of Campbell," *The New York Review of Books* (28 September): 16–19.

Gill, Sam (1994). "The Academic Study of Religion," *Journal of the American Academy of Religion* 62/4: 965–975.

—— (1998). "No Place to Stand: Jonathan Z. Smith as *Homo ludens*, the Academic Study of Religion *Sub specie ludi*," *Journal of the American Academy of Religion* 66/2: 283–312.

—— (2000). "Play." In Willi Braun and Rusell T. McCutcheon (eds.), *Guide to the Study of Religion*, 451–462. London: Cassell Academic Press.

Goody, Jack (1961). "Religion and Ritual: The Definitional Problem," *The British Journal of Sociology* 12: 142–164.

Greeley, Andrew M. (1995). *Sociology and Religion: A Collection of Readings.* New York: HarperCollins College Publishers.

Green, Garrett (1995). "Challenging the Religious Studies Canon: Karl Barth's Theory of Religion." *Journal of Religion* 75: 473–486.

Green, William Scott (1996). "Religion within the Limits," *Academe* 82/6: 24–28.

Griffiths, Paul J. (1994). *On Being Buddha: The Classical Doctrine of Buddhahood.* Albany: State University of New York Press.

—— (1998a). Review of *Manufacturing Religion. First Things: A Monthly Journal of Religion and Public Life* 81 (March): 44–48.

—— (1998b). "Some Confusions about Critical Intelligence: A Response to Russell T. McCutcheon," *Journal of the American Academy of Religion* 66/4: 893–895.

—— (1999). *Religious Reading: The Place of Reading in the Practice of Religion.* New York: Oxford University Press.

—— (2000). "The Very Idea of Religion," *First Things: A Monthly Journal of Religion and Public Life* 83 (May): 30–35.

Grimes, Ronald (ed.) (1996). *Readings in Ritual Studies.* Upper Saddle River, NJ: Prentice Hall.

Gross, Rita M. (1996). *Feminism & Religion.* Boston: Beacon Press.

Grottanelli, Cristiano, and Bruce Lincoln (1985). "A Brief Note on (Future) Research in the History of Religions," *Center for Humanistic Studies Occasional Papers.* Center for Humanistic Studies, University of Minnesota, 4: 1–15. Reprinted in *Method & Theory in the Study of Religion* 10/3 (1998): 311–325.

Guthrie, Stewart (1993). *Faces in the Clouds: A New Theory of Religion.* New York: Oxford University Press.

—— (1996). "Religion: What Is It?" *Journal for the Scientific Study of Religion* 35/4: 412–419.

—— (2000). "Projection." In Willi Braun and Russell T. McCutcheon (eds.), *Guide to the Study of Religion,* 225–238. London: Cassell Academic Press.

Harris, Marvin (1979). *Cultural Materialism: The Struggle for a Science of Culture.* New York: Vintage.

—— (1987). *Cultural Anthropology.* New York: Harper and Row.

Harrison, Peter (1990). *"Religion" and the Religions in the English Enlightenment.* Cambridge: Cambridge University Press.

Hart, Darryl G. (1999). *The University Gets Religion: Religious Studies in American Higher Education.* Baltimore: Johns Hopkins University Press.

Headland, Thomas N., Kenneth L. Pike, and Marvin Harris (eds.) (1990). *Emics and Etics: The Insider/Outsider Debate.* London: Sage Publications.

Hewitt, Marsha A. (1993). "Cyborgs, Drag Queens, and Goddesses: Emancipatory-Regressive Paths in Feminist Theory," *Method & Theory in the Study of Religion* 5: 135–154.

—— (1996). "How New Is the 'New Comparativism'? Difference, Dialectics, and World-Making," *Method & Theory in the Study of Religion* 8/1: 15–20.

Hick, John (1989). *An Interpretation of Religion: Human Responses to the Transcendent.* New Haven: Yale University Press.

Hinnells, John (1984). *The Penguin Dictionary of Religions*. New York: Penguin Books.

Holm, Jean, and John Bowker (eds.) (1994a). *Myth and History*. London: Pinter Publishers.

—— (1994b). *Rites of Passage*. London: Pinter Publishers.

Horowitz, S. R. (1997). "But Is It Good for the Jews? Spielberg's Schindler and the Aesthetics of Atrocity." In Y. Loshitzky (ed.), *Spielberg's Holocaust: Critical Perspectives on Schindler's List*. Bloomington: University of Indiana Press.

Hoy, David (1978). *The Critical Circle: Literature, History, and Philosophical Hermeneutics*. Berkeley: University of California Press.

—— (1991). "Is Hermeneutics Ethnocentric?" In David Hiley, James Bohman, and Richard Shusterman (eds.), *The Interpretive Turn: Philosophy, Science, Culture*, 155–175. Ithaca, NY: Cornell University Press.

Hubbard, Jamie (1992). "Premodern, Modern, and Postmodern Doctrine and the Study of Japanese Religion," *Japanese Journal of Religious Studies* 19/1:3–27.

—— (1998). "Embarrassing Superstition, Doctrine, and the Study of New Religious Movements," *Journal of the American Academy of Religion* 66/1:59–92.

Idinopulos, Thomas A. and Edward Yonan (eds.) (1994). *Religion and Reductionism: Essays on Eliade, Segal, and the Challenge of the Social Sciences for the Study of Religion*. Leiden: E. J. Brill.

—— (1996). *The Sacred and Its Scholars. Comparative Methodologies for the Study of Primary Religious Data*. Leiden: E. J. Brill.

Idinopulos, Thomas A., and Brian C. Wilson (eds.) (1998). *What Is Religion? Origins, Definitions, and Explanations*. Leiden: Brill.

Inden, Ronald (1990). *Imagining India*. London: Blackwell.

Jameson, Frederic (1988). "The Ideology of the Text." In *The Ideologies of Theory: Essays, 1971–1986*. Vol 1. *Situations of Theory*, 17–71. Minneapolis: University of Minnesota Press.

Jay, Martin (1996). "For Theory," *Theory and Society* 25: 167–183.

Jay, Nancy (1992). *Throughout Your Generations Forever: Sacrifice, Religion, and Paternity*. Chicago: University of Chicago Press.

Jensen, Jeppe Sinding, and Armin Geertz (1991). "Tradition and Renewal in the Histories of Religions: Some Observations and Reflections." In Jeppe S. Jensen and Armin W. Geertz (eds.), *Religion, Tradition, and Renewal*, 11–27. Aarhus, Denmark: Aarhus University Press.

Jensen, Tim (1998). "The Scholar of Religion as a Cultural Critic: Perspectives from Denmark," *Bulletin of the Council of Societies for the Study of Religion* 27/2: 40–43.

Johnston, Robert K. (1997). Review of Joel W. Martin and Conrad E. Ostwald, *Screening the Sacred. Journal of the American Academy of Religion* 65/2: 496–498.

Juschka, Darlene (1997). "Religious Studies and Identity Politics: Mythology in the Making," *Bulletin of the Council of Societies for the Study of Religion* 26/1: 8–11.

—— (1998). "'Whose Turn Is It to Cook?' Victor Turner's *Communitas* and Pilgrimage Questioned." Unpublished paper presented to the Eastern International Region of the American Academy of Religion.

Karabel, Jerome (1996). "Towards a Theory of Intellectuals and Politics," *Theory and Society* 25: 205–233.

Kershaw, Ian (1999). *Hitler, 1889–1936: Hubris.* New York: W. W. Norton.

King, Richard (1999). *Orientalism and Religion: Postcolonial Theory, India, and "The Mystic East."* London: Routledge.

Krymkowski, Daniel, and Luther H. Martin (1998). "Religion as an Independent Variable: Revisiting the Weberian Hypothesis," *Method & Theory in the Study of Religion* 10/2: 187–198.

La Barre, Weston (1972). *The Ghost Dance: The Origins of Religion.* London: George Allen & Unwin Ltd.

Larrington, Carolyne (ed.) (1992). *The Feminist Companion to Mythology.* London: Pandora Press.

Larson, Gerald (1995). *India's Agony over Religion.* Albany: State University of New York Press.

Lawson, E. Thomas (1994). Review of John Cumpsty, *Religion as Belonging. Journal of the American Academy of Religion,* 62: 184–186.

—— (1996). "Theory and the New Comparativism, Old and New," *Method & Theory in the Study of Religion* 8/1: 31–35.

Lawson, E. Thomas, and Robert N. McCauley (1990). *Rethinking Religion: Connecting Cognition and Culture.* Cambridge: Cambridge University Press.

—— (1993). "Crisis of Conscience, Riddle of Identity: Making Space for a Cognitive Approach to Religious Phenomena," *Journal of the American Academy of Religion* 61: 201–223.

Lease, Gary (1994). "The History of 'Religious' Consciousness and the Diffusion of Culture," *Historical Reflections / Réflexions Historiques* 20: 453–479.

—— (guest ed.) (1995). "Pathologies in the Academic Study of Religion: North American Institutional Case Studies," *Method & Theory in the Study of Religion* 7/4: 295–416.

—— (1998). "What Are the Humanities and Why Do They Matter? The Case of Religion and Public Life," *Bulletin of the Council of Societies for the Study of Religion* 27/4: 91–95.

—— (2000). "Ideology." In Willi Braun and Russell T. McCutcheon (eds.), *Guide to the Study of Religion,* 438–447. London: Cassell Academic Press.

Lehmann, Arthur C., and James E. Myers (eds.) (1993). *Magic, Witchcraft, and Religion: An Anthropological Study of the Supernatural.* 3rd edition. Mountain View, CA: Mayfield Publishing.

Lentricchia, Frank (1985). *Criticism and Social Change.* Chicago: University of Chicago Press.

Lessa, William A., and Evon Z. Vogt (eds.) (1979). *Reader in Comparative Religion: An Anthropological Approach.* 4th edition. New York: HarperCollins.

Lightstone, Jack (1997). "Whence the Rabbis? From Coherent Description to Fragmented Reconstruction," *Studies in Religion* 26: 275–295.

Lincoln, Bruce (1986). *Myth, Cosmos, and Society: Indo-European Themes of Creation and Destruction*. Cambridge: Harvard University Press.

—— (1989). *Discourse and the Construction of Society: Comparative Studies of Myth, Ritual, and Classification*. New York: Oxford University Press.

—— (1991). *Death, War, and Sacrifice: Studies in Ideology and Practice*. Chicago: University of Chicago Press.

—— (1994). *Authority: Construction and Corrosion*. Chicago: University of Chicago Press.

—— (1996a). "Theses on Method," *Method & Theory in the Study of Religion* 8: 225–227. Reprinted in McCutcheon 1998b: 395–398.

—— (1996b). "Mythic Narrative and Cultural Diversity in American Society." In Laurie Patton and Wendy Doniger (eds.), *Myth and Method*, 163–176. Charlottesville: University Press of Virginia.

—— (2000a). "Culture." In Willi Braun and Russell T. McCutcheon (eds.), *Guide to the Study of Religion*, 409–422. London: Cassell Academic Press.

—— (2000b). *Theorizing Myth: Narrative, Ideology, and Scholarship*. Chicago: University of Chicago Press.

Llewellyn, J. E. (1998). "The Center Way Out There: A Review Article of Recent Books on Hindu Pilgrimage," *International Journal of Hindu Studies* 2/2: 249–265.

—— (forthcoming). "'Pilgrimage as a Bounded Entity': A Review Essay," *Religious Studies Review*.

Lodge, David (1981) [1965]. *The British Museum Is Falling Down*. New York: Penguin Books.

—— (1995) [1984]. *Small World*. New York: Penguin Books.

Long, Charles (1986). *Significations: Signs, Symbols, and Images in the Interpretation of Religion*. Philadelphia: Fortress Press. [Reprinted, Colorado: The Davies Group, 1999.]

—— (1987). "Cosmogony." In Mircea Eliade (ed.), *Encyclopedia of Religion*. Vol. 4: 94–100. New York, Macmillan.

Lopez, Donald S. (1995). *Curators of the Buddha: The Study of Buddhism Under Colonialism*. Chicago: University of Chicago Press.

Lyden, John (1995). *Enduring Issues in Religion*. San Diego: Greenhaven Press.

Lyotard, Jean-François (1984). *The Postmodern Condition: A Report on Knowledge*. Geoff Bennington and Brian Massumi (trans.). Minneapolis: University of Minnesota Press.

Macaulay, David (1979). *Motel of the Mysteries*. Boston: Houghton Mifflin Co.

Mack, Burton L. (1988). *The Myth of Innocence: Mark and Christian Origins*. Philadelphia: Fortress Press.

—— (1989). "Caretakers and Critics: On the Social Role of Scholars Who Study Religion." Unpublished paper presented to the Seminar on Religion in Society, Wesleyan University.

—— (1995). *Who Wrote the New Testament? The Making of the Christian Myth*. New York: HarperCollins.

—— (1996). "On Redescribing Christian Origins," *Method & Theory in the Study of Religion* 8/3: 247–269.

—— (2000). "Social Formation." In Willi Braun and Russell T. McCutcheon (eds.), *Guide to the Study of Religion*, 283–296. London: Cassell Academic Press.

MacKendrick, Kenneth G. (1999). "The Aporetics of a Tennis-Playing Brontosaurus, or a Critical Theory of Religion: A Rejoinder to Russell T. McCutcheon and William E. Arnal," *Studies in Religion* 28/1 (1999): 77–83.

MacQueen, Graeme (1988). "*Whose* Sacred History? Reflections on Myth and Dominance," *Studies in Religion* 17: 143–157.

Mamet, David (1996). *Make-Believe Town: Essays and Remebrances*. Boston: Little, Brown and Company.

de Man, Paul (1986). *Resistance to Theory* . Minneapolis: University of Minnesota Press.

Manganaro, Marc (1992). *Myth, Rhetoric, and the Voice of Authority: A Critique of Frazer, Eliot, Frye, and Campbell*. New Haven, CT: Yale University Press.

Mannheim, Karl (1985). *Ideology & Utopia: An Introduction to the Sociology of Knowledge*. New York: Harcourt Brace Jovanovich.

Marsden, George (1994). *The Soul of the American University: From Protestant Establishment to Established Nonbelief*. New York: Oxford University Press.

—— (1997). *The Outrageous Idea of Christian Scholarship*. New York: Oxford University Press.

Martin, Joel W. (1997). Review of Margaret Miles, *Seeing and Believing*. *Journal of the American Academy of Religion* 65/2: 498–501.

Martin, Joel W., and Conrad E. Ostwald (eds.) (1995). *Screening the Sacred: Religion, Myth, and Ideology in Popular American Film*. Westview Press.

Martin, Luther (1996). "Introduction: The Post-Eliadean Study of Religion: The New Comparativism," *Method & Theory in the Study of Religion* 8/1: 1–3.

Marty, Martin E. (1989). "Committing the Study of Religion in Public." *Journal of the American Academy of Religion* 57/1: 1–22.

—— (1996). "You *Get* to Teach and Study Religion," *Academe* 82/6: 14–17.

—— (1997). *The One and the Many: America's Struggle for the Common Good*. Cambridge: Harvard University Press.

—— (1998). "Rejoinder." *Bulletin of the Council of Societies for the Study of Religion* 27/2: 43–45.

Masuzawa, Tomoko (1993). *In Search of Dreamtime: The Quest for the Origin of Religion*. Chicago: University of Chicago Press.

—— (1998). "Culture." In Mark C. Taylor (ed.), *Critical Terms for Religious Studies*, 70–93. Chicago: University of Chicago Press.

McCauley, Robert N., and E. Thomas Lawson (1996). "Who Owns 'Culture'?" *Method & Theory in the Study of Religion* 8/2: 171–190.

McCutcheon, Russell T. (1990). "Naming the Unnameable: Theological Language and the Academic Study of Religion," *Method & Theory in the Study of Religion* 2: 213–229

—— (1991). "Ideology and the Problem of Naming," *Method & Theory in the Study of Religion* 3: 245–256.

—— (1995). "The Category 'Religion' in Recent Publications: A Critical Survey," *Numen* 42/3: 284–309.

—— (1997a). "Classification and the Shapeless Beast: A Critical Look at the AAR Research Interest Survey," *Religious Studies News*, September 12/3: 7, 9.

—— (1997b). "A Default of Critical Intelligence? The Scholar of Religion as Public Intellectual," *Journal of the American Academy of Religion* 66/2: 443–468.

—— (1997c). *Manufacturing Religion: The Discourse on Sui Generis Religion and the Politics of Nostalgia.* New York: Oxford University Press.

—— (1997d). "'My Theory of the Brontosaurus . . .': Postmodernism and 'Theory' of Religion," *Studies in Religion* 26/1: 3–23.

—— (1998a). "The Economics of Spiritual Luxury: The Glittering Lobby and the Parliament of Religions," *Journal of Contemporary Religion* 13/1: 51–64.

—— (ed.) (1998b). *The Insider/Outsider Problem in the Study of Religion: A Reader.* London: Cassell Academic Press.

—— (1998c.) "Methods and Theories in the Classroom: Teaching the Study of Myths and Rituals," *Journal of the American Academy of Religion* 66/1: 147–164.

—— (1998e). "Redescribing 'Religion and . . .' Film: Teaching the Insider/Outsider Problem," *Teaching Theology and Religion* 1/2: 99–110.

—— (1998f). "Redescribing 'Religion' as Social Formation: Toward a Social Theory of Religion." In Thomas A. Idinopulos and Brian C. Wilson (eds.), *What Is Religion? Origins, Definitions, and Explanations*, 51–71. Leiden: E. J. Brill.

—— (1998g). "Returning the Volley to William E. Arnal," *Studies in Religion* 27/1: 67–68.

—— (1998h). "Talking Past Each Other: Public Intellectuals Revisited," *Journal of the American Academy of Religion* 66/4: 911–917.

—— (1999). "Of Strawmen and Humanists: A Reply to Bryan Rennie," *Religion* 29: 91–92.

—— (2000). "Myth." In Willi Braun and Russell T. McCutcheon (eds.), *Guide to the Study of Religion*, 190–208. London: Cassell Academic Press.

—— (forthcoming). "Autonomy, Unity, and Crisis: Rhetoric and the Invention of the Discourse on *Sui Generis* Religion." *Pre/Text.*

—— (forthcoming). "Theorizing at the Margin: Religion as Something Ordinary," *ARC: Journal of the Faculty of Religious Studies*, McGill University.

McLuhan, Eric, and Frank Zingrone (eds.) (1995). *Essential McLuhan.* Concord, Ontario: Anansi Press Ltd.

McMullin, Neil (1989). "Historical and Historiographical Issues in the Study of Pre-Modern Japanese Religion," *Japanese Journal of Religious Studies* 16/1:3–40.

—— (1992). "Which Doctrine? Whose 'Religion'?—A Rejoinder," *Japanese Journal of Religious Studies* 19/1:28–39.

Merod, Jim (1987). *The Political Responsibility of the Critic.* Ithaca, NY: Cornell University Press.

Miles, Margaret (1996). *Seeing and Believing: Religion and Values in the Movies*. Boston: Beacon Press.

Miner, Horace (1956). "Body Ritual among the Nacirema," *American Anthropologist* 58: 503–507.

Morris, Brian (1987). *Anthropological Studies of Religion: An Introductory Text*. Cambridge: Cambridge University Press.

Murphy, Tim (1997). "Taking the Bull by the Tail: Responses to the *Lingua Franca* Article," *Bulletin of the Council of Societies for the Study of Religion* 26/4: 78–85.

—— (1998). "The 'One' behind the 'Many'," *Bulletin of the Council of Societies for the Study of Religion* 27/2: 39–40.

Neusner, Jacob (1997). "Scholarship, Teaching, Learning: Three Theses for the Academic Study of Religion," *Religious Studies Review* 12/3: 21, 48.

Niebuhr, G. (1996.) " Finding a Religious Quilt That Is a Patchwork," *The New York Times* (Saturday, November 23): 13.

O'Connor, June (1998). "The Scholar of Religion as Public Intellectual: Expanding Critical Intelligence," *Journal of the American Academy of Religion* 66/4: 897–909.

O'Flaherty, Wendy Doniger (1985). "The Uses and Misuses of Other People's Myths," *Journal of the American Academy of Religion* 54: 219–239.

Oxtoby, Willard (ed.) (1996a). *World Religions: Eastern Traditions*. New York: Oxford University Press.

—— (1996b). *World Religions: Western Traditions*. New York: Oxford University Press.

Paden, William (1992). *Interpreting the Sacred: Ways of Viewing Religion*. Boston: Beacon Press.

—— (1994). *Religious Worlds: The Comparative Study of Religion*. Boston: Beacon Press.

—— (1996a). "Elements of a New Comparativism," *Method & Theory in the Study of Religion* 8/1: 5–14.

—— (1996b). "A New Comparativism: Reply to Panelists," *Method & Theory in the Study of Religion* 8/1: 37–49.

—— (2000). "World." In Willi Braun and Russell T. McCutcheon (eds.), *Guide to the Study of Religion*, 334–347. London: Cassell Academic Press.

Pals, Daniel (1996). *Seven Theories of Religion*. New York: Oxford University Press.

Payne, Rodger M., and Briane K. Turley (1999). "Navigating a New Landscape: Religious and Technological Pluralism in Diana Eck's *On Common Ground*," *Journal of the American Academy of Religion* 67/3: 637–647.

Penner, Hans (1994). "Holistic Analysis: Conjectures and Refutations," *Journal of the American Academy of Religion* 62/4: 977–996.

Perkins, Judith (1995). *The Suffering Self: Pain and Narrative Representation in the Early Christian Era*. New York: Routledge.

Pike, Kenneth L. (1967) [1954]. *Language in Relation to a Unified Theory of the Structure of Human Behavior*. Berlin: Mouton.

Popper, Karl R. (1962). *Conjectures and Refutations: The Growth of Scientific Knowledge*. New York: Basic Books.

Prakash, Gyan (1995). "*Orientalism* Now," *History and Theory* 34/3: 199–212.
Preus, J. Samuel (1987). *Explaining Religion: Criticism and Theory from Bodin to Freud*. New Haven, CT: Yale University Press.
Pye, Michael (ed.) (1994). *The Continuum Dictionary of Religion*. New York: Continuum Publishing Co.
Queenan, Joe (1998). *Red Lobster, White Trash, and the Blue Lagoon: Joe Queenan's America*. New York: Hyperion.
Rai, Milan (1995). *Chomsky's Politics*. London: Verso.
Raschke, Carl (1986). "Religious Studies and the Default of Critical Intelligence," *Journal of the American Academy of Religion* 54/1: 131–138.
Remus, Harold (1997). "By the Skin of Our Teeth," *Bulletin of the Council of Societies for the Study of Religion* 26/1: 12–17.
Remus, Harold, William C. James, and Daniel Fraikin (1992). *Religious Studies in Ontario: A State-of-the-Art Review*. Waterloo: Wilfrid Laurier University Press.
Rennie, Bryan S. (1998). "Forum," *Religion* 29: 413–414.
Resch, Robert Paul (1992). *Althusser and the Renewal of Marxist Social Theory*. Berkeley: University of California Press.
Ricoeur, Paul (1987). "Myth and History." In Mircea Eliade (ed.), *Encyclopedia of Religion*. Vol. 10: 273–282. New York, Macmillan.
Roberts, Richard H. (1995). "Globalized Religion? The 'Parliament of World's Religions' (Chicago 1993) in Theoretical Perspective," *Journal of Contemporary Religion* 10: 121–137.
——— (1998). "The Dialectics of Globalised Spirituality: Some Further Observations," *Journal of Contemporary Religion* 13/1: 65–71.
Rohr, Janelle (ed.) (1988). *Science and Religion*. San Diego: Greenhaven Press.
Rosenau, Pauline Marie (1992). *Postmodernism and the Social Sciences: Insights, Inroads, and Intrusions*. Princeton, NJ: Princeton University Press.
Rosenbaum, Ron (1995). "A Reporter at Large: Explaining Hitler," *The New Yorker* 71/10 (May 1): 50–70.
——— (1998). *Explaining Hitler: The Search for the Origins of His Evil*. New York: Random House.
Rudolph, Kurt (1985). *Historical Fundamentals in the Study of Religion*. Joseph Kitagawa (intro.). New York: Macmillian Publishing Company.
Ryan, Michael (1984). *Marxism and Deconstruction: A Critical Articulation*. Baltimore: Johns Hopkins.
Said, Edward (1978). *Orientalism*. New York: Random House.
——— (1993). *Culture and Imperialism*. New York: Alfred A. Knopf.
——— (1996). *Representations of the Intellectual*. New York: Vintage Books.
——— (1999). "Public Spectacle, Public History," *Al-Ahram Weekly* (February 18–24): http://www.ahram.org.ed/weekly/1999/417/op2.htm.
Saler, Benson (1993). *Conceptualizing Religion: Immanent Anthropologists, Transcendent Natives, and Unbounded Categories*. Leiden: E. J. Brill.
Scocca, Tom (1999). "Going Public," *Lingua Franca* 9/2: 8–9.
Scott, Joan Wallach (1991). "The Evidence of Experience," *Critical Inquiry* 17: 773–797.
Segal, Robert A. (ed.) (1996). *Theories of Myth: From Ancient Israel and Greece to Freud, Jung, Campbell, and Lévi-Strauss*. New York: Garland Publishing.

Sharf, Robert H. (1998). "Experience." In Mark C. Taylor (ed), *Critical Terms in Religious Studies*, 94–115. Chicago: University of Chicago Press.

Sharma Arvind (ed.) (1993). *Our Religions: The Seven World Religions Introduced by Preeminent Scholars from Each Tradition*. New York: HarperCollins.

Sharpe, Eric J. (1971). *Fifty Key Words: Comparative Religion*. Richmond, VA: John Knox Press.

Sigal, Pierre André (1987). "Roman Catholic Pilgrimage in Europe." In Mircea Eliade (ed.), *Encyclopedia of Religion*. Vol. 11, 330–332. New York: Macmillan Publishing Co.

Skinner, Quentin (1987). "Introduction," *The Return of Grand Theorizing in the Human Sciences*, 3–20. New York: Cambridge University Press.

Smart, Ninian (1989). *The World's Religions: Oral Traditions and Modern Transformations*. Cambridge: Cambridge University Press.

——— (1994). "Retrospect and Prospect: The History of Religions." In Ugo Bianchi (ed.), *The Notion of "Religion" in Comparative Research: Selected Proceedings of the XVI IAHR Congress*. 901–903. Rome: "L'Erma" di Bretschneider.

Smith, Brian K. (1989). *Reflections on Resemblance, Ritual, and Religion*. New York: Oxford University Press.

Smith, Jonathan Z. (1975). "The Social Description of Early Christianity," *Religious Studies Review* 1/1: 19–25.

——— (1978). *Map Is Not Territory*. Leiden: E. J. Brill.

——— (1982). *Imagining Religion: From Babylon to Jonestown*. Chicago: University of Chicago Press.

——— (1988). "'Religion' and 'Religious Studies': No Difference At All," *Soundings* 71/2–3: 231–244.

——— (1990a). "Connections," *Journal of the American Academy of Religion* 58/1: 1–15.

——— (1990b). *Drudgery Divine: On the Comparison of Early Christianities and the Religions of Late Antiquity*. Chicago: University of Chicago Press.

——— (1991). "The Introductory Course: Less Is Better." In Mark Jurgensmeyer (ed.), *Teaching the Introductory Course in Religious Studies: A Sourcebook*, 185–192. Atlanta: Scholars Press.

——— (1995a.) "Afterword: Religious Studies: Whither (Wither) and Why?" *Method & Theory in the Study of Religion* 7/4: 407–414.

——— (ed.) (1995b). *The HarperCollins Dictionary of Religion*. New York: HarperCollins Publishers.

——— (1996a). "A Matter of Class: Taxonomies of Religion," *Harvard Theological Review* 82/4: 387–403 [Excerpted in *Harvard Divinity School Bulletin* 25/4 (1996): 26].

——— (1996b). "Social Formations of Early Christianities: A Response to Ron Cameron and Burton Mack," *Method & Theory in the Study of Religion* 8/3: 271–278.

——— (1997). "Are Theological and Religious Studies Compatible?" *Bulletin of the Council of Societies for the Study of Religion* 26/3: 60–61.

——— (2000) "Classification." In Willi Braun and Russell T. McCutcheon (eds.), *Guide to the Study of Religion*, 35–43. London: Cassell Academic Press.

Smith, Wilfred Cantwell (1991) [1963]. *The Meaning and End of Religion*. Minneapolis: Fortress Press.

Sperber, Dan (1996). *Explaining Culture: A Naturalistic Approach*. Oxford: Blackwell.

Staal, Frits (1993) [1989]. *Rules without Meaning: Ritual, Mantras, and the Human Sciences*. New York: Peter Lang.

Stark, Rodney (1996). *The Rise of Christianity: A Sociologist Reconsiders History*. Princeton, NJ: Princeton University Press.

———— (1997). "Bringing Theory Back In," In Lawrence Young (ed.), *Rational Choice Theory and Religion: Summary and Assessment*, 3–23. New York: Routledge.

Stark, Rodney, and William S. Bainbridge (1987). *A Theory of Religion*. New York: Peter Lang.

Strenski, Ivan (1987). *Four Theories of Myth in Twentieth-Century History*. Iowa City: University of Iowa Press.

———— (1998a). "On 'Religion' and Its Despisers." In Thomas A. Idinopolus and Brian C. Wilson (eds.), *What Is Religion? Origins, Definitions, and Explanations*, 113–132. Leiden: E. J. Brill.

———— (1998b). "Religion, Power, and Final Foucault," *Journal of the American Academy of Religion* 66/2: 345–367.

Taylor, Daniel (1999). "Are You Tolerant? (Should You Be?)," *Christianity Today* 43/1 (January 11): 42–52.

Taylor, Mark (ed.) (1998). *Critical Terms for Religious Studies*. Chicago: University of Chicago Press.

Thompson, E. P. (1991) [1963]. *The Making of the English Working Class*. New York: Penguin.

Trouillot, Michel-Rolph (1995). *Silencing the Past: Power and the Production of History*. Boston: Beacon.

Turner, Edith (1987). "Pilgrimage." In Mircea Eliade (ed.), *Encyclopedia of Religion*. Vol. 11, 327–330. New York: Macmillan.

Wach, Joachim (1967). "The Meaning and Task of the History of Religions (*Religionswissenschaft*)." In Joseph Kitagawa (ed.), *The History of Religions: Essays on the Problem of Self-Understanding*. Karl Luckert (trans.). Chicago: University of Chicago Press.

Wagner, Roy (1981) [1975]. *The Invention of Culture*. Chicago: University of Chicago Press, 1975.

Weber, Max (1993) [1922]. *The Sociology of Religion*. Talcott Parsons (intro.) and Ephraim Fischoff (trans.). Boston: Beacon Press.

Wiebe, Donald (1983). "Theory in the Study of Religion," *Religion* 13: 283–309.

———— (1984a). "Beyond the Sceptic and the Devotee: Reductionism and the Scientific Study of Religion," *Journal of the American Academy of Religion* 52:157–165.

———— (1984b). "The Failure of Nerve in the Academic Study of Religion," *Studies in Religion* 13/4: 401–422.

———— (1989). "History of Mythistory in the Study of Religion? The Problem of Demarcation." In Michael Pye (ed.), *Marburg Revisited: Institutions and Strategies in the Study of Religion*,31–46. Marburg: Diagonal Verlag.

———— (1994a). "From Religious to Social Reality: The Transformation of 'Religion' in the Academy." In Ugo Bianchi (ed.), *The Notion of "Religion" in Comparative Research: Selected Proceedings of the XVI IAHR Congress*, 837–845. Rome: "L'Erma" di Bretschneider.

———— (1994b). Review of Peter Byrne, *Natural Religion and the Nature of Religion* and Peter Harrison, *"Religion" and the Religions in the English Enlightenment. Method & Theory in the Study of Religion* 6/1: 92–104.

———— (1994c). "Transcending Religious Language: Towards the Recovery of an Academic Agenda." In Ugo Bianchi (ed.), *The Notion of "Religion" in Comparative Research: Selected Proceedings of the XVI IAHR Congress*, 905–912. Rome: "L'Erma" di Bretschneider.

———— (1996). "Is the New Comparativism Really New?" *Method & Theory in the Study of Religion* 8/1: 21–29.

———— (1997). "A Religious Agenda Continued: A Review of the Presidential Addresses to the AAR." *Method & Theory in the Study of Religion* 9/4: 353–375.

———— (1999). *The Politics of Religious Studies.* New York: St. Martin's Press.

Wilken, Robert L. (1989). "Who Will Speak for the Religious Traditions?" *Journal of the American Academy of Religion* 57/4: 699–717.

Williams, Raymond (1990) [1977]. *Marxism and Literature.* New York: Oxford.

Wilson, John F. (1964). "Mr. Holbrook and the Humanities, or Mr. Schlatter's Dilemma," *The Journal of Bible and Religion* 32: 252–261.

Wintonick, Peter, and Mark Achbar (1993). *Manufacturing Consent: Noam Chomsky and the Media.* (Film and Video) Montreal, Quebec: Necessary Illusions.

Wolf, Naomi (1992). *The Beauty Myth: How Images of Beauty Are Used against Women.* New York: Doubleday.

Wolfe, Alan (1996). "Higher Learning," *Lingua Franca* 6/3: 70–77.

Zipes, Jack (1994). "Breaking the Disney Spell." In *Fairy Tale as Myth. Myth as Fairy Tale*, 72–95. Lexington: University Press of Kentucky.

INDEX

Thanks to Ryan Garrett for his assistance in preparing this index.